Linguistics and Deaf Children

Linguistics and Deaf Children

Transformational Syntax and Its Applications

By

W. Keith Russell
Stephen P. Quigley

Institute for Child Behavior and Development
University of Illinois
Urbana-Champaign

Desmond J. Power

Institute of Special Education
Burwood State College
Burwood, Australia

Alexander Graham Bell Association for the Deaf
Washington, D.C.

Contents

Preface

The purpose of this book is to introduce teachers of deaf children to some recent linguistic thinking on the structure of language, and to illustrate with research findings and examples from writings of deaf children how that thinking might help in understanding the ways in which the **syntax** of deaf children's written language differs from the syntax of Standard English. In order to understand the syntactic structure of the written language of deaf students; in order to detect the rules that generate that structure and understand where and how they deviate from the rules of Standard English; in order to modify or develop reading materials for deaf students in relation to the students' knowledge of syntax; and in order to teach Standard English to deaf students, the teacher needs a thorough knowledge of methods of linguistic analysis, of language acquisition by hearing children, and of language acquisition by deaf children. The result of better understanding of these matters, hopefully, will be better teaching of English.

When we say that the book is concerned with language structure, with syntax, we reveal that our unit of concern is the sentence and that we are interested in the ways in which sentences are constructed. Having identified the sentence as our unit of concern, the temptation is strong to immediately offer a definition. We shall refrain from doing so, however, and assume that all readers know what an English sentence is, even if they might not be able to provide a definition. Rather than a definition, we offer a few examples of sentences to show the diversity of the seemingly simple unit with which we are concerned:

> So they stopped and get a dog brought to the picnic with them.
>
> *(deaf student, age 18 years)*
>
> Mike and Pat had a race to see who could get done eating the fastest and Mike won because he had a big mouth.
>
> *(hearing student, age 8 years)*

It is a light blue moonless summer evening, but late, perhaps ten o'clock, with Venus burning hard in daylight, so we are certainly somewhere far north, and standing on this balcony, when from beyond along the coast comes the gathering thunder of a long many-engined freight train, thunder because though we are separated by this wide strip of water from it, the train is rolling eastward and the changing wind veers for the moment from an easterly quarter, and we face East, like Swedenborg's angels, under a sky clear save where far to the northeast over distant mountains whose purple has faded, lies a mass of almost pure white clouds, suddenly, as by a light in an alabaster lamp, illumined from within by gold lightning, yet you can hear no thunder, only the roar of the great train with its engines and its wide shunting echoes as it advances from the hills into the mountains: and then all at once a fishing boat with tall gear comes running round the point like a white giraffe, very swift and stately, leaving directly behind it a long silver scalloped rim of wake, not visibly moving inshore, but now stealing ponderously beachward toward us, this scrolled silver rim of wash striking the shore first in the distance, then spreading all along the curve of beach, its growing thunder and commotion now joined to the diminishing thunder of the train, and now breaking reboant on our beach, while the floats, for there are timber diving floats, are swayed together, everything jostled and beautifully ruffled and stirred and tormented in this rolling sleeked silver, then little by little calm again, and you see the reflection of the remote white thunderclouds in the water, and now the lightning within the white clouds in deep water, as the fishing boat itself with a golden scroll of travelling light in its silver wake beside it reflected from the cabin vanishes around the headland, silence, and then again, within the white white distant alabaster thunderclouds beyond the mountains, the thunderless gold lightning in the blue evening, unearthly
. . .*

Each of these is a sentence. At least, each was considered a sentence by its author: an 18-year-old deaf student, an 8-year-old hearing student, and an author of a great novel, respectively. The sentence by the 18-year-old deaf student unfortunately typifies the written language of deaf persons of that age. It is readily apparent that the most striking feature of the sentence is the manner in which its structure differs from

---

*From *Under the Volcano* by Malcolm Lowry. Copyright 1947 by Malcolm Lowry. Reprinted by permission of J. B. Lippincott Company.

a similar sentence by the 8-year-old hearing student. The contrast in language structure, and in age of the authors, helps emphasize the great difficulty deaf students have in acquiring Standard English.

These sentences serve to illustrate two things: (1) the acquisition of English syntactic structure presents particular problems for the deaf child, and (2) the teacher must have extensive knowledge of syntactic structure and methods of analyzing it to successfully teach language to deaf children. That teachers of deaf children often lack such knowledge is indicated by the curricula used in teacher preparation programs where preparation in language often is concentrated on methods devised specifically for use with deaf children, such as Wing's Symbols, the Barry Five Slate, and the Fitzgerald Key. Although these methods are effective for certain purposes, they in themselves are not sufficient for analyzing or teaching English syntax; as evidence we offer the sentence from Malcolm Lowry's novel, *Under the Volcano*. The sentence is long: 348 words long. It is a beautiful sentence. And it is not a simple, declarative sentence, the virtues of which are often preached to teachers of deaf children. It defies analysis, or teaching, by means of the Fitzgerald Key and similar devices used in structuring language for deaf students. It would seem from this that any curriculum for preparing teachers of deaf children needs to contain much more information on language structure and acquisition than most curricula now contain. It is probably a fair analogy to state that teachers of deaf children should be expected to know as much about language as a teacher of chemistry is expected to know about chemistry.

This book, then, is about syntax: that is, the study of sentences and their internal structures and relationships. Specifically, we will be concerned with a theory of syntax known as "transformational," because we feel that this is the most promising of the various competing syntactic theories. In the following chapters, we will attempt to formalize the various types of knowledge which a native speaker has "internalized" (learned about his language); for it is obvious that, although most such speakers can tell whether or not a sentence is "good English," (i.e., if it is grammatical), whether or not a sentence is ambiguous, and whether or not a set of sentences are synonymous, and what functions the various parts of the sentence perform, he is not likely to be able to tell *why*. In completing this book, the reader will find out more about the *why*. More specifically, he will also know how certain types of English sentences such as negatives, questions, and passives are related to others. Because we will concentrate on those structures which research has shown are often deviant in the language of deaf children, the teacher will perhaps be able to recognize more readily not only the specific difficulties of deaf students, but also the systematic nature of their errors, and perhaps gain some insight into what might be done to help correct those errors. Finally, through introduction to the terminology and methods used in this text, the reader should be in a better position to explore further the enormously wide-ranging field of transformational grammar by continuing on to those books listed in the References.

And now, a few cautions. First of all, this book is basically a text on syntax. Little will be said about semantics (the study of meaning) or phonology (the study of sound systems). These are, of course, both extremely important aspects of a native speaker's knowledge of his language. Nevertheless, we have here restricted ourselves to syntax because (1) research has demonstrated that syntactic structure is an area of great difficulty for deaf students (see, for example, Quigley, Smith, and Wilbur, 1974), and (2) the major part of innovative work in transformational grammar has taken place in the area of syntax, and therein lies its major promise for teachers.

The material in this book is not intended to be taught to deaf students, but to increase the teacher's ability to teach English effectively because of increased understanding. There is little evidence to show that systematic teaching of linguistic structures and terminology to hearing students in the classroom has any beneficial effect at all on their use of language, and this may be the case for deaf students also. This, however, should not lead one to believe that formal study of grammar is not valuable for teachers, if it is remembered that any teacher of mathematics, chemistry, or sociology has absorbed a tremendous amount of abstract understanding of his subject which is not conveyed to his students, yet which assists greatly in enabling him to impart that knowledge which is necessary. So it should be with an increased understanding of language. Last of all, the emphasis in this book is on learning methods for linguistic analysis and on gaining understanding, not memorizing facts. Exposure to the particular language processes discussed here should help the reader to generalize to other areas of syntax, and to look objectively at various alternative types of analysis, and to apply the results in a teaching situation.

This book is an outgrowth of an extensive study of syntactic structure in the language of deaf students which was supported by the Bureau of Education for the Handicapped and the National Institute of Education. Major results of the research program lie in four areas: (1) evaluation of syntactic skills; (2) description of syntactic development and of consistent deviations from Standard English; (3) syntactic analysis of reading materials; and (4) preparation of materials for training teachers of deaf students in transformational grammar and its application to the teaching of language. The results of the research have been disseminated in a series of research articles and in a final report. These documents are listed in the References of the book. Preparation of teacher training materials involved development of a program on PLATO, the computer-assisted instruction program at the University of Illinois. That program became a partial basis for the present book.

The first two chapters of the book provide a brief introduction to linguistics, to transformational generative grammar, and to some problems and methods of teaching language to deaf children. Chapter 3 deals with phrase structure rules, and chapters 4 through 8 with various transformational rules. In most of the chapters, the linguistic theory of the syntactic structure under examination is presented first, followed by sections discussing research findings relating to the development of the structure in the language of both hearing and deaf persons. The treatment of syntactic structures is not exhaustive, but is restricted to those structures about which substantial information is available for deaf pupils. This does include most of the structures necessary for reasonably mature usage of the English language. Finally, Chapter 9 presents some applications of linguistics, psycholinguistics, and sociolinguistics to the problems of developing language in deaf children.

Chapters 4 through 8 also contain sections describing the frequency of occurrence of certain syntactic structures in a commonly used series of school readers, consisting of 11 books ranging from primers to 6th-grade level. Comparisons are made between the grade level at which particular syntactic structures appear in the texts and the age level at which deaf students begin to understand them. These data are emphasized in Chapter 9 to illustrate how severe the reading problem of prelingually deafened persons really is. It is, in fact, even more severe than is indicated by scores on standard reading tests which, although very low in comparison to those of hearing pupils, are still spuriously high estimates of the prelingually deafened pupil's reading ability. The comparative data on the syntax of the language of deaf students and that of commonly used reading materials should supply the teacher with some knowledge to develop and modify language materials for deaf students, and the linguistic sections of the book should supply him with the methods for doing this.

Appendix A is a chapter on morphology which is needed for understanding some of the material in the body of the book. Appendix B provides information on very recent developments in linguistics and related fields which will likely become increasingly important to teachers of language. Finally, the Glossary following the appendixes is provided to supply the reader with a basic terminology of the topics covered in this book.

The authors would like to express their gratitude to the many people without whose assistance this book would not have been possible. Several persons read earlier drafts and provided many valuable suggestions: among these were Marlyn O'Neill and Julie Summers. Jeannie Jones performed the difficult task of drawing the many linguistic trees and diagrams. Ruth Quigley provided invaluable help in preparing the References; RevaBeth Russell provided assistance with the Glossary. Finally, we thank Joyce Fitch for supervising the typing and organization of the book, and others who assisted in the typing of the manuscript, especially Barbara Carmichael, Mary Huls, and Mary Lou Sparbell.

CHART OF
PHONETIC SYMBOLS USED IN APPENDIX A

Vowels

i	pit	iy	feet
ɛ	pet	ey	ate
æ	pat	uw	boot
ɨ	Butch	ow	tone
ə	horses	aw	sound
ʌ	nut		
a	father		

Consonants

č	chip	ǰ	jet
š	ship	ž	measure
θ	thin	ð	this
		ŋ	sing

All other consonants have their regular sound values.

CHAPTER 1

Introduction

Any normal speaker of a language is able to use that language in talking about various objects, ideas, and qualities. If one were to ask a native English speaker to precisely define "bitter," "lavender," "sincere," or even "idea," he would likely have great difficulty; nevertheless, he could use any of these words in conversation and use them correctly, without any such difficulty. But the linguistic knowledge of a native speaker is much more complex than even this understanding of vocabulary. Suppose he was given the following list, and asked to comment on the "Englishness" of each word:

    (1) frak   **(4)** hello
    (2) strill   **(5)** haj
    (3) fgrup   **(6)** saeiod

He would be able to point out not only that most of these words have no meaning in English, but also that among those which do not have meaning, some could, nevertheless, simply by the nature of their structure, possibly be good English words. For example, if a speaker of English were to invent an electric sundial, he might choose to call it a "strill" or a "frak," but never a "fgrup" or a "saeiod"—it would be difficult enough even to pronounce the latter two words.

A native speaker can display this same ability with sentences, as well as words. For example, he would be able to tell us that sentences **(7)**, **(9)**, and **(10)** below are "good English sentences" (even though he would not know the meanings of some of the words), but that **(8)** and

1

(11) are not. (Linguists have adopted a convention that an asterisk before a sentence implies that it is "ungrammatical.")

(7)   Books are fun to read.

(8)   *Fun to read are books.

(9)   Kroofs are murp to heeg.

(10)   The mungus nated the kritch very snitly.

(11)*Snitly very the mungus nated kritch the.

This knowledge is known to linguists as the ability to judge the **grammaticality** of sentences.

What else does the native speaker "know" about his language? Consider the well-known nursery rhyme:

(12) *This is the house that Jack built,*

This is the malt that lay in the house that Jack built.

This is the rat that ate the malt that lay in the house that Jack built.

This is the cat that chased the rat that ate the malt that lay in the house that Jack built.

These four sentences are enough to indicate the pattern; it is easy to see what would happen if we were to continue. Would we be forced to stop after producing a hundred sentences of this type?—a thousand?—a million? Obviously not; theoretically, at least, we could go on adding new elements forever. Any speaker of English is capable of producing a theoretically infinite number of sentences of just this one type. We can achieve similar results by simply adding one sentence after another and inserting the word "and." Again there is no limit to the number of sentences we could produce.

The same results can be accomplished in other ways as well. Because of this capability, a speaker of English encounters sentences every day which he has never seen or heard before, yet can easily understand: for example, "Anteaters eat flies when ants aren't available." (Notice that we are making no claim about the truth of this statement. The fact remains that it is perfectly reasonable for a nonzoologist to make such a statement.) Similarly, a speaker can use sentences which he has never before used, as with the above sentence, for example.

Still considering our "native speaker of English," we will find that he knows yet more about his language. For example, consider the following sentence:

(13) The shooting of the gangsters frightened me.

You may recognize this as an **ambiguous** sentence—one which has more than one meaning. (Even if you did not see the ambiguity immediately, it will become clear that the interpretation of the sentence would be different depending on whether you thought of the gangsters as doing the shooting or as being shot.)

Now look at the following group of sentences:

(14a) That English is complex can be disputed by no one.

(14b) No one can dispute that English is complex.

(14c) That English is complex cannot be disputed by anyone.

(14d) It cannot be disputed by anyone that English is complex.

(14e) It can be disputed by no one that English is complex.

(14f) The complexity of English cannot be disputed by anyone.

(14g) What cannot be disputed by anyone is that English is complex.

. . .and so forth. . .

You will recognize that, although the order of words in each sentence varies a great deal, and although the sentences differ somewhat even at the level of the words they contain, *they all mean essentially the same thing*—and the list is not complete. Any native English speaker knows that these sentences are **synonymous**.

Finally, a native speaker of English recognizes not only *meanings, grammaticality, synonymity,* and *ambiguity,* but also the internal functions of sentences. You know that in the sentence "Mathematicians detest numbers," the first and third words, though of the same type, are different in function—one performs the "detesting," while the other is the object of the detesting. We see, then, that there is a lot more to a person's knowledge of English than having simply, like an automaton, learned a huge set of sentences and repeating them on some suitable cue. What is surprising is that a normal-hearing child gains this knowledge in just the first few years of his life, without, in most cases, any formal study, but merely through exposure to nothing but the myriad of linguistic structures in the conversation surrounding him.

Linguistics

Linguistics, as a field of scholarly research, is the scientific study of natural language. Linguistics is scientific in that empirical methods of analysis are applied to the structures of language to arrive at hypotheses about the way language works. Linguistics is said to be a "science" by virtue of just this empirical method. An empirical science is one which sets up hypotheses and then tests the "truth" of these hypotheses against data carefully collected under controlled conditions. The "data" for linguistics are sets of similar and contrasting sentences. In this book we are going to be concerned only with **natural language.** By a natural language (as opposed to artificial ones, including computer programming languages like FORTRAN) we mean one that is used by human beings, many of whom learned it in infancy without being formally taught.

A linguist, in describing a language, attempts to write a **grammar** of that language. Such a grammar consists of a set of statements, or **rules,** about how a language works. (Notice that the word "rule" is used by most modern linguists as the word "law" is used by physicists.) A complete grammar will consist of *semantic rules defining meaning, syntactic rules dealing with the structure and organization of sentences, and phonological rules describing the sound system of the language*. As stated previously, this book is going to be concerned mainly with the syntactic component of the grammar.

Subfields of Linguistics

The writing of grammars is the realm of **descriptive linguistics.** The true theoretical descriptivist is a practitioner of pure science; he studies a language because it is interesting and exciting, and because of the contribution his findings will make to human knowledge. Many of his results may later find practical application, but this is not his concern. **Historical linguistics** is concerned with studying the relationships between the different stages of a language over long periods of time, and the processes by which languages change through time. The goal of **comparative linguistics,** closely related to historical linguistics, is, obviously, comparison—the comparison of two or more language systems, usually with the goal of determining **genetic or historical relationships,** and of reconstructing early stages of these languages, and ultimately the parent language from which the languages in question have developed.

Linguistics has relevance to many seemingly unrelated fields. This can perhaps be exemplified by listing a few interdisciplinary areas: **anthropological linguistics**—the study of language in its cultural setting; **psycholinguistics**—the study of the connection between man's use of language and his psychological processes, as well as the study of language acquisition; **sociolinguistics**—the investigation of language in its social context; and **mathematical linguistics**—which deals with the formal aspects of linguistic description. **Phonetics** examines the physical characteristics of speech sounds: articulatory, acoustical, and perceptual. **Applied linguistics** is just what the term implies: the application of the results of linguistic research in practical areas, such as language teaching, stylistics, and machine translation.

Because language is unique to man, it holds special interest for nearly everyone. Through understanding language we understand ourselves. Probably no field of study has had so much informal attention devoted to it as has language. Everyone feels that he is an expert on his own language because, of course, he speaks it fluently, and, as we have seen, this is no small accomplishment. But if everyone knows so much about his native language, why the need for a distinct field of science concerned with investigating language? Hopefully, the answer to this question will become clear to you as we progress.

Language Studies Through History

Although it is only within the past few years that linguistics has been recognized as a distinct area of study and that linguistics departments have appeared in universities, for many centuries philosophers, anthropologists, language specialists, historians, and others have devoted themselves to language studies. Pāṇini, an Indian grammarian who lived about the fifth century B.C., was the author of a grammar of Sanskrit, an ancient language of India used to record the holy Hindu writings. In the 2400 years since, no one has been able to improve upon this brilliant work. The Greeks and Romans also produced detailed linguistic analyses beginning several centuries before Christ. The Greeks concerned themselves with questions such as the "naturalness" of language, and whether a word such as "fish" actually has some inherent relationship to the object it represents or whether it is simply an arbitrary representation. They also expended a great deal of effort defining word classes like "noun," "verb," etc. which have continued in linguistic tradition to the present. The Romans similarly produced detailed descriptions of their own language, Latin.

European linguistics was based for a long time on the Latin model. In fact, this tradition still manifests itself in the teaching of English grammar in school. Students are taught verb conjugations comparable to the Latin pattern: "I see, you see, he sees, we see, you see, they see." While this verb did indeed have six forms in the present tense in Latin ("video, vides, videt, videmus, videtis, vident"), it is obvious that there are only *two* forms in English—"see" and "sees."

As these linguistic traditions continued, profound insights into the nature of language were achieved by scholars such as Descartes, von Humboldt, and a group of French scholars known as the Port Royal Grammarians. Among this last group's perceptive insights were the ideas of grammatical "transformations" and "universals" in language. These concepts were ignored for a period of time, and have only recently regained our attention. They will play a major role in later chapters in this book.

With the coming of the 19th century, linguistic attention was focused on relationships among languages. The beginning of this tradition was the realization that not only Greek and Latin, but also such seemingly "exotic" languages as Sanskrit and Anatolian, belong to the same language family as English, namely **Indo-European.** The major accomplishment of this period was the development of scientific procedures for determining whether or not any two languages are genetically related (i.e., whether they evolved from the same "parent" language) and for applying methods of **internal reconstruction**—analysis of a single language to reconstruct its hypothetical parent language. The

19th-century philologists also discovered that sound changes which take place over time are regular and predictable rather than idiosyncratic and random, which enabled phonologists more and more to apply scientific methods in their research.

A few decades ago a new movement began in linguistics, known today as **structuralism.** Influenced strongly by the philosophical theory of logical positivism which was in vogue at the time, and by the behavioristic psychological claim that only externally observable phenomena should be accepted as evidence in scientific investigation, the structuralists emphasized the outward, and especially the spoken, forms of language. Because of these restrictions, the preponderance of research during this period dealt with phonology, resulting in syntax and semantics being largely ignored. Nevertheless, a few linguists such as Charles Fries (1952) and Eugene Nida (1960) did concern themselves with syntax, and their methods of analysis are still widely accepted.

As a result of the restrictions placed on linguistic research by the structuralists, the field of linguistics became much more scientific and systematic. Linguists of this period emphasized the structure of language: that is, the interrelatedness of the elements of languages as members of language systems, rather than as isolated units. All of this resulted in great progress, and structuralism held sway past the middle of the century. But in 1957, a new perspective on the workings of language was achieved with the publication of *Syntactic Structures* by Noam Chomsky. The basic concepts of this book (namely those of "transformational grammar") and their implications will be discussed in detail in Chapter 2.

Linguistics in the Education of Deaf Students

The methods that teachers apply in developing language in deaf students usually reflect prevailing theories of grammar. (Schmitt, 1966, has presented a review of the history of teaching language to deaf children.) Prior to the 1920's, teachers of deaf students used methods based largely on classical grammar models. Teaching was formal and "analytic"; that is, it tended to start with words (parts of speech) as elements and build sentences by combining single words into phrases, phrases into simple sentences, and simple sentences into more complex ones. Emphasis was placed on rote memorization of sentences and working through grammar books and formal systems of language development. As Schmitt (1966) says, "The grammatical orientation of the time is apparent in Clerc's complaint that of the 44 verb inflections and modes, each containing affirmative, negative, and interrogative forms, most deaf children were able to 'rehearse' only 15 to 20." (This complaint was made in 1851 by Laurent Clerc, the first known deaf teacher of deaf pupils in the United States.)

The grammatical formalism was evident also in the sets of symbols for grammatical categories and structures developed by several teachers. One of the best known was that of George Wing of the Minnesota School for the Deaf, which was published as the **Wing Symbols** in 1887. Schmitt describes it thus:

> The Wing symbols . . . consist of letters, numbers, and other symbols placed over words to represent their forms and functions in a sentence. The eight "essential symbols" were S=Subject; V=Verb (with three modifications of the V to specify the verb as transitive, intransitive, or passive); O=Object; AC=Adjective Complement; N=Noun and pronoun complement. The system also included numbers from one to seven for modifying forms, six connective symbols, and fourteen special symbols for such things as verb tense, types of objective cases, and so forth.

In 1926 Edith Fitzgerald produced a system for developing sentence patterns in deaf children's language, which is still widely used. The **Fitzgerald Key** was first described in her book *Straight Language for the Deaf*. Schmitt (1966) describes it as follows:

> The Key itself consists of six columns headed by interrogative words and symbols indicating parts of speech and sentence functions: (1) subject (who:, what:); (2) verb and predicate words; (3) indirect and direct objects (what:, whom:); (4) phrases and words telling where; (5) other phrases and word modifiers of the main verb (for:, from:, how:, how often:, how much:, etc.); (6) words and phrases telling when:. Phrases and dependent clauses may be fitted into appropriate places in the column, and the use of connective symbols allows for compound sentences. Young deaf children begin language development by classifying words according to the more basic headings, such as who:, what:, and ═══════ (verb). The child's first few years in school are spent "building the Key." New language patterns and principles are explained in terms of the Key, and it serves as a reference and a self-correction device for the children to use in live and written language work. In her book Fitzgerald gives numerous suggestions for building the Key. Although a sequence of language development is indicated, Fitzgerald states that the actual order of introduction of language structures should depend upon the needs of the children.

The whole structure of Fitzgerald's system is very much in keeping with the tenets of the structuralist linguists that words are the basic building blocks of sentences and that sentences are formed by a left-to-right combination of words into strings. Such an approach implies that sentences can be accounted for entirely in terms of their "surface structure" (the words we see or hear). We will see in later chapters that the surface structure view of language has severe limitations. However, to a considerable extent, structuralist theories of sentence building still hold sway among teachers of deaf children, although they are often heavily tempered by such **natural approaches** as that advocated by Mildred Groht (1958). Recently, additional naturalist notions have been advocated by van Uden (1968), Simmons (1967), and Moog (1970). These writers are questioning the utility of traditional approaches. They argue that it is not until a child has a sound basis of early language that one should begin to introduce teaching via formal grammatical notions such as parts of speech, sentences, clauses, and so forth, and that most stress must always be placed on **reflective conversational approaches.**

We stated previously that native speakers of English have "internalized" a set of rules of grammar which enable them to understand implications of sentences which are not apparent in the surface structure signal of the sentence (whether this signal is visual or auditory); that is, we can *understand sentence meaning, detect grammatical and ungrammatical utterances*, know when sentences are *synonymous* or *ambiguous*, and understand the internal *relationships between parts of sentences*. The broadest generalization one might make about the results of recent research dealing with deaf children's syntax is that deaf children apparently do not adequately internalize this knowledge (see Quigley, Smith, and Wilbur, 1974). In the terminology of van Uden (1968), their language is not "transparent" to them and they are unable to break through its surface forms to an understanding of the meaning of any but the most simple sentences. Van Uden feels that this is due to the grammatical formalism of much of our teaching of deaf children. He has characterized traditional approaches as **constructivist** in that they take words ("parts of speech") as ingredients, put them together (in "Keys" or even just in speech and writing in less formal ways), and "bake" them hard into sentences which are rote-learned by the child, resulting in the deaf child's failure to attain the flexible internalization of rules that most hearing children acquire even before they start school.

Let us stress once more that the information presented in this book, on syntax and on language development, is for the benefit of the *teacher* rather than the *pupil*. The teacher needs this kind of information to understand both Standard English structure and the deaf child's deviations from that structure, and to enable her to structure language materials and techniques to aid the deaf child in acquiring mature language usage. As stated in the Preface, formal teaching of grammar to hearing students produces little or no improvement in their language, and a like situation probably applies to deaf pupils.

CHAPTER 2

Transformational Generative Grammar: A New Viewpoint

As do all scientists, linguists continue to build on the work of their predecessors. Researchers throughout the centuries, since the time of the ancient Greek and Indian philosophers, have achieved linguistic insights which still seem innovative today. Nevertheless, science continues to grow, and so it is with linguistics—theories of the past must be modified and improved if progress is to be made.

For linguistic science, the year 1957 is a landmark in this process of growth. For it was in that year that two different publications proposed the "new" (to linguists at that time) idea of "linguistic transformations." One of these was an article by Zellig Harris entitled "Co-occurrence and Transformation in Linguistic Structure"; the other was the book *Syntactic Structures*, by Harris's former student Noam Chomsky. Chomsky's work received the greater recognition of the two, and he is now widely known as the father of **transformational generative grammar**, commonly called **transformational grammar** or **generative grammar**.

Chomsky, deviating from the then prevalent emphasis on phonology, based his early work almost entirely on syntax, and attempted to display the failure of the structuralists to truly account for many of the syntactic phenomena of language. Chomsky's novel point of view assumed that, regardless of the depth of understanding a person may have of the meaning of words or morphemes in a language, and of their pronunciation, his understanding of sentences—which Chomsky

9

claimed are the basic units of communication in language—could still be completely inadequate. This can easily be observed if we compare the following two seemingly "simple" sentences.

(**1a**)   The deep-sea diver killed the sharks.

(**1b**)   The sharks killed the deep-sea diver.

It is easy to imagine how an editor might react if a reporter were to replace (**1b**) by (**1a**)! Notice, however, that although the meanings of the two sentences differ radically, the meanings of the individual component words *and* their pronunciations are identical.

Of course, it might be claimed that *order* is the crucial criterion of meaning. A native speaker of English knows, "obviously," that the word or phrase preceding the verb is the subject (which performs the action) and the one following it is the object (or recipient of the action). But one would then be forced to consider sentences like (**2a**) and (**2b**), which are synonymous.

(**2a**)   The deep-sea diver was killed by the sharks.

(**2b**)   The sharks killed the deep-sea diver.

Such examples would force either the retraction of the original claim that word order is *the* crucial element in meaning, or a refining of the definition of "the subject of a sentence." (Linguists often make a distinction between the **grammatical** and **logical subject** of a sentence. "The sharks" is the logical subject of both the above sentences, but the grammatical subject of (**2a**) is "the deep-sea diver.") Even more perplexing would be examples like sentence (**3**).

(**3**)   The deep-sea diver, who was diving for the treasures pirates had hidden centuries ago, killed the sharks.

Notice that here the subject-object pair, "the deep-sea diver—the sharks," is separated by several verbs and several nouns. These nouns themselves can be characterized as subjects or objects of the different verbs, and the relevant decisions cannot be made on the basis of word order alone. It is evident from these examples that something much more complex than word order is necessary to determine the structural functions and relationships of the various sentence parts.

The Structuralist Approach

Although the emphasis of structuralist linguistic study was on phonology, some structuralists, notably Charles Fries and Eugene Nida, developed means of describing the various classes of sentence structures. We will briefly discuss some of their methods and findings, and then some of the arguments of Chomsky and other transformationalist theorists which display the inability of these structuralist formulations to adequately explain some of the facts of language.

One possible way to proceed (actually attempted by some structuralists) is to appeal to word order, as we have already suggested. In addition to the difficulties already described, there are still more serious ones for this solution. With this procedure, structuralists simply attempted to list all the possible types of sentences based on possible sequences of word classes. For example, *Art N V Art Adj N N* (where Art = Article, Adj = Adjective, N = Noun, V = Verb) is a possible sentence pattern of English, as evidenced by sentence **(2b)**. One difficulty arises with a pattern such as *Art Adj Adj N V*. That this is a possible English sentence word order is evidenced by sentence **(4)**.

(4) The big red ball bounced.

However, the same pattern also predicts that a sentence like **(4a)** should also be grammatical—and it clearly is not. It is highly unlikely that any native speaker of English would produce the adjectives in this order:

(4a) The red big ball bounced.

More serious is the fact that the ambiguity of sentences such as **(5)**, for example, is not distinguishable in structuralist systems.

(5) The shooting of the hunters disturbed me.

In this case both meanings of this sentence could only be represented by *Art N Prep Art N V Pron* (Prep = Preposition, Pron = Pronoun). Also, while sentences like **(6a)** and **(6b)** are obviously synonymous, their formulae are entirely different and word order provides no clue to this fact.

(6a) It was a donut that he ate.

(6b) What he ate was a donut.

And finally, such an explanation does not take into account the infinite capabilities of language. No matter how many sentence formulae we might list, we would still have only a finite (countable) number of possible structures. There would always be at least one more sentence not characterized by our formulae, since as we have shown (in Chapter 1 in our "house that Jack built" example), English consists of an *infinite* number of sentences.

In order to produce word-order formulae of the above type, it was necessary for the structuralists to define the word classes ("parts of speech") which might enter into such formulae. There were several criteria for such a definition: (1) *meaning*: simply define the classes according to meaning (as did the traditionalists), as in "a noun is the name of a person, place, or thing"; (2) *inflection*: that is, classify words according to their possible inflective endings: e.g., "a noun is a word that can be made plural"; (3) *syntax*: e.g., "a noun is a word which can substitute for another noun." Criterion (1) was excluded by the structuralists, because of their belief in the "separation of (linguistic) levels." That is to say, because of their particular empirical orientation, syntactic results could only be valid when obtained through the use of syntactic (and sometimes morphological) evidence; any appeal to semantics or phonology was not allowed. It is also clear that purely semantic definitions are extremely difficult to formulate. Are, for example, the words "idea" or "homogeneity" really the names of "persons," "places," or "things"? The second criterion (inflection) also failed to properly define class membership. For example, considering the above-cited example ("a noun is a word that can be made plural"), it is apparent that words like "magic," "pants," and "everyone," since they cannot normally be pluralized, would be excluded from the class of "nouns."

Criterion (3), therefore, was the most extensively applied of the three listed. Typically, the structuralists used this criterion by constructing **frames**—sentences with "blank spaces" into which words could be substituted one for another. Any word which could be substituted for another in a given frame and still produce a grammatically correct sentence was considered to be a member of the same class as the word for which it was substituted. Thus, for example, one structuralist definition might characterize a **nominal** as "any noun or expression which substitutes for a noun" in the following sentence frame:

(7) _____ destroyed the nation.

Thus the words "wickedness," "war," "strife," and "elephants" are all members of the same class since they can all fit into the same empty slot. If one is a nominal, then they all are. Notice, however, that "the wickedness," "the war," "the strife," and "the elephants" fit equally well into the above frame, showing that they also are "nominals," since they can substitute for a noun.

Now consider frame (8).

(8) The _____ destroyed the nation.

This is a nominal slot, as shown by the acceptability of such sentences as "The *strife* destroyed the nation." However, none of our second list of nominals as defined by the first frame above can fit into this slot. (They would produce "The *the strife* destroyed the nation," and so forth.) Hence "the strife" cannot be a nominal, thus contradicting our first test!

Now consider the expressions "wickedness may have"; "politicians ravaged and"; and "marble players completely." Each of *these* three phrases can be substituted into either of the above frames with perfectly good results! However, it would clearly be ridiculous to call them "nominals."

One of the major problems with the approach we mentioned above is its failure to differentiate the two meanings of sentences like (9).

(9) They are visiting Russians.

This is because words are not isolated units in English, but form natural groupings within the sentence. In one meaning of the above sentence "visiting" and "Russians" form a unit; in the other, "are" and "visiting" are most clearly related. The structuralists' usual solution to this problem is known as **diagraming**, or **parsing**, sentences. One method for accomplishing this, developed in the traditional period (the 1880's), is known as the **base-and-modifier technique**. Without going into details, this approach emphasizes the interrelationship of the words of a sentence, at the same time deemphasizing the order. The two senses of the above sentence would be diagramed, respectively, in the following two ways:

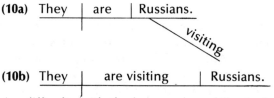

(10a) They | are | Russians.

(10b) They | are visiting | Russians.

A major difficulty with the base-and-modifier technique is that it does disregard word order; thus, "He looked up the number" and "He looked the number up" would both be diagramed as **(11)**.

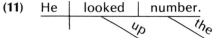

(11) He | looked | number.

Another problem with this approach is that it is unable to demonstrate what are called **hierarchies** in the word relationships in sentences. "Hierarchy" is the technical term for our knowledge that words in sentences fall into certain groups, and that there can be groups within groups. For instance, we are all aware that in a sentence like "John threw his books in the fire," "threw his books in the fire" is a natural grouping ("his books in" is not), and that within this group is another—"in the fire," within which is still another group—"the fire." These groups constitute a linguistic hierarchy and this knowledge of ours about sentence structure clearly must be accounted for in any adequate grammar, but the base-and-modifier technique of sentence analysis is unable to handle its expressions. For these reasons, **Immediate Constituent Analysis** was devised and elaborated by Eugene Nida (1960) and other structuralist linguists. This method succeeds in maintaining the surface word order while at the same time indicating many of the hierarchical relationships of the sentence. So, for our ambiguous sentence **(9)**, we have the following two analyses.

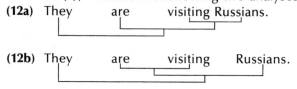

(12a) They   are   visiting Russians.

(12b) They   are   visiting   Russians.

The first diagram shows clearly that "visiting Russians" is a unit in this case, and that "are visiting Russians" is a higher (more complex) unit. (Note that this phrase corresponds to the traditional "predicate" of the sentence.) On the other hand, in the second diagram, "are visiting" is a lower unit, with again "are visiting Russians" forming a higher one. The diagrams show clearly that, although the words and their order are the same, the structures (and consequently the meaning) of the two sentences are very different, something that the base-and-modifier technique could not demonstrate.

However, even the Immediate Constituent Analysis inherits some of the problems of a simple word-order analysis. First of all, sentence **(4)** ("The big red ball bounced"—grammatical) and **(4a)** ("*The red big ball bounced"—ungrammatical) would have exactly the same structure under Immediate Constituent Analysis. Secondly, there is still the difficulty of accounting for the possibility of an infinite number of English sentences. That is, we can list a hundred, a thousand, or a million immediate constituent structures, but there would always be many sentences which did not match any of these structures. And finally, while Immediate Constituent Analysis manages to account for the kind of ambiguity resulting from differing hierarchical relationships, it still cannot explain certain other ambiguities, such as "Visiting relatives can be fun," which can be diagramed only one way:

(13) Visiting relatives can be fun.

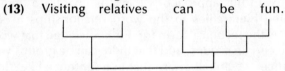

Sentences with entirely different structures but very similar meanings (such as "It was a donut that he ate" and "What he ate was a donut") are also outside the bounds of explanation for a system of Immediate Constituent Analysis. There is no reasonable way in which Immediate Constituent Analysis diagraming can show that these two sentences are closely related; that they are, in fact, "transformations" of an underlying meaning, "He ate a donut."

The Goals of Transformational Grammar

Chomsky in *Syntactic Structures* (1957) displayed many other inadequacies of structuralist syntax similar to the ones discussed above, but using much more formal and mathematical methods than we have, and at much greater length. He then presented a completely new framework which he claimed could account for these difficulties. His goals were quite different from those of the structuralists. Rather than simply attempting to *describe* the structure of language as the structuralists had, Chomsky wanted to *explain* it, and for this reason proposed a "generative" model of syntax which employed "transformations" to link the underlying meaning of a sentence to the sentence as it was actually pronounced (or written; the general principles are the same). (See Figure I, below.)

Figure 1

Chomsky argued that even if it could be shown that Immediate Constituent Analysis could adequately *describe* grammars (which is, as we have seen, far from simple), certain facts about the manner in which a speaker of the language understands sentences would still remain unexplained. At the same time, grammars developed from Immediate Constituent Analysis would have to be enormously complicated and clumsy in handling the problems we have discussed above. One of Chomsky's major contributions was to provide simple and elegant solutions to these problems. Some of these difficulties have already been pointed out; as another example, Chomsky says:

> We will have to place many restrictions on the choice of [the verb] in terms of subject and object in order to permit such sentences as: "John admires sincerity," "sincerity frightens John," "John plays golf," "John drinks wine," while excluding the 'inverse' non-sentences "sincerity admires John," "John frightens sincerity," "golf plays John," "wine drinks John."

He then points out that each of these sentences corresponds to a sentence with the verb "is" + the past participle of the verb (i.e., a passive sentence). However, notice that "Sincerity is admired by John," "John is frightened by sincerity," "Golf is played by John," and "Wine is drunk by John" are grammatical, while "*John is admired by sincerity," "*Sincerity is frightened by John," "*John is played by golf," and "*John is drunk by wine" are not. We can see that under an Immediate Constituent Analysis for the corresponding passive sentences, all the subject-verb-object restrictions (that is, restrictions on what subjects and objects can occur with what verbs) of the original active sentences will have to be restated, but *in the opposite order* (with subjects replacing objects, and vice versa). This is clearly the type of complexity and redundancy in a grammar that should preferably be avoided.

Any native speaker understands that an active sentence and its corresponding passive mean the same thing (ignoring some qualifications to be discussed later). For example, consider the following.

(14a) The hunters found Bigfoot's footprints.

(14b) Bigfoot's footprints were found by the hunters.

Any theory which emphasizes word order will fail to explain the manner in which the native speaker understands these sentences to be the same.

Competence and Performance

Chomsky made an important distinction between what he called **competence** and **performance**. Listening to a speaker in a normal speaking situation, one becomes rapidly aware of the imperfection of everyday speech, laden as it is with ungrammatical sentences, false starts, hesitations, repetitions, and so forth. Similarly, the hearer often makes temporary errors in understanding and subsequent changes in his interpretations. According to Chomsky, such errors can all be explained through situational influences (e.g., momentary distractions) and physical (e.g., tiredness) or mental (e.g., memory) limitations of human beings. A musician may know the score of a piece of music perfectly, yet perform it imperfectly in a particular instance; an accountant may make errors in his arithmetic, although obviously he has long since learned all the rules of addition, subtraction, multiplication, and division. In an analogous manner, Chomsky said, "a native speaker of English 'knows' all the 'rules' of his language perfectly, but unintentionally violates them in actual 'performance'—speaking a sentence." (Remember that linguistic "rules" are not decrees about what should be said, but formulas for determining which sentences are grammatical and which are not.) Therefore, Chomsky's grammar was concerned with defining the "internalized" set of rules of an "ideal" native speaker (or hearer) or competence, as opposed to the sometimes inconsistent language as it is outwardly used, referred to as performance. Thus, Chomsky (1965) says:

> Linguistic theory is concerned primarily with an ideal speaker-listener, in a completely homogeneous speech-community, who knows its language perfectly and is unaffected by such grammatically irrelevant conditions as memory limitations, distractions, shifts of attention and interest, and errors (random or characteristic) in applying his knowledge of the language in actual performance.

We thus make a fundamental distinction between competence (the speaker-hearer's knowledge of his language) and performance (the actual use of language in concrete situations). Only under the idealized conditions set forth by Chomsky is performance a direct reflection of competence. By dealing only with an ideal speaker-hearer's underlying competence, the goal of providing a systematic description of language becomes much more feasible. (More recent theory is tending to enlarge the realm of competence so that it includes many aspects of what were formerly considered under the category of performance. However, the point of separation is not what interests us; the important point is that the two are distinct.)

Transformations

In attempting to describe the competence of an ideal speaker-hearer, while at the same time seeking to overcome some of the problems of a structuralist description such as have been mentioned, and to explain the way the speaker-hearer "understands" sentences of his language, Chomsky proposed a new mechanism, the **transformation**. Transformations apply to what is known as the **deep structure** (sometimes called **"underlying" structure**) of a sentence to "derive" the **surface structure**, or that entity to which the phonological rules (rules for pronunciation) will apply. Let us now consider what is meant by the term "deep structure."

We earlier discussed the synonymity of certain related sentence structures, one classic example being the active-passive pair. For example, the following active sentence **(15a)** and its passive counterpart **(15b)** have basically the same meaning.

(15a) John admires sincerity.

(15b) Sincerity is admired by John.

As a more extreme example, consider sentences **(14a-g)** in Chapter 1, all of which are synonymous. This is where the concept of deep structure enters linguistic theory. *The deep structure of a sentence is the level at which the grammatical relationships are preserved.* To see what this means, let us look for a moment at two famous sentences presented by Chomsky:

(16) John is easy to please.

(17) John is eager to please.

A native speaker of English knows that in **(16)** John is the person who is pleased, and in **(17)** he is the person who does the pleasing. Yet the surface structures of these sentences are identical. Our knowledge of the relationships between "John" and "pleasing" in these sentences cannot be contained in the surface structure. It resides somewhere else: in the deep structure, "where the grammatical relationships are preserved," i.e., where the "sentences" are very abstractly represented.

Deep structures are often formally represented by means of **tree** diagrams, which are simply a notational device for representing the hierarchical structure and internal relationships of sentences. Thus, in the framework of Chomsky's early book, *Syntactic Structures*, the deep structure of the active-passive pair **(15a-b)** would be roughly as follows. (We have omitted many details in this tree for the sake of clarity. In this case the deep structure is very much like the eventual surface active version of the sentence, but we will see later that this is not always so.)

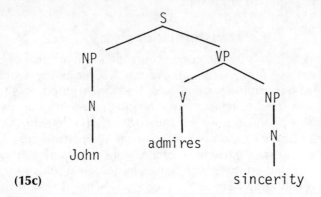

(15c)

Similarly, the deep structure underlying all of the sentences **(14a-g)** of Chapter 1 would be something like **(18)**. (Triangles will be used in trees to represent structure whose detail is irrelevant to the point in question.)

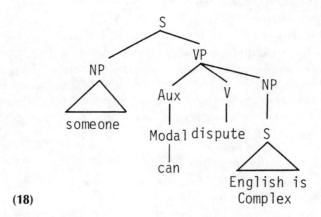

(18)

A series of "transformational rules" would then be applied to change this deep structure into the set of surface structure sentences in our list—a slightly different set for each sentence.

It is easy to see that in order to account for all the various relationships within a sentence, deep structures in some cases are necessarily quite complex. We will not attempt to explain all the details of these tree diagrams at this time; they will become clearer later. The crucial point is that one deep structure may result in one, two, or even many superficially different surface structures, and that the mechanism which accounts for this is the system of syntactic transformations. Thus, our first deep structure meets the conditions for the application of the passive transformation, which (in very simple terms) exchanges the subject and object of the sentence, at the same time inserting some additional **morphemes** which change the form of the verb, as follows. (The double-bladed arrow is the symbol to indicate application of a transformation.)

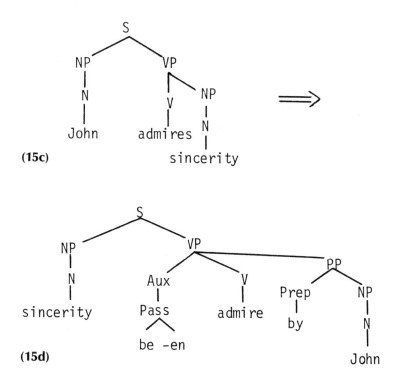

(15c)

(15d)

Several other rules will then apply to tree **(15d)** to result in the passive sentence **(15b)**, "Sincerity is admired by John." These same rules, if applied to tree **(15c)** (without the application of the passive transformation), will result in the active sentence **(15a)**, "John admires sincerity."

Similarly, in our second example, one deep structure corresponds to at least seven different surface structures, each of which is the result of the application of a slightly different series of transformations to the one deep structure tree. (Notice that one transformation which must apply in all seven cases is Negation, which makes a sentence negative. Without its application, our deep structure would give us sentences meaning "Someone can dispute that English is complex.")

We have given examples of cases for which *one* deep structure corresponds to *several* surface structures. Similarly, it is possible for *one sur-*

face structure to result from *several different deep structures*. As an example, consider the following sentence, with which you are already familiar.

(19)   The shooting of the gangsters frightened me.

There are at least two possible deep structures for the above sentence, as follows:

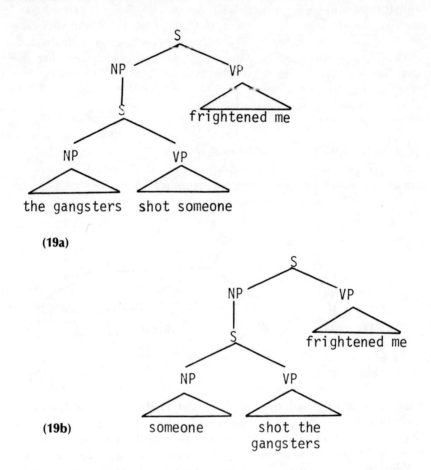

(19a)

(19b)

Notice that in the two possible interpretations of the sentence, the shooting is performed in one case by the gangsters, and in the other by someone else. This information is displayed by deep structures **(19a)** and **(19b)**, respectively, the distinction being lost in surface structure. Recall again that deep structure is the level at which the underlying relationships of the parts of a sentence are represented.

Earlier it was pointed out that one of Chomsky's arguments for the necessity of transformational rules (and thus a level of deep structure) was the desire to characterize a native speaker's understanding of, and about, sentences. Consider the following two sentences.

(20) The teacher asked the student to leave the room.

(21) The teacher promised the student to leave the room.

It should be clear that the surface structures of the two sentences are identical; yet it is equally clear that the internal relationships are different. If the requested (or promised) action of leaving is carried out, in the first sentence it will be the student who leaves; in the second example it will be the teacher. Any native speaker understands the difference. This can only be conveyed by the deep structures: the deep structure subject of "leave" will be "the student" in the first case, but "the teacher" in the second.

A very similar concept was often represented in traditional grammar, where it was often stated that a command such as "go home" has an "understood" subject, "you." The deep structure analogue to this claim is tree **(22)**, as contrasted to the surface structure tree **(23)**, which has no explicit subject. In this case, we say that we have a transformational rule which "deletes" the occurrence of "you" in deep structure to produce the surface structure, which has no subject.

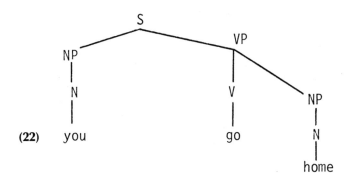

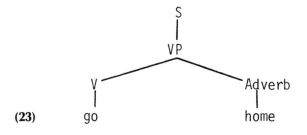

The Components of a Grammar

Now let us consider a model of the levels of a transformational grammar.

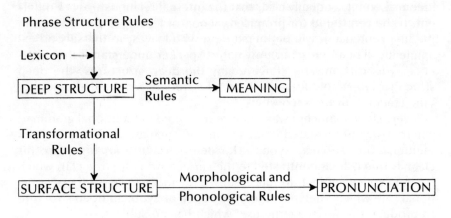

Figure 2

The above diagram demonstrates the important role played by the deep and surface structures. It is often said that the function of a grammar (or set of linguistic "rules") is to connect sound and meaning. As indicated in the diagram, meaning is integrally associated with deep structure, and sound with surface structure.

Phrase Structure

The purpose of the **phrase structure** (P-S) rules of a grammar is to create the deep structure, which is a representation of the internal relationships of a sentence. The result of the application of phrase structure rules is a **linguistic tree** (although other notational variants, i.e., alternative ways of writing the rules, are possible); the rules themselves define membership in the various grammatical classes of the language. For example, the P-S rule $S = NP + VP$ simply states that a sentence consists of a noun phrase plus a verb phrase, and the result in tree form is the following:

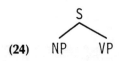

(24)

Note carefully the meaning of the equal sign; it might be interpreted variously as "consists of," "is realized as," or "is written as," but *never* as "becomes." It is necessary to make this point so as not to fall into the trap of believing that a speaker literally, before producing an utterance, begins with an *S* and changes it to an *NP* plus a *VP*. The model we are presenting is a linguistic model, not a psychological one; the relation between the two will be discussed more fully later on.

Following is a simple set of phrase structure rules which "define" or **generate** a small set of English sentences:

1. S (Sentence) = NP (Noun Phrase) + VP (Verb Phrase)
2. NP = N (Noun)
3. NP = Det (Determiner) + N
4. VP = V (Verb) + NP
5. VP = V

One sentence structure (illustrated in tree form) generated by the above set of rules is the following:

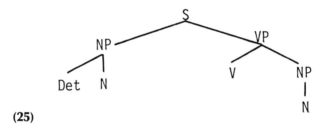

(25)

A step-by-step illustration of the "generation" of this tree is as follows:

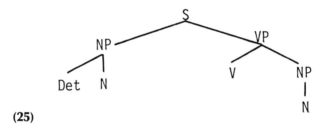

Derivation 1

Notice that there are other ways of applying the rules to generate the same structure. Rule 4, for example, could have applied *before* rule 3, with the same results. On the other hand, rule 1 *must* apply before rule 4; otherwise there would be no VP to rewrite. We say that the rules are **partially ordered** with respect to each other.

The Lexicon

The **lexicon** of a language could be defined roughly as its dictionary; it contains the vocabulary of the language. Listed with each item will be syntactic, semantic, and phonological information about that item. It is important to realize, however, that the lexicon consists not of words, but of morphemes. A morpheme is the minimal unit of grammatical structure and, in most cases, manifests a single constant meaning. The class of morphemes and the class of words overlap, but many morphemes are not words and many words are not morphemes. Appendix A presents a more detailed treatment of morphemes.

The lexicon contains, in addition to morphemes, rules for inserting these morphemes into the deep structures of sentences (that is, **lexical insertion**). For example, after lexical insertion into the structure **(25)** produced by our phrase structure rules, above, we might get **(26)**.

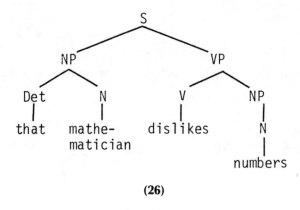

(26)

Of course, "The dog eats artichokes," or "The Huns prefer bologna," would also be generated, as well as sentences with different structures produced by the same set of rules applied differently, such as "Henrietta loves the acupuncturist," or "Barracudas swim."

In Chomsky's early theory as presented in *Syntactic Structures*, the lexicon was not a separate component of the grammar; its functions were performed by the phrase structure component, through the use of rewriting rules such as N→ *boy, dog, teacher, donut, Zinjanthrop-*

ist . . .; Det → a, an, the, . . .; V → walks, believes, circum-navigates . . ., and so forth. This approach, however, cannot account for the fact that lexical items are restricted in occurrence by the characteristics of the structure into which they are to be inserted. For example, there is no reason why the rules above would not generate sentence **(27)**.

(27)   The donut circumnavigates the teacher.

One influencing factor in lexical choice is the syntactic structure of the sentence. For example, choice of verb depends upon whether a noun phrase follows, in which case a **transitive verb** like "hit," "deploy," or "circumnavigate" would be used; or whether no noun phrase follows the verb, in which case an **intransitive verb** like "swim," "stammer," or "soliloquize" would be chosen. This would be indicated in the lexicon by **features** on the lexical items. For example, a transitive verb like "deploy" would be marked [__NP] (where a blank indicates insertion of "deploy"); indicating that V can be rewritten as "deploy" only if there is a noun phrase following.

Lexical insertion is also restricted by word combinations in the sentence. We saw earlier that while a sentence like "Sincerity frightens John" is perfectly acceptable, the corresponding sentence with subject and object interchanged, "*John frightens sincerity," is strange and unnatural, to say the least (except perhaps when used in some metaphorical sense). This is a result of the empirically demonstrable fact that "frightens" occurs only before *animate* objects. John can frighten the dog, the elephant, or the aardvark, but not sincerity, the tree, an idea, or the ace of spades.

To account for "cooccurrence restrictions" of the first type, called by Chomsky **strict subcategorization features**, and the second type, called by Chomsky **selectional restrictions,** items in the lexicon must be marked by both syntactic and semantic features. Thus, for example, if + represents presence of a quality and – its absence, "John" would be represented as [N, + animate, + human, + male], and "sincerity" as [N, + abstract]. The verb "frighten" would have the features [V, [__NP], [__ + animate]]. This would be interpreted as saying " 'frighten' is a verb; it is a transitive verb which occurs before noun phrases, and it can occur only with animate objects." Notice that there is a hierarchy of selectional restriction **features,** so that [+ human] is automatically subsumed under [+ animate], and thus any verb which occurs with [+ animate] objects can occur with [+ human] objects.

In *Syntactic Structures*, Chomsky introduced the now-famous sentence "Colorless green ideas sleep furiously." He claimed that, although this sentence is semantically strange, it is *syntactically* "grammatical," and most native speakers would concur with this judgment. Notice that with selectional restrictions such a sentence will be ruled out as "ungrammatical." Selectional restrictions are of necessity dependent upon lexical features for their definition; whether they themselves are actually a part of the syntactic component, or of the semantic component, is open to debate.

The Transformational Component

Joint application of the phrase structure and lexical rules results in the deep structure of a sentence. This deep structure is subject to transformational rules of the language. We have already discussed one such transformational rule, the Passive transformation. A transformation, in simple terms, applies to one linguistic tree to change it into another. The structure may be changed in various ways: through insertion of new elements, deletion of old elements, or movement of existing elements of a tree.

When Chomsky first introduced transformations, a significant concept was that of **kernel sentences**. In order to understand this term, it is necessary to realize that Chomsky allowed for both **obligatory transformations** (those which *must* be applied if their conditions are met), and **optional transformations** (which may or may not be applied). An example of an obligatory transformation would be "Subject-Verb Agreement," which gives us, for example, "John goes" rather than "John go." Optional transformations include those which form passives, or negative sentences or questions.

Kernel sentences, then, were those which resulted from application of the obligatory rules, and no optional rules, to a deep structure representation. Consider, for example, the following deep structure:

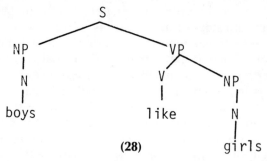

(28)

If the obligatory transformations only are applied, we obtain the kernel sentence "Boys like girls." If we apply the (optional) Passive transformation (as well as the obligatory ones), the result is "Girls are liked by boys." Application of the (optional) Negative transformation gives us "Boys do not like girls," and the (optional) Yes-No Question transformation gives "Do boys like girls?" We might even apply all three of these optional transformations, resulting in "Are not girls liked by boys?"

Chomsky also introduced the idea of **generalized transformations**. These transformations are those which combine two or more deep structures into either **compound sentences** joined by "and," "but," "or," etc., or **complex sentences** with, for example, relative clauses (such as "The man who the dog bit bit it back"). Transformations which are not generalized (and which thus apply to a single deep structure) Chomsky called **singulary transformations**.

We see, then, that kernel sentences are basically simple, affirmative, declarative sentences of the language—those which most native speakers would consider to be most basic.

With the publication of Chomsky's *Aspects of the Theory of Syntax* in 1965, the power of transformations was greatly reduced, this being accompanied by an increase in the complexity of deep structures. This was accomplished in the following ways.

First, all transformations became obligatory; the deep structure tree contained all information necessary for determining which rules would apply. (Remember that deep structures result from application of the phrase structure rules.) Thus, the declarative, passive, negative, and question forms of example **(28)** would differ in the deep structure as follows:

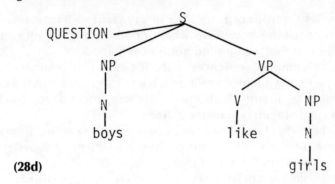

(28d)

All the transformations discussed earlier would still be necessary, but they would now all be obligatory, and in some cases reformulated somewhat. Applications of all obligatory transformations would result in the sentences "Boys like girls," "Girls are liked by boys," "Boys do not like girls," and "Do boys like girls?", corresponding to **(28a)**, **(28b)**, **(28c)**, and **(28d)** above.

The reason for this revision was the desire to simplify and constrain the grammar by adding the requirement that "all transformations preserve meaning." If the deep structure, for example, contained no marking for negation (negation being introduced by an optional transformation), then the Negative transformation would be adding semantic information which was absent in the deep structure. By adding this requirement, the deep structure became a well-defined input for those rules determining the meaning of the sentence.

The second major change was that all transformations became singulary; complexities such as coordination and relativization were now generated by the phrase structure rules. Deep structures such as the following were now possible.

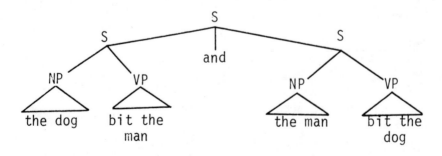

(29)

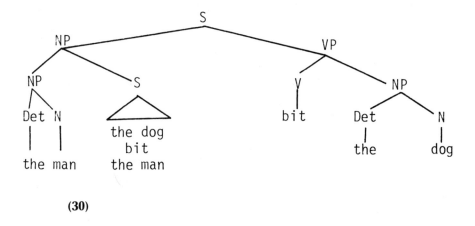

(30)

These deep structures would be acted upon by the transformational component to produce **(29a)** and **(30a),** respectively.

(29a) The dog bit the man and the man bit the dog.

(30a) The man who the dog bit bit the dog.

It has been necessary to explain both the older and newer transformational concepts because, although most theoretical research and much of the applied now relies on the *Aspects* model (or still more recent models), many non-linguists still work with kernel sentences and generalized transformations.

The Semantic, Morphological, and Phonological Components

Those components of the grammar which we have been discussing (phrase structure, lexical, and transformational components) comprise the syntactic portion of the grammar, and, in Chomsky's framework, the core of the grammatical structure. The three remaining components, the semantic, morphological, and phonological, are **interpretive components** which interpret structures generated by the syntax. Meaning is derived through the application of what have been called **semantic interpretation** or **semantic projection rules** to the *deep structure;* pronunciation of the sentence is determined by the application of morphological and phonological rules to the *surface structure* of the sentence. "Morphological rules" are those which determine how morphemes are combined; for example, that which tells us that "take" + PAST = "took" after the phonological rules have also applied.

Generative Semantics

The theory developed in *Aspects* is known as the **Standard Theory.** In more recent years a new framework has been developed known as **Generative Semantics.** The basic difference between the two is that the generative semanticists, rather than considering the semantics and phonology to be interpretive components, prefer to integrate them with the syntactic component. At the same time, they disclaim the existence of a level of deep structure separate from the level of meaning. The result is an essentially linear model:

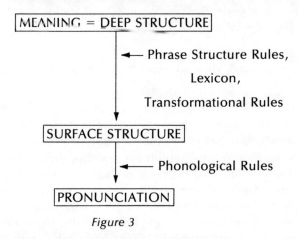

Figure 3

Making the deep structure equivalent to the meaning of the sentence has resulted in extremely abstract deep structures. Following is a deep structure (or **conceptual structure,** or **underlying structure,** or **abstract representation**) proposed by one generative semanticist (McCawley, 1968).

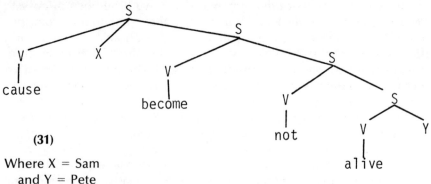

(31)

Where X = Sam
    and Y = Pete
This extremely abstract deep structure represents **(31a)**!
    (31a)   Sam killed Pete.

It is not at all clear yet what the implications of generative semantics are for applied areas and we will not be any more concerned with it in this book. As a theory, however, it is gaining wide acceptance among linguists, and more will probably be heard of it. Without arguing the relative merits of the two schools, we have chosen to work with relatively concrete deep structures, since for our practical purposes we feel that it would only be unnecessarily complex, as well as confusing, to be overly concerned with still-disputed theoretical issues. Our emphasis on the "Standard Theory" (that based on the *Aspects* Model) should not be taken to indicate a theoretical preference on our part.

The Value of Transformational Grammar

Now that we have introduced the basic concepts of transformational grammar, let us reconsider the various areas of linguistic knowledge which a native speaker possesses, and examine how the addition of a transformational component assists in explaining them.

1. A native speaker's ability to distinguish grammatical utterances from ungrammatical ones is easily accounted for. Grammatical utterances are simply those which are generated by rules of the grammar; ungrammatical sentences are not generated.

2. The infinite number of sentences available in a language (i.e., the capacity of native speakers to produce or understand **novel utterances**) can be transformationally generated in two different ways. In the *Syntactic Structures* framework, this is accomplished through the generalized transformations, which can join any number of deep structures to create increasingly more complex structures endlessly. In the more recent theory, complexity is generated early, in the phrase structure component. As an example, consider the following phrase structure rule:

(32) S → S and S

Repeated application of this rule would result in a **derivation** such as the following. (A derivation is a sequence of trees resulting from the step-by-step application of rules):

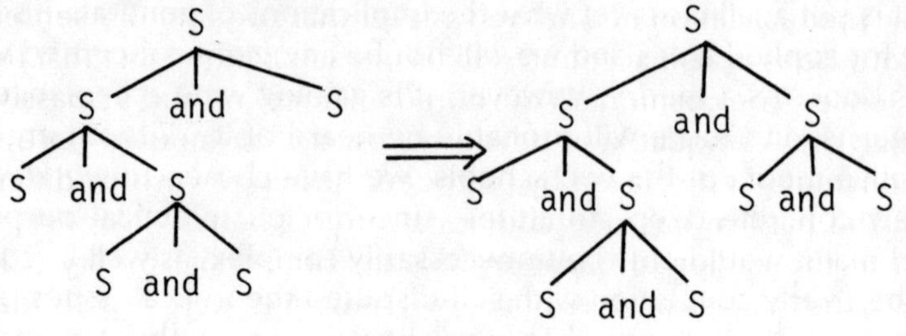

(tree diagrams)

, and so on.

Derivation 2

Obviously, this process could be continued indefinitely, because any *S* can *always* be rewritten again as *S and S*. As a second example, consider the following rules.

(33)   S → NP + VP
(34)   NP → Det + N + S

A sample derivation is as follows:

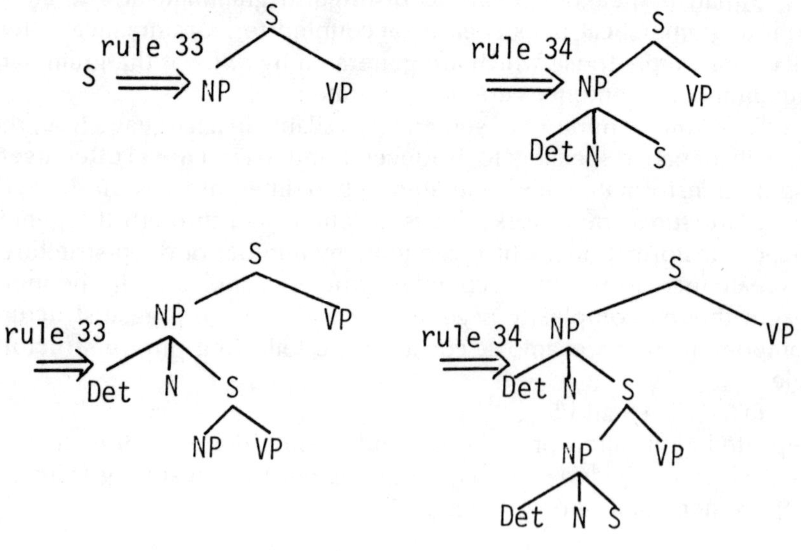

(tree diagrams)

Derivation 3

And so on.

Again, the possibilities for extension are theoretically infinite. This quality of Chomsky's phrase structure rules of being able to generate sentences within sentences indefinitely is known as **recursion** (i.e., the rules can be repeated endlessly).

3. The realization of a native speaker that two or more sentences are synonymous is also accounted for. For example, the fact that the active sentence "The cosmonaut devoured a kumquat" and its passive counterpart "A kumquat was devoured by the cosmonaut" are virtually synonymous is displayed by their deep structures, which differ only in that the passive has one additional node labeled "PASSIVE." (Recall that in the earlier formulation of transformational theory (Chomsky, 1957), the deep structures of the two sentences were exactly identical.)

4. Understanding of ambiguity is also accounted for. The ambiguous sentence "They are visiting Russians" has already been shown to have two distinctly represented surface structures in terms of constituent structure, and can thus be accounted for by the surface analysis of the structuralists. However, as we have seen, "The shooting of the gangsters frightened me" can be represented only one way on the surface. The ambiguity can be accounted for by postulating two different deep structures which merge into one and the same surface structure.

5. Functioning of the internal constituents of a sentence and their relationships can easily be defined at the level of deep structure. For example, an *NP* (noun phrase) directly "below" an *S* (sentence) node functions as the *subject* of that sentence; an *NP* directly "below" a *VP* (verb phrase) node acts as the *object* of the sentence. Thus, in the deep structure **(35)**, "boys" is the subject, and "girls" is the object, of the sentence.

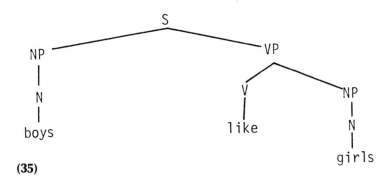

(35)

Summary

We see, therefore, that a transformational view of syntax is able to formally account for the way in which a native speaker understands his language. The question of whether or not a transformational grammar (a set of syntactic, semantic, morphological, and phonological rules) is a psychologically real model of how a speaker (or hearer) uses his language is still unresolved. Chomsky and other linguists have claimed that it is not; psychological studies have come to varying conclusions. It is probably fairly safe to say, however, that a transformational grammar is a fairly good model of a speaker-hearer's competence (that is, what he knows about his language). We must remember, though, that the *notation* of transformational grammar (arrows, trees, etc.) is simply a means of writing the rules down; various other notations would work just as well. Also, although such a grammar may describe a speaker-hearer's knowledge, it probably does not describe well how he actually uses his language.

To reiterate what has already been said in Chapter 1, our goal is to explain the manner in which transformational linguists believe English to be understood and produced by its speakers, and help teachers to be better able to analyze deaf students' language in order to understand the rules comprising their grammatical systems, rather than to teach rules (in the non-linguistic sense) about the proper way to use English. Again, we are teaching *concepts* and *methods* of analysis, rather than linguistic facts.

Research Applications of Transformational Grammar

Our concern so far has been mostly with theory, and it may be thought that all this seems very remote from the concerns of teachers in the classroom. We hope to show, however, that transformational grammar can be useful in helping teachers to understand the language problems of deaf children, but first we shall give some examples of how the ideas of transformational generative grammar theory have been applied in a number of areas.

1. The theory of transformational grammar has now been widely used for more than a decade in research into language development in hearing children. Some well-known works in this area are Paula Menyuk's *Sentences Children Use* (1969) and Lois Bloom's *Language Development: Form and Function in Emerging Grammars* (1970). The Harvard University group of psycholinguists led by Roger Brown have published many papers about their prolonged and intensive study of a small number of children. Several of their reports can be found in Brown's *Psycholinguistics: Selected Papers* (1970). Of particular interest to teachers of young deaf children is a paper co-authored by Roger Brown, Courtney Cazden, and Ursula Bellugi (1969) entitled "The Child's Grammar from I to III," where the authors examine the kinds of conversational interactions between mothers and children which may facilitate children's language acquisition. Ferguson and Slobin (1972) have provided a collection of the more important papers in develop-

mental psycholinguistics and Cazden (1972) an interesting introductory text.

2. Transformational grammar notions have also been effectively used to describe the language of children who are delayed beyond normal limits in acquiring it (Lee, 1966; Lee and Canter, 1971), and the language of children who grow up speaking a **dialect** that is not the "Standard English" used by most children in our culture (Labov, 1970), and the language of mentally retarded children (Schiefelbusch, 1972).

3. Some aspects of the theory have also been applied to teaching English as a second language (Jakobovits, 1970; Diller, 1971), to the analysis of written and spoken language of elementary and high school age children (Loban, 1963; Hunt, 1965; O'Donnell, Griffin, and Norris, 1967), and to the teaching of English syntax to high school students (Bateman and Zidonis, 1966; Mellon, 1969).

4. Several studies have used the ideas and terminology of transformational grammar as a theoretical framework for the analysis of deaf children's language. Schmitt (1968), Power and Quigley (1973), Quigley, Smith, and Wilbur (1974), and others have presented reports of "controlled" studies of deaf children's comprehension of complex syntactic structures. Taylor (1969) has presented an extensive transformational analysis of the written language of deaf children. The findings of these and other studies will be examined in detail in later chapters of this book.

We noted in Chapter 1 that methods of teaching language to deaf children usually reflect prevailing theories in linguistics. There are signs that the theory of transformational grammar is beginning to be reflected in curriculum development and teaching methods for deaf children. Hamel (1971) has produced a language curriculum which uses some notions of transformational grammar, and McCarr (1973 a,b) has produced a set of "Lessons in Syntax" based on the theory. Streng (1972) has published a text on transformational generative theory oriented toward "teachers of children with language and hearing disabilities" and has provided two "grammars" of different levels of complexity which she feels should represent the minimum linguistic competence of deaf students. All of these are directly applied studies and procedures, but transformational grammar theory also has much to offer educators of deaf children in a more general sense.

McNeill (1970) and others have advanced the notion that the productions of young hearing children should not be judged in comparison with the adult grammar of Standard English but as productions appropriate to the grammars of young children. The two-year-old child who produces such sentences as "All gone shoe," and "All gone milk," and "Big a truck" is not speaking "bad adult English" but "good two-year-old English"; the grammar of a two-year-old is simply different in many respects from that of adults. As the child matures and interacts verbally with adults around him, his grammar and his verbal productions approximate more and more the adult model. Thus, psycholinguists study child language as the productions of child grammars rather than as deviations from Standard English, and the study of language development becomes the study of the stages through which child language passes on the way to adult grammar, rather than merely a cataloging of language errors. Similarly, sociolinguists study variations in dialect, such as Black English, as appropriate rather than as undesirable deviations from Standard English.

It could be argued that this might all be very true for the hearing child, but that the handicap of severe prelingual deafness is such that the language of deaf children is often so deviant and so unlike Standard English that it could not possibly be produced by a set of rules; likewise, that the deaf child could not possibly be using a grammar to produce the sometimes almost uninterpretable written language that even many older deaf adolescents do indeed produce.

However, some impressive evidence for the existence of consistent rules of grammar in the language of deaf children which deviate from Standard English rules was presented by Taylor (1969). She performed a transformationally oriented analysis of the written language of deaf children which we will be looking at in some detail in later chapters. What concerns us at the moment is her demonstration of the existence of rules of grammar in the language of deaf children. She agrees with what we have outlined above, that the best evidence for a system of rules

> comes in the form of repeated non-grammatical constructions occurring consistently in the writing of a single child. Such structures suggest that a rule or rules idiosyncratic to that child's grammar are operating to produce predictable deviant structures in certain environments, deviant that is in terms of the target or adult grammar, not in terms of the child's grammar. One example of such idiosyncratic rules is provided by a congenitally deaf third grader whose [phrase structure] grammar apparently included only one rule expanding the verb phrase VP→ V + NP. Thus for producing sentences of the subject-verb-object pattern, e.g., *The man saw a bird*, his grammar was adequate. However, when he attempted constructions involving verbs normally intransitive in English, his rule invariably produced such deviant structures as *The ant fell a water* or *The ant sleep a bed*, sentences in which necessary prepositions have been omitted. Moreover, in attempting to produce sentences involving intransitive verbs without prepositional phrases, this student still applied the rule VP→ V + NP; however, he treated the main verb as the NP and inserted *have* as a place-holding pro-verb. The results were such anomalies as the following: *The ant have a*

swimming for *The ant swam* and *The bird have a fly* for *The bird flew*.

Examples of such idiosyncratic rules were also found on the transformational and morphological levels. One example of an idiosyncratic transformational rule is provided by a fifth grader whose grammar apparently included a rule of the following form: Given two strings of the form $NP_1 + VP_1$ and $NP_2 + VP_2$, where $NP_1 = NP_2$, then delete NP_2 and juxtapose VP_2 immediately after VP_1. This rule results in such ungrammatical predicate coordinations as *Ant walk found animals* and *Ant run get pin*. This student produced five of these compound predicates coordinated by juxtaposition, and no instance of a predicate coordinated with a conjunction, suggesting that at this particular stage in her language development her grammar included a different rule for coordinating predicates from that of the adult model.

Idiosyncratic rules at the morphological level are exemplified by a student who apparently had his own rules for inflecting verbs. This student seemed to have an exceedingly primitive system of morphological rules, as the bulk of the verbs in his corpus were of the form *is* + the uninflected verb stem, e.g., *Ant is jump on snail back*, *Ant is keep ball at home*, and *Father is go now*.

Taylor concludes that

the deaf children's language at the four grade levels not only implies the presence of internalized rules but further indicates that their language development is a process of gradually bringing these rules into closer and closer conformity to the adult model.

Such a conclusion is in agreement with the findings of the research which we will report in later chapters of this book. Deaf children do, in fact, possess a set of grammatical rules which frequently deviate from those of Standard English. They do, in general, bring these rules into closer and closer conformity to the adult model, although, as the evidence from this study indicates (and as teachers of deaf children already know), most deaf children have not achieved Standard English competence in many language structures even by 18 years of age.

CHAPTER 3

Phrase Structure

In Chapter 2, phrase structure rules and their place in the grammar were discussed. As a reminder, here again is the diagram of the components of a grammar. One additional bit of terminology which needs to be added here is that of the **base**, which is comprised of the phrase structure and lexicon together. The purpose of the base component of the grammar, as previously discussed, is to provide a deep structure

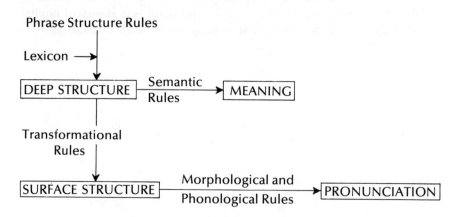

Phrase Structure Rules

Lexicon ⟶

DEEP STRUCTURE — Semantic Rules ⟶ MEANING

Transformational Rules

SURFACE STRUCTURE — Morphological and Phonological Rules ⟶ PRONUNCIATION

Figure 1

38

representation to which the semantic and syntactic rules can apply. Transformationalists have traditionally referred to the base as "generating" deep structure trees, and, coupled with the practice of "expanding" trees step by step, this commonly leads to the misconceived notion of the native speaker himself, each time he speaks, "thinking" of an *S* node, expanding it into an *NP* and a *VP*, then expanding the *NP*, then the *VP*, etc. A more realistic manner of viewing the base component has been proposed by McCawley, 1968. Attributing the original concept to the linguist Richard Stanley, McCawley states:

> the base component is a set of *node admissibility conditions*, for example, the condition that a node is admissible if it is labeled A and directly dominates [i.e., appears directly above] two nodes, the first labeled B and the second labeled C.

Thus, McCawley's hypothetical **node admissibility condition** says that the node A in a deep structure tree is *accepted* as well-formed by the phrase structure only if it appears in the following form:

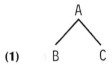

(1)   B   C

It follows that the node A is rejected if it appears in any of the following constituents:

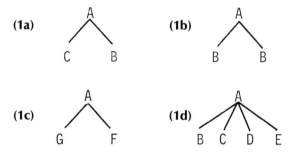

(1a) — C   B   **(1b)** — B   B

(1c) — G   F   **(1d)** — B C D E

To give a more concrete example, a node S is accepted by the phrase structure of English only if it dominates an NP node and a VP node, in that order, as follows:

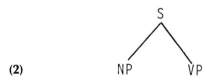

(2)   NP   VP

This is simply a more formal way of saying that in English, any sentence (S) must consist of a noun phrase (NP) followed by a verb phrase (VP). Assume, then, that an English deep structure tree contains the following subtree:

(2a)

The phrase structure will then reject this deep structure as ill-formed for English, on the basis of node-admissibility condition **(2)**.

Considered in this manner, the function of the phrase structure and lexical rules of the language is simply to examine each node in a deep structure tree to see whether it meets the conditions placed on it by the base and thereby qualifies as a well-formed deep structure tree. We shall accept this premise in what follows; however, since new ideas must be taught "step by step," and because past traditions have had a strong effect on linguistic formalization, it will be frequently necessary to use terms like "generate" or "produce" and to give examples of step-by-step derivations. It will be important to constantly keep in mind the ideas of "node admissibility conditions," and to remember that no claim is being made about the psychological mechanisms of real-life, real-time sentence production or comprehension.

The **expansion** of a node A to nodes B and C we shall represent as $A = B + C$. This is simply a shorthand version of the node admissibility condition **(1)**. The "+" symbol indicates that B appears to the left of C, and C to the right of B. Many nodes can be expanded in more than one possible way. (For example, a noun phrase may consist of a single noun [e.g., "Zulus"] or of a noun preceded by an article [e.g., "the Zulu"].) This is represented notationally by means of parentheses. For example, suppose that an A can consist either of $B + C$ or of B only. One way of representing this would be listing two rules:

    (3a)   Either $A = B + C$
    (3b)   or $A = B$

Another, shorter, way of saying the same thing is as follows:

    (3) $A = B + (C)$

The parentheses around the C mean that it is optional; it may appear in the tree below A or may not. The B is obligatory; it must appear.

Now consider rule **(4)**.

    (4) $A = (B) + C$

It should be clear that this is an abbreviation of two rules:

    (4a) $A = B + C$
    (4b) $A = C$

These, in turn, represent the following two tree representations:

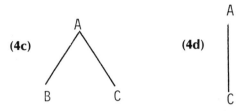

(4c)

(4d)

The pair of rules **(3a)** and **(3b)** could be abbreviated in one additional way, as follows:

(3c) $A = \begin{Bmatrix} B + C \\ B \end{Bmatrix}$

The "curly brackets" mean "choose one"; that is, either $A = B + C$ or $A = B$. Curly brackets are not often used in this way; parentheses are preferred where possible. However, there are cases in which it is impossible to use parentheses, yet simplification is desired. An example might be the following two rules:

(5a) $A = B$

(5b) $A = C$

These two rules can be abbreviated, using curly brackets, as **(5)**.

(5) $A = \begin{Bmatrix} B \\ C \end{Bmatrix}$

Similarly, the rule **(6)** is an abbreviation of **(6a)** and **(6b)**.

(6) $A = B + \begin{Bmatrix} C \\ D \end{Bmatrix}$

(6a) $A = B + C$

(6b) $A = B + D$

Thus we have two means of representing a choice between two or more alternative expansions of a single node (such as A): parentheses (when some elements are optional) and curly brackets.

Sentence Constituents

Now that we have our notation set out, we can proceed to discuss the phrase structure rules of English. The first rule (already referred to) relates the sentence to its **immediate constituents**. (A **constituent** is all the material dominated by a common node. Immediate constituents are those constituents of which a higher constituent is directly formed; they will be the nodes directly below and joined to the upper constituent in a tree.)

The rule is as follows:

(7) $S = NP + VP$

Recall that the rule as we have written it is simply an abbreviation for the following node admissibility condition.

(7a)

That is, a sentence consists of a noun phrase followed by a verb phrase. Consider now the following deep structure trees:

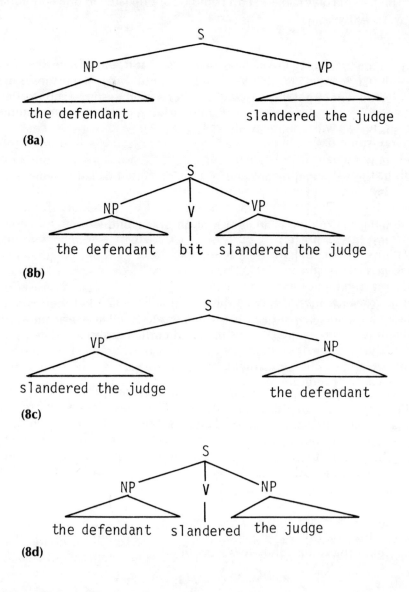

(8a)

(8b)

(8c)

(8d)

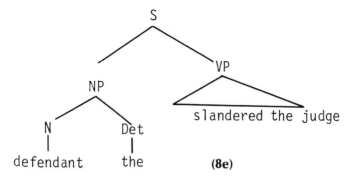

(8e)

Of the five trees above, only **(8a)** is well-formed. Notice that the structure **(7a)** occurs as a subtree of **(8a)**. Tree **(8b)** is ill-formed because the S node has an extra constituent, *V*, between the *NP* and the *VP*. The S node in **(8c)** has the correct constituents, *NP* and *VP*, but in the wrong order, resulting in an obviously un-Englishlike sentence.

Now study **(8d)** carefully. The string of words at the bottom of the tree is grammatical in English, but our node admissibility condition tells us there is something wrong. The point is this: The problem is not with the words themselves and their order, but rather with the tree. Recall that the reason trees (or similar devices) are necessary is that the words of a sentence are not all of equal status with respect to the other words in the sentence. The purpose of a tree, then, is to represent the relationships of the words in a sentence and to represent the sentence's various constituents. The problem with **(8d)** is that it tells us that the sentence "The defendant slandered the judge" consists of three constituents: "the defendant," "slandered," and "the judge." But a native speaker of English will recognize intuitively that the verb "slandered" and the object "the judge" are actually closely related and should form a constituent, as is the case in **(8a)**, where the *V* and the *NP* both belong to the constituent *VP*. (This constituent is traditionally known as the **predicate** of the sentence.) Thus tree **(8d)** does not properly represent a speaker's intuitions as to what the constituents are in this sentence. From a more formal and empirical point of view, it can be shown that there are transformations (for example, Conjunction Reduction, which will be discussed in a later chapter) which must refer to the verb and its object together, *as a constituent*. Tree **(8d)**, then, is ill-formed (as our node admissibility condition predicts), despite the seeming grammaticality of the string of words at the bottom of the tree.

Finally, let us consider tree **(8e)**. Although our rule (*S* = *NP* + *VP*) does not rule out this tree as ill-formed, "Defendant the slandered the judge" is clearly ungrammatical; and the ungrammaticality obviously arises from the ill-formedness of the first (or subject) *NP*. This leads us to our next phrase structure rule, that which deals with noun phrases.

Noun Phrase Constituents

Each **noun phrase** in English must contain a noun. Each of the following nouns is also a noun phrase:

begonias	John
elephants	Grinelda
lasagna	Samarkand

Often, however, a noun occurs with a preceding word which serves to "determine" the definiteness, indefiniteness, location, or some other quality of the noun. Some such classes of words, which are often collectively called **determiners**, follow.

Articles	Demonstratives	Genitives (Gen)
a/an	this	my
the	that	our
any	these	your
every	those	his
each		her
some		its
		their

So in addition to noun phrases like "lasagna," "begonias," or "Grinelda," we can also have "the lasagna," "a begonia," "those stalactites," or "his appendectomy." These facts can be captured by a noun phrase phrase structure rule (node admissibility condition):

   (9)   NP = (Det) + N,

where *Det* represents *Determiner* and *N* stands for *Noun*. Remember that the parentheses indicate optionality of an element; some noun phrases contain determiners and others don't, but all must contain at least a noun. Again the rule is an abbreviation, this time representing two different subtrees.

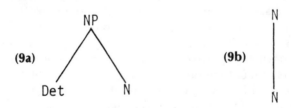

Now consider again trees **(8a)-(8e)**. The noun phrases of all trees but **(8e)** are well-formed; the subject noun phrase of **(8e)** contains the subtree **(8f)**, where the *N* incorrectly precedes the *Det*.

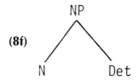

(8f)

And, although the NP subtrees of **(8b)**, **(8c)**, and **(8d)** are well-formed, we have already seen that the trees themselves are ill-formed by virtue of the fact that the immediate constitutents of the *S* are illegal in each case. The only tree remaining is **(8a)**, in which the *S*-subtree and the *NP*-subtree, as well as others we have not yet studied, are all well-formed.

Now notice the following additional trees:

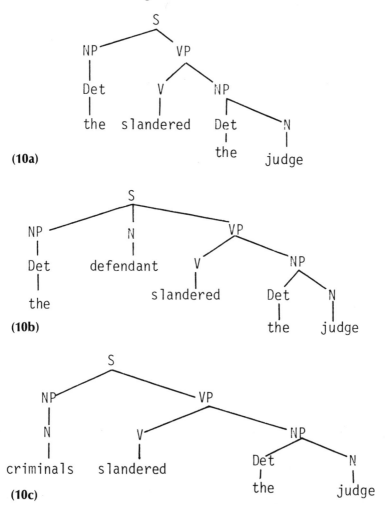

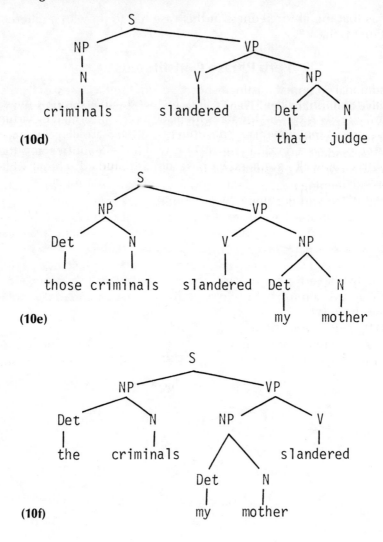

(10d)

(10e)

(10f)

Trees **(10a)** and **(10b)** above are clearly ill-formed, since an *NP* appears in each which dominates only *Det*; recall that node admissibility condition **(9)** requires a noun, as in **(9a)** or **(9b)**. Notice also that in **(10b)** the word order is correct; the structure is ruled out only by the NP rule. But again, this is intuitively correct. Tree **(10b)** implies that "the," "defendant," and "slandered the judge" are all of equal status, while it is intuitively clear that "the defendant" should be a constituent. Trees **(10c)**, **(10d)**, and **(10e)** are well-formed. In addition to the *S* constituents being well-formed, each *NP* constituent displays a form corresponding to either **(9a)** or **(9b)**. Finally, **(10f)** is ungrammatical, and it should be obvious that the ill-formedness in this case has to do with a different constituent, the *VP*.

Verb Phrase Constituents

Traditional grammar distinguishes two different classes of verbs: **transitive** and **intransitive.** Transitive verbs are those which take an object (a noun phrase); intransitive verbs cannot take an object. Some examples of transitive verbs are "bit" ("That boy bit *a girl*"), "slander" ("The defendant slandered *the judge*"), and "adore" ("Siegfried adores *Eleanor*"). As examples of intransitive verbs, we can consider "sleep" ("Sleeping Beauty slept"), "crawl" ("Some babies crawl"), and "shine" ("The sun is shining"). Many verbs in English can be either transitive or intransitive. For example, "paint" can be either transitive (as in "I painted *my wastebasket*") or intransitive (as in "Painters paint"). Other such verbs are "read," "write," "believe," and "eat."

Another way of saying that verbs can be transitive or intransitive is to indicate that a **verb phrase** consists of at least a verb and sometimes, but not always, a noun phrase (object). In our node admissibility notation, we have **(11)**.

    (11)   VP = V + (NP)

Following are trees for some of the above examples. Study them carefully, recalling our earlier rules *S = NP + VP* and *NP = (Det) + N.*
Intransitive:

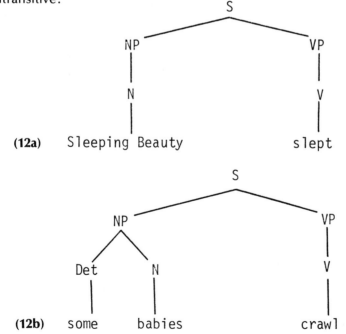

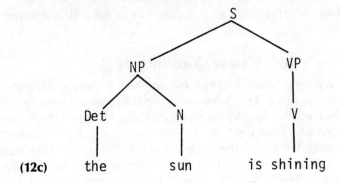

(12c)

Transitive:

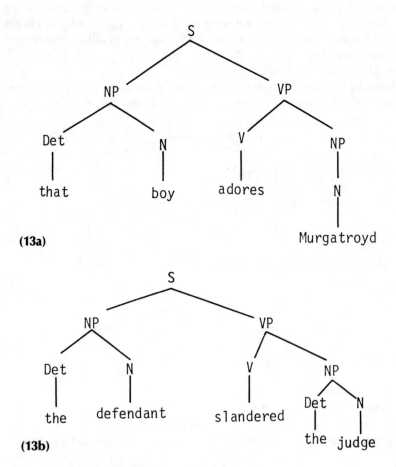

(13a)

(13b)

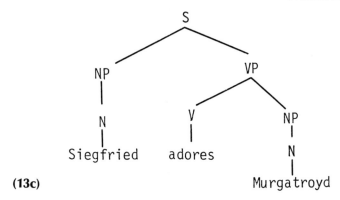

(13c)

More About Noun Phrases

Consider the following sentences:

(14) *The dog that bit the mailman* eats Wheaties.

(15) *People who water-ski* like water.

The italicized portions of these sentences appear intuitively to be constituents, but what kind? As will be seen as transformations are introduced later in this book, there are various syntactic tests which can be applied to resolve questions like these. We shall not go into a formal proof, but rather point out one simple test which offers some help here. Recall the PASSIVE transformation, which is described informally as applying to a transitive sentence like *"Some chimps* are learning NP_1

language" to interchange the subject noun phrase and the object noun NP_2

phrase—in this case giving *"Language* is being learned by NP_2

some chimps." (The differing subscripts on the two *NP*'s indicate that NP_1

the two noun phrases are different.) Now notice the following sentences:

(14a) *Wheaties* are eaten by *the dog that bit the mailman.*

(15a) *Water* is liked by *people who water-ski.*

It is clear that **(14a)** is related to **(14)**, and **(15a)** to **(15)**, by the PASSIVE transformation, indicating that the phrases "the dog that bit the mailman" and "people who water-ski" are noun phrases.

Recall now, however, our original formulation of the noun phrase rule, repeated below as **(16)**.

(16) NP = (Det) + N

If we attempt to structure the noun phrases under consideration by means of this rule, we notice that the formulation is not exhaustive:

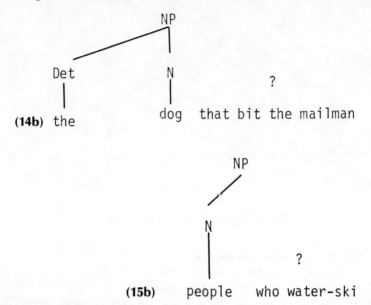

(14b) the   dog that bit the mailman

(15b)   people who water-ski

Phrases like the questioned ones above are known (both traditionally and in modern treatments) as **relative clauses**. Relative clauses are related to sentences in that they always involve a subject and a predicate. In the examples above, it is apparent that the one who *bit the mailman* is *the dog*, and that the ones who *water-ski* are *people*. In traditional terms, "that" stands for "the dog," and "who" stands for "people." In a transformational grammar, this relationship is captured quite straightforwardly, since, as you will recall, the deep structure of the sentence is very close to the actual meaning of the sentence. The result is that surface structure *relative clauses* are represented as *sentences* in deep structure. In this framework, the deep structures of **(14)** and **(15)** are the following:

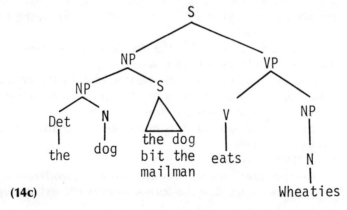

(14c)

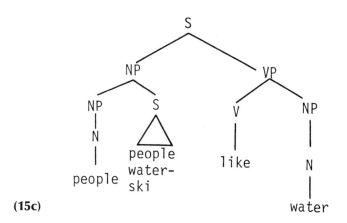

(15c)

The sentences inside the uppermost NP's are known as **embedded sentences**. (We have not specified the phrase structures of these embedded sentences; you should be able to do so on the basis of the rules presented thus far.) Now certain transformations, which will be considered in later chapters, apply to these deep structures to produce the surface structure sentences, with "the dog" and "people" being relativized to "that" and "who," respectively. In order to incorporate relative clauses into noun phrases, it is necessary for us to add an additional noun phrase rule:

(**17**)   NP = NP + S

Curly brackets can be used to combine the two NP expansion rules (**9**) and (**17**) as follows:

$$NP = \begin{Bmatrix} (Det) + N \\ NP + S \end{Bmatrix}$$

Notice that if an NP is expanded in the second way, a new NP, embedded in the first, results; this then must be expanded in turn. The result is a structure like that of (**14c**) or (**15c**).

In both examples presented above, the relativized word serves as subject of the embedded sentence. However, **relative words** can also replace sentence objects, as demonstrated by the following two sentences and their deep structure trees:

(**18**)   The house which the agent sold us had termites.
(**19**)   The man who Mary loves plays the saw.

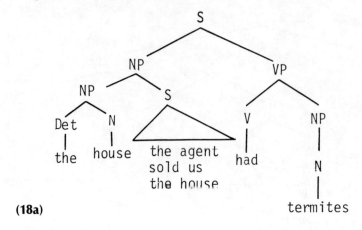

(18a)

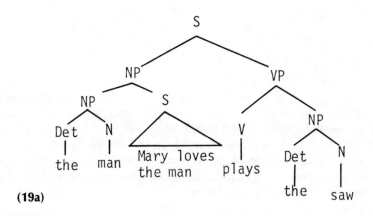

(19a)

More About Verb Phrases

Our verb phrase rule above does not account for sentences like the following:

    (20)   Vincent gave Millicent strychnine.

    (21)   The reporters asked the President questions.

In each of the above sentences, the verb is followed by two noun phrases, each of which seems to be in some sense an object of the verb. The traditional names for the two types of object are **direct object** ("strychnine," "questions") and **indirect object** ("Millicent," "the President"). The two deep structures will be represented as follows.

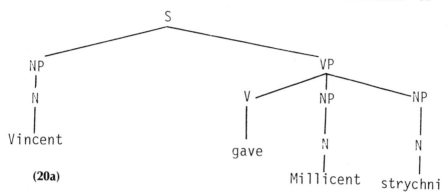

(20a)

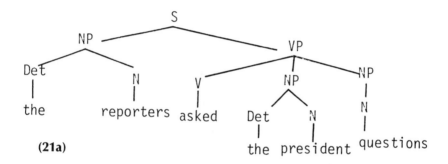

(21a)

This, of course, entails another revision of the verb phrase rule to incorporate an additional optional noun phrase:

    (22)   VP = V + (NP) + (NP)

Our verb phrase rule is still incomplete. Recall that in deep structure a relative clause like "that bit the mailman" is represented by an embedded sentence, in this case "the dog bit the mailman." Sentences are often embedded in the verb phrase as well as the noun phrase, as evidenced by the sentence "Superman likes *to snorkel*." There should be no disagreement that "likes to snorkel" is a constituent, and, in fact, a verb phrase. It is also intuitively correct to assume that the subject of "snorkel" is "Superman." (Notice that the subject of the embedded sentence is not always evident from the surface structure, as shown by "Herman asked Hermina to yodel" vs. "Herman promised Hermina to yodel," where the understood subject of "yodel" is different in each case.) Also, the "to" in "to snorkel" has no meaning, indicating that it is probably not present in deep structure. Thus, we will represent the deep structure of "Superman likes to snorkel" as follows:

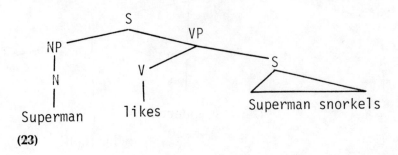

(23)

Finally, consider the shape of the verb in the examples we have seen. We have "crawl," "slandered," "is shining," and "adores," among others. Of these verbs, the only one which comprises a single morpheme (see Appendix A for more on morphemes) is "crawl." ("slandered" = "slander" + "ed," etc.) Now recall that the phrase structure component generates single morphemes rather than words; it is clear that *-ed* in "slandered," *is -ing* in "is shining," *-s* in "adores, "etc. must originate from a node separate and distinct from the *V* node. This node is called *Aux*, and such morphemes (some of them abstract ones, like PAST) are known as **auxiliaries**. Thus our verb phrase rule must be rewritten as follows.

   (24)   VP = Aux + V + (NP) + (NP) + (S).

Notice that the *Aux* node is obligatory, even though in certain cases ("crawl," for example) it may not have any effect on surface pronunciation. Also observe that the *Aux* node is generally considered to appear to the left of *V*, producing structures such as **(25)**.

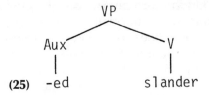

(25)   -ed   slander

Although there are theoretical arguments for such a treatment, we shall not consider them here. You will see later how transformations apply to give the surface structure **(26)**.

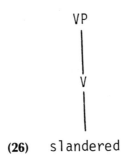

(26) slandered

Auxiliary Constituents

We have just seen that the auxiliary comprises several different types: *-s, -ed, is -ing* are some examples we have seen of surface auxiliaries. These morphemes may be categorized into three different classes, as follows:

Modals

Modals, or **modal auxiliaries,** comprise a set of words which precede the main verb and modify its meaning. There are several in English, a few of which follow:

can	may
could	might
shall	will
should	would

Modals function in many different ways, as will be clear from the following sentences:

Pearl *can* swim. (ability)
Pearl *could* swim if she knew how. (conditional)
Pearl *could* not swim until she was 30. (ability)
You *may* go if you wish. (permission)
He *may* go if he has time. (possibility)
He *will* go tomorrow. (future time)

Modals will be represented in our trees by nodes labeled *Modal*. For example:

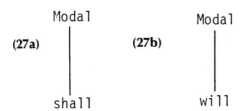

(27a) Modal | shall

(27b) Modal | will

Lexical insertion accounts for which particular modal will appear on the surface.

Tense

The concept of **Tense** has to do with time. However, although most of us think in terms of three basic time periods (past, present, and future), English has only two grammatical tenses: PAST and NONPAST. This can be demonstrated by considering the first person singular (i.e., "I") forms of the verb "believe".

Tense Time	PAST	NONPAST
Past	I believed	XXXXXXXXX
Present	XXXXXXXXXX	I believe
Future	XXXXXXXXXX	I will believe

Notice that, although the PAST morpheme is realized as -*d* attached to the verb, the form of the verb is the same in the present and future, with the only indication of future tense being the *modal* "will." (In cases other than the first person, things are not so clear; but this is the result of **agreement rules** rather than tense.) All underlying trees will contain a Tense node, and since Tense can be either PAST or NON-PAST, we need the following node admissibility condition:

(28)   Tense $= \left\{ \begin{array}{l} \text{PAST} \\ \text{NONPAST} \end{array} \right\}$

Aspect

The final auxiliary class we will consider is **Aspect**, which is one means English utilizes to make complex differentiations with respect to time relationships. The two Aspects of concern to us are **PROGRESSIVE** and **PERFECTIVE**. The main purpose of the PROGRESSIVE Aspect is, as the term implies, to indicate a continuing action; its basic elements are the verb *be* (in one of its various forms) and the **Present Participle** of the verb identified by the suffix -*ing*. Some examples follow:

(29)   Siegfried *is* play*ing* tiddlywinks.
(30)   Ferdinand *was* teas*ing* the bull.
(31)   The professor *will* be read*ing* a paper.

The PERFECTIVE Aspect signifies a period of time in relation to some other time specified in the context. In the PRESENT Tense, the PERFECTIVE appears on the surface as a present form of the verb *have* plus the **Past Participle** of the verb, which usually ends in -*ed* or -*en*. The **Present Perfective** refers to an action which took place an unspecified number of times at any time previous to the present. Although its meaning is difficult to put into words, the following examples should help to clarify its use.

(32)   Mother *has* cook*ed* breakfast.

(33)   He *has* beat*en* every opponent he ever played.

(34)   The case *has* gone to court.

The **Past Perfect** (i.e., the combination of PAST Tense and PER-FECTIVE Aspect) is used to refer to an action which occurred previous to some point of time in the past—the point of reference is specified in the context. It consists of the past tense of *have*, plus the Past Participle. For example:

(35)   Mother *had* cook*ed* breakfast before anyone else so much as stirred.

(36)   He *had* beat*en* every opponent he ever played, right up to his death.

(37)   The case *had gone* to court by the time the new evidence became available.

The two aspects, PROGRESSIVE and PERFECTIVE, can occur alone in a sentence, as in our examples thus far, or both can occur together, as in the following sentence.

(38)   Mary Jane has been drinking too much moonshine.

In this example, "been" is the Past Participle of *be* (indicating PER-FECTIVE Aspect), and "drinking" is the Present Participle of "drink" (indicating PROGRESSIVE Aspect). The tense is NONPAST, resulting in the form "has." The above factors can be summarized by rule (39).

(39)   Aspect = (PERF{PROG)

(We use interlocking parentheses to indicate that while both PERF and PROG are optional, one or the other must be chosen; that is, the node *Aspect* must always dominate *PERF, PROG*, or both.)

If we incorporate the three different types of auxiliaries into a phrase structure rule, the result is the following:

Aux = (Modal) + Tense + (Aspect)

Tense (either PAST or NONPAST) is necessary in every sentence; *Modal* and *Aspect* are optional. Following are some examples of sentences incorporating the various types of auxiliaries, in each case accompanied by their deep structure trees:

(40)   Penelope gave Ichabod a toad.

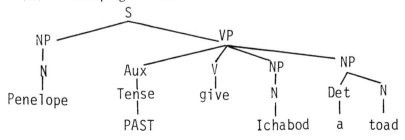

(41)   The judges will award the prize.

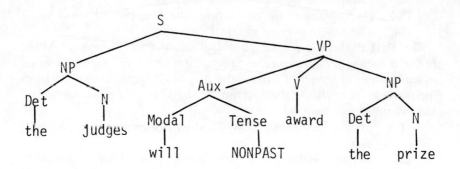

(42)   John had decided to transfer.

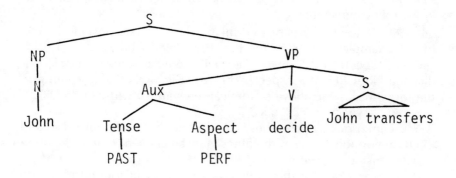

(43)   Axel has been forgetting lunch.

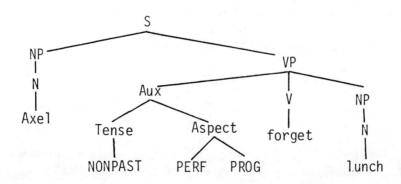

(44) Eleanor must have cried.

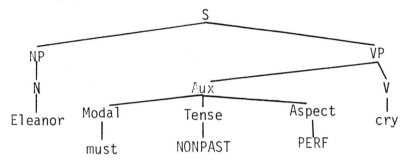

(45) Jacob might have been sculpting.

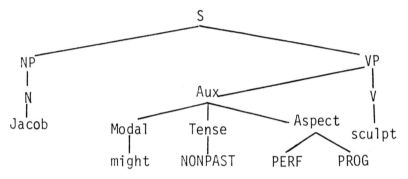

Some Additional Structures

So far we have the following list of phrase structure rules:

$$S = NP + VP$$
$$NP = \begin{bmatrix} (Det) + N \\ NP + S \end{bmatrix}$$
$$VP = Aux + V + (NP) + (NP) + (S)$$
$$Aux = (Modal) + Tense + (Aspect)$$
$$Tense = \begin{bmatrix} PAST \\ NONPAST \end{bmatrix}$$
$$Aspect = (PERF)(PROG)$$

There are still a few structures unaccounted for. We shall consider the following: conjunctions, adjectives, and prepositions.

In Chapter 2 it was pointed out that treatment of **conjunction** has varied since the publication of *Syntactic Structures*. Most linguists now consider the majority of conjoined structures to be related to conjoined sentences in underlying structure. For example, "Johnny and Billy like rattlers" is represented in deep structure by **(46)**.

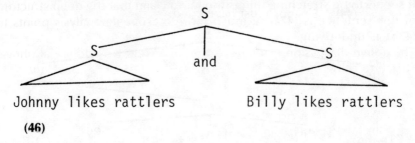

(46)

Tho surface structure results from a transformation known as Conjunction Reduction, to be discussed later. The following types of conjoined elements are generally derived from underlying conjoined sentences as well.

Conjoined Verb Phrases: Helen *ate her kumquat and drank her eggnog.*

Conjoined Verbs: The hunter *shot and killed* his prey.

Conjoined Adjectives: Fearless Fosdick is *big and strong.*

Conjoined Adverbs: The headhunters ran *quickly but silently.*

There are some conjoined noun phrases, however, which apparently cannot be derived from sentence conjunction. Consider, for example, sentence **(47)**:

   (47)   Lettuce and cabbage are similar.

(47a)

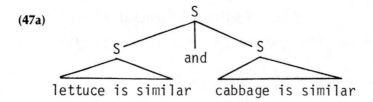

(47b)

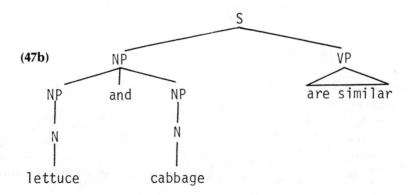

It seems to be stretching things too far to claim that the deep structure of this sentence is **(47a)**; a much more reasonable analysis points to **(47b)** as underlying.

The above discussion leads us to the following two additional phrase structure rules:

(48) $S = S + \begin{bmatrix} \text{and} \\ \text{but} \\ \text{or} \end{bmatrix} + S$

(49)   NP = NP + and + NP

Using brackets to combine these with our earlier S and NP rules, we have **(50)** and **(51)**.

(50) $S = \begin{bmatrix} S + \begin{bmatrix} \text{and} \\ \text{or} \\ \text{but} \end{bmatrix} + S \\ NP + VP \end{bmatrix}$

(51) $NP = \begin{bmatrix} NP + \text{and} + NP \\ (\text{Det}) + N \\ NP + S \end{bmatrix}$

Predicate Adjectives like those in sentences **(52)** and **(53)** have traditionally been considered to be a major syntactic category.

(52) The werewolves were *gruesome*.

(53) Prunes are *nutritious*.

Early transformational theory generated phrase structures like the following:

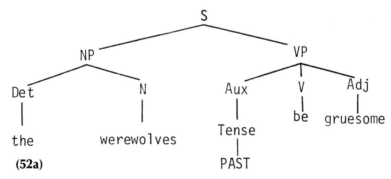

(52a)

Notice that if we were to take this position, we would be forced to revise our *VP* rule. However, recent theory has shown that main verbs and adjectives act very much alike. (See Appendix A in Lakoff (1970).) In addition, *be* in such sentences is virtually semantically empty; in fact, in some languages (Russian or Japanese, for example) a form of *be* does not occur in such constructions at all (giving sentences comparable to "The werewolves gruesome" and "Prunes nutritious"). All of the above suggests that we might consider adjectives to comprise a sub-

class of verbs in the deep structure, with *be* being inserted by a transformational rule (in English, but not in languages like Russian and Japanese). The deep structure of the two example sentences above would
then be:

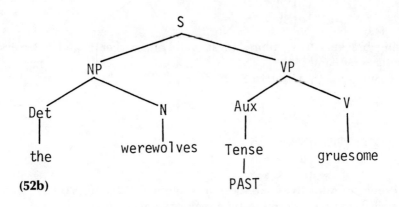

(52b)

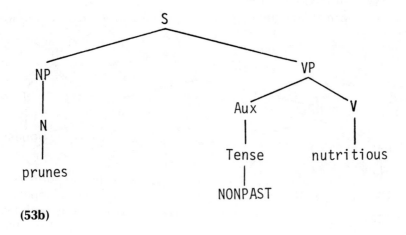

(53b)

In the concrete treatments of early transformational grammar, **Prepositional Phrases** consisting of noun phrases preceded by prepositions
("on the wagon," "at the hoedown," "by the mailman") were generated directly by the phrase structure rules to give deep structures like
the following (where *PP* represents *Prepositional Phrase* and *Prep*
stands for *Preposition*):

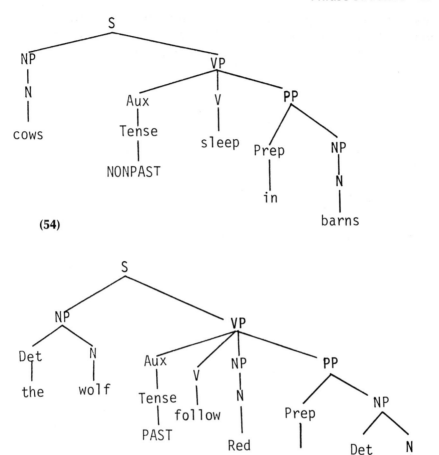

(54)

(55)

More recently, two conflicting proposals have been put forth concerning prepositions. The first says that prepositions do not appear in the deep structure at all, but are inserted by transformations, with features on the noun determining the choice of preposition. The other proposal, presented and developed by Fillmore (1968) in a more complete theory known as **Case Grammar**, considers all nouns to have attached prepositions in deep structure, many of them being deleted by general rules.

Partially because both of these proposals still have problems, but mostly because they would lead to greater abstractness than we desire here, we will assume that prepositions are generated directly in the base as components of prepositional phrases. This requires another change in our verb phrase expansion rule, as well as an additional rule for Prepositional Phrases.

(56) VP = Aux + V + (NP) + (NP) + (S) + (PP)

(57) PP = Prep + NP

Summary

We have been discussing the phrase structure rules which characterize the deep structures of sentences. We have explained that, although terms like "generate" and "derive" are common in referring to the base component, phrase structure expansions are probably not real-life processes. We have therefore considered phrase structure rules to be "node admissibility conditions" determining the well-formedness of constituent structures. For example, our first rule was **(58)**, which is an abbreviation for a node admissibility condition which matches the constituent **(59)** to trees to see if they are well-formed.

(58) S = NP + VP

(59)

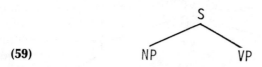

To avoid confusion, up to this point we have used = to indicate branching in our rules. The normal practice, however, is to use→: *S→NP + VP*. Remember, however, that even when an arrow is used, it is to be interpreted as *consists of*, and not as indicating any real-time process. Following is the complete set of rules introduced in this chapter, but now with arrow notation.

$$S \rightarrow \begin{bmatrix} S + \begin{Bmatrix} \text{and} \\ \text{but} \\ \text{or} \end{Bmatrix} + S \\ NP + VP \end{bmatrix}$$

$$NP \rightarrow \begin{Bmatrix} NP + \text{and} + NP \\ (\text{Det}) + N \\ NP + S \end{Bmatrix}$$

VP→ Aux + V + (NP) + (NP) + (S) + (PP)

Aux→ (Modal) + Tense + (Aspect)

$$\text{Tense} \rightarrow \begin{bmatrix} \text{PAST} \\ \text{NONPAST} \end{bmatrix}$$

Aspect→ (PROG)(PERF)

PP→ Prep + NP

Hearing Children's Acquisition of Phrase Structure Rules

The literature on hearing children's acquisition of the basic structures of English is now so vast that we cannot hope to do more than indicate some areas of interest. The detailed survey already produced by Brown (1973), and the volumes he has forecast present a fascinating account of the developments in this field through the 1960's and also present many of the important issues of theory and empirical research. Many studies (typical of which is Menyuk, 1969) have shown that most hearing children have the basic aspects of the phrase structure rules of their language well under control after a year or so at school, except perhaps for the more complex aspects of embedding further sentences into the *NP* or *VP* via the recursive rules already discussed (that is, relativization; conjunction; and complementation, which will be discussed later). Various complications that disturb the normal surface structure word order also seem to cause problems to a more advanced age (C. Chomsky, 1969).

For our purposes, it is sufficient to summarize early development by saying that hearing children go through the stages (not necessarily mutually exclusive) of **babbling** (relatively "meaningless" concatenations of sounds, mainly vowels), and **vocalization** (where recognizable intonation contours appear similar to adult declarative sentences, questions, and other forms). Shortly after this (usually somewhere around the first birthday) the first "words" appear, though initially the phonetic shape of these reference utterances may bear little resemblance to the usual adult form. Although multi-morpheme utterances may appear earlier (usually in the form of "lexicalized" rote-learned items that would seem to be really one word to the child [e.g., "wadat?"]), most children also go through what is called the **holophrastic** stage, where one-word utterances appear to have different semantic intentions, discernible in terms of the context of action of child and observer, and often, applied to the word. ("Milk" may mean "That's my milk," "Give me milk!" or "Is that my milk?" depending on the stress and intonation.)

At about the second birthday or a little earlier, the first multiword "sentences" begin to appear. This stage has been perhaps the most extensively investigated of all, and various hypotheses have been put forward to explain the characteristics of these, the child's first attempts at expressing his needs and feelings in English syntax. Essentially, the facts are that the child at this age produces two-word utterances and the distribution of words in these utterances is such that a relatively small number occur infrequently and in seemingly fixed positions, whereas members of a larger (and more rapidly growing) class are more freely used. These characteristic distributions produced what is known as the "Pivot-Open" hypothesis, which claims that the child has a relatively small number of **pivot words** (roughly akin to adult function words like determiners and prepositions) and an increasing store of **open words** (similar to open class words like nouns and verbs in adult speech), and that these are generic to the adult "parts of speech" categories in the sense that the adult classes evolve from them via a process of differentiation (McNeill, 1970). In his examination of this issue, Brown (1973) has marshalled a wide range of evidence which indicates that the $P + O$ hypothesis does not fit the facts of early language use, and that it is necessary to go beyond the distributional analyses of the surface structure of the "sentences" to take into account the semantics (via context and action) of the utterance. His method of "rich interpretation" of the data indicates that "there is a deep structure for each sentence that is more complex than the surface structure, and this deep structure is closer to adult English than the surface structure is. . . . [Hence] Pivot grammars do not correctly characterize the sentences of children at [this stage]."

In the later parts of this stage of language development and beyond, structure begins to appear that can be accounted for, at least in part, by the phrase structure rules we have outlined. Menyuk (1969) has reported an intensive body of developments from nursery school to kindergarten and Grade 1 ages, and since her results seem typical, they will be followed here. Essentially, Menyuk found that, as early as nursery school, most of her subjects were using all the parts of speech as categorized by adult grammars. She notes that subject noun phrases are often not present at the earliest points of this stage; pronouns are rarely used; tense and number marking of verbs only gradually appears, as does the use of auxiliary and modal verbs.

One interesting aspect of Menyuk's findings is that, while all her subjects used correct sentences, they also occasionally produced deviations from the standard adult rules. These fell into a number of different categories: (a) miscategorization ("I see the hungries"); (b) violations of subcategorization rules ("He's a bigger"); (c) violations of word order ("Some more cat I make"); (d) non-expansion of a symbol, which appears in surface structure as an *omission*—of nouns ("I want the bigger"), verb phrases ("Mark a good boy"), prepositions ("I go New York"), determiners ("I see boy"), and particles ("You put the hat"); (e) violations of selectional restrictions—with pronouns ("He's a big train"), determiners ("A blue leaves"), and prepositions ("He'll be 3 in June 10th"), and (f) further expansion of a terminal symbol (*redundancy* in surface structure)—nouns ("She took it the hat"), verb phrases ("He'll might get in jail"), determiners ("I want some lots of flour"), particles ("She put on the dress on"), and prepositions ("I shop in over there").

Menyuk found variations in the incidence of occurrence of these phenomena, but generally speaking, deviations decreased and correct structures increased in number throughout the age-range she studied. By the time most children are ready to go into Grade 2, they are capably using most aspects of standard adult phrase structure rules, and, as we shall discuss later, many aspects of the recursive rules that embed sentences within one another to produce complex syntactic structure.

Deaf Children's Acquisition of Phrase Structure Rules

Deaf children appear to have relatively little difficulty in learning the more general phrase structure rules of English, but very great difficulty indeed in learning their more subtle manifestations in surface structure, to the extent that there are aspects of the use of, for example, the determiner system that have not been fully mastered by 18-year-old deaf students, and which they seem to have made virtually no progress in acquiring in their last 10 or so years of schooling. Since very little research has yet been done on the earlier stages of deaf children's acquisition of these rules, we will concentrate here on the later stages. Several reported studies have examined various aspects of deaf students' acquisition of phrase structure rules: O'Neill (1973), Power (1973), Taylor (1969), and others. We noted previously that the simplest phrase structure rule takes the form $S \rightarrow NP + VP$. All the above-mentioned studies agree that this rule is the earliest acquired by deaf children, and that it is usually mastered completely by age 10 or so. Power found that some children below this age tended to interpret the simple sentences produced by this rule ("The dog chased the cat") more in terms of their experience of the world than in terms of the word order constraints imposed by the rule. For some children, subject and object *NP*'s could be exchanged, seemingly depending on their (perhaps idiosyncratic) experience of whether, in the real world, dogs tend to chase cats more than cats chase dogs, or vice versa. Schmitt (1968) reported a similar phenomenon.

In her examination of the written language of deaf children, Taylor found that "Topic-Comment" constructions, such as those Gruber (1967) found in the earliest speech of hearing children, frequently preceded the correct use of the $S \rightarrow NP + VP$ rule. She found three constructions of this type to be common: $S \rightarrow NP + Locative$ ("The bird away"), $S \rightarrow NP + Adjective$ ("The ant happy") and $S \rightarrow NP + NP$ ("The ant idea"). These are, of course, similar to Menyuk's category of Omission. Many errors of omission also seemed to be due to problems of deciding whether or not a verb was transitive, as in "The dove dropped. It put on the water." Determiners were also very commonly omitted, often inconsistently. The overall frequency of omission errors appears to decline with age.

Redundancy errors occurred mainly with prepositions for Taylor's deaf students, as in "The ant walked to home. He thanked to the dove." Order errors were relatively infrequent in the writing she obtained. Taylor felt that English sentence order may have been mainly mastered by age 10, the youngest age represented in her sample, but this has been due to problems involved in the type of data obtained from the analysis of a "free" corpus of writing. Analyses of *test* results from other studies indicate many errors of order in children considerably older than 10 years. These indicate that Taylor's results should not be generalized beyond simple active declarative sentences.

Deaf children have great difficulty in acquiring the standard rules of English usage for expanding the *NP* and *VP* nodes. The expansion of an *NP* or a *VP* by means of embedded *S* to form a complement or a relative clause is extremely difficult for them; separate chapters are devoted to these structures, and their discussion will be deferred till then. Within the *NP* and *VP* expansion rules of the main sentence, deaf students have particular difficulty in two areas, the determiner and auxiliary systems—aspects of English structure which are particularly complex and subtle in their use. O'Neill (1973) examined deaf students' use of some aspects of the determiner system. Taylor had found that in the writing of deaf students, determiner omissions were the most frequent kind of omission at the age levels she studied and that students as old as 16 years showed no improvement in this area. In a study in which students were required to judge the acceptability of correct and incorrect sentences, O'Neill confirmed these findings, as well as discovering that deaf students accepted redundant use of determiners ("some the trucks") to an advanced age. Both studies found confusion as to the correct determiner to use with "mass" nouns (as in "a water"), and Taylor found confusion as to what conditions called for the use of the definite article ("the") or the indefinite article ("a/an"). Problems in the ordering of determiners and adjectives ("big a truck") have also been reported.

Quigley, Montanelli, and Wilbur (1975) reported a study of the development of the verb system in the language of deaf children, including the auxiliary system. It was found that deaf students were confused about what form of auxiliary verb should be used to form progressives and perfectives. They often omitted the auxiliary altogether or incorrectly used a part of the verb *be* for both progressive and perfective ("The boy was hit the girl" as well as "The boy was hitting the girl"). The misuse of auxiliaries was also prevalent in questions and in negative sentences, as was confusion over the rule which requires obligatory placement of some form of *do* in questions and negatives in sentences containing no other auxiliary (Quigley, Montanelli, and Wilbur, 1975). Problems similar to all of the above were also displayed by deaf students in their use of modal verbs such as "can," "will," and so forth. Substitution of *be* for *have* and vice versa was also found to be common in young deaf students, with only 60 per cent of 18-year-olds being able to reject such sentences as "John is a ball" and "John has sick."

In summary, it can be seen that deaf students have considerable difficulty mastering many subtle aspects of the use of the determiner and auxiliary systems of English, and that as many as 30 to 40 per cent of them leave school not having gained control of their use in Standard English constructions. However, the broad aspects of word order and word use come under increasing control and are mastered reasonably well by many deaf children by the age of 12.

CHAPTER 4

Transformations I: Passivization and Relativization

Transformations

Previous chapters have discussed the relationships of the components of a grammar and the "generation" of deep structure by means of phrase structure rules and lexical insertion. The component which has provided a name for "transformational grammar" is the one which relates the deep structure to the surface syntactic structure of the sentence: the **transformational component.** The transformational component is made up of **transformational rules:** rules which apply to

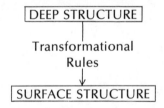

linguistic trees (recall that a tree is not a psychologically real structure, but a notational device used to represent psychologically real structure) to *delete, insert*, or *transpose* elements.

1. An example of a deletion rule is the one which forms **imperatives** in English. For example:

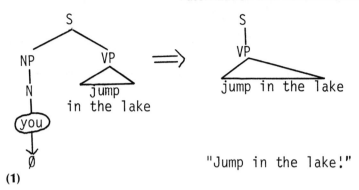

(1)

"Jump in the lake!"

(Notice the $\Longrightarrow$ notation for transformations, as compared to the $\longrightarrow$ used in phrase structure notation.)

2. One rule of insertion is that which inserts *do* into certain nega-tivized and questioned sentences.

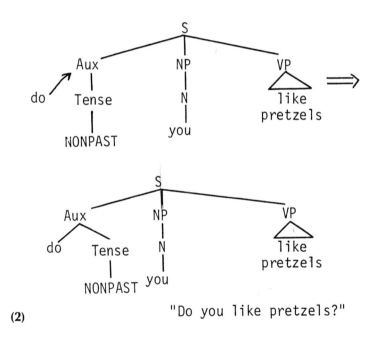

(2)

"Do you like pretzels?"

Notice that another rule must first apply to move the *Aux* node to the left of the sentence (as in the leftmost tree above) before *do* is in-serted.

3. We have already presented a rule which transposes, or exchanges, elements: the PASSIVE transformation.

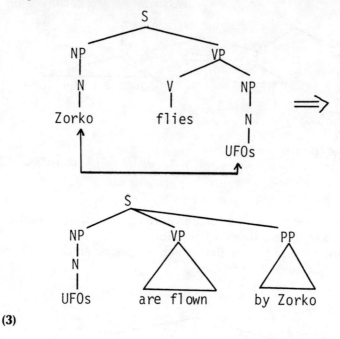

(3)

Before it will be possible to discuss specific transformations it will be necessary to introduce **bracketing**, which is a means of abbreviating trees. As a first example, consider the subtree **(4)** and its bracketing, **(4a)**.

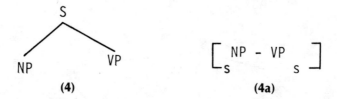

The bracketing tells us that we have a constituent *S*, whose limits are defined by the leftmost and rightmost brackets labeled *S*, and which consists of an *NP* and a *VP*. Now consider the following more complex bracketing:

(5) $[_{VP} Aux - V [_{NP} Det - N \ _{NP}] \ _{VP}]$

The above bracketing tells us that the *VP* in this case consists of *Aux*, a *V*, and an *NP* (in that left-to-right order), and that the *NP*, in turn, consists of a *Det* and an *N*. An alternative representation of the above facts is **(5a)**.

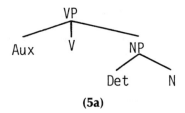

(5a)

Now notice the following points about bracketing:
1. Labels are subscripted to the bracket to distinguish them from branches of the node which do not serve the function of labeling; see the *X*'s in the following.

(6) $\left[_X Y - Z _X\right]$

2. Nodes of the tree which do not branch into lower categories, or whose branching is not significant, are written on the line between brackets; those which do branch appear only as labels on brackets:

(7)

$$= \quad [_{VP} \text{Aux} - \text{V} - \underline{\text{NP}} _{VP}]$$

$$= \quad [_{VP}\text{Aux} - \text{V} [_{NP}\text{Det} - \text{N}_{NP}] _{VP}]$$

(8)

3. In reading or producing bracketing, it is probably easiest to start with the innermost brackets (or lowest level of tree) and work outward (or upward).

As an exercise, determine the corresponding subtree for each of the following bracketed sequences:

1.$[_{NP} \text{NP} - \text{S} _{NP}]$

2.$[_{Aux} \text{Tense} [_{Aspect} \text{PROG} _{Aspect}] _{Aux}]$

3.$[_S [_{NP} \text{N} _{NP}] [_{VP} \text{Aux} - \text{V} [_{NP} \text{Det} - \text{N} _{NP}] [_S \text{NP} - \text{VP} _S] _{VP}] _S]$

4.$[_{Aux} \text{Modal} - \text{Tense} _{Aux}]$

Passivization

The first transformation we shall deal with relates the active and passive "versions" of a sentence. For example:

(9a)   The quarterback trains tadpoles.

(9b)   Tadpoles are trained by the quarterback.

Recall that in the earliest versions of the theory, **(9a)** and **(9b)** were considered to be two different outputs of the same deep structure, differing only in that **(9b)** had undergone the optional PASSIVE transformation, while **(9a)** had not. Recent formulations have proposed different

(10a)

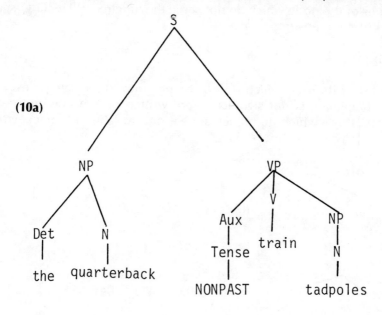

(10b)

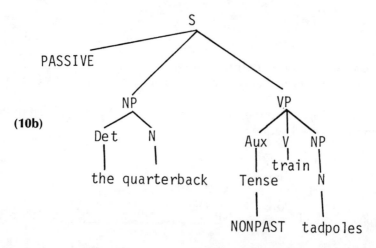

deep structure sources for active and passive sentences, with the two deep structures differing quite radically in some cases. Since the purposes of this book do not require extreme abstractness, we shall take an intermediate position (both theoretically and historically), and consider the two deep structures to be identical except for a marker on the deep structure of the passive sentence which specifies it as a passive. Thus the deep structures of **(9a)** and **(9b)** will be **(10a)** and **(10b)**, respectively.

Application of all the relevant transformations to **(10b)** results in a surface representation something like **(10c)**.

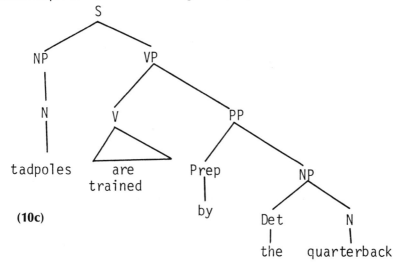

(10c)

It is apparent that **(10b)** and **(10c)** differ in several ways. The most obvious difference is probably in the location of the *NP*'s. The first part of the PASSIVE transformation applies to **(10b)** as follows:

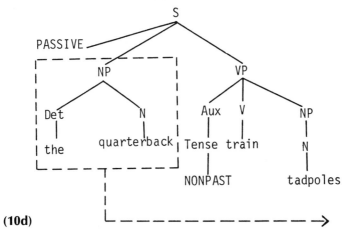

(10d)

The second part moves the other NP:

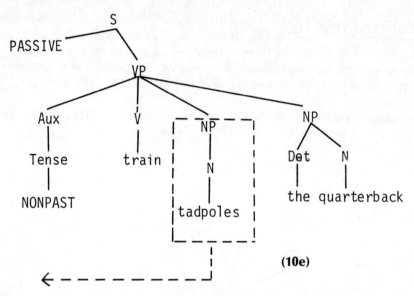

(10e)

The cumulative effect of the above two changes is to interchange the subject and object noun phrases. This is the reason for the confusion that often arises with the traditional definition of "subject of a sentence": that is, the noun phrase which "performs the action of the verb." Of course, in both **(9a)** and **(9b)**, the action is performed by "the quarterback," even though structurally the subject of **(9b)** is "tadpoles." Notice, however, that the traditional definition is satisfied in the deep structure, where the subject is in both cases "the quarterback." This shows the necessity for distinguishing between the **deep** (or **logical**) **subject** (or object) and the **surface** (or **grammatical**) **subject**. Application of the PASSIVE transformation thus results in the logical object becoming the grammatical subject of the sentence.

Of course, the PASSIVE transformation is a general one, which applies not only to structure **(10b)**, but to any tree with a PASSIVE node. In addition, the transformation (as we have considered it thus far) need refer only to the *NP* nodes; the internal structure of the *NP*'s has no

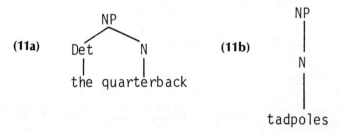

effect whatever on the application of the PASSIVE. Thus, the rule "moves" not only *NP* nodes like **(11a)** and **(11b)**, but also those like **(12a)**, **(12b)**, **(12c)**, **(12d)**, and so forth.

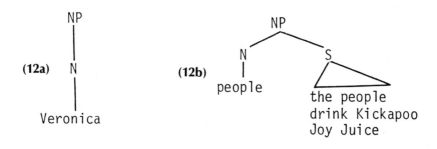

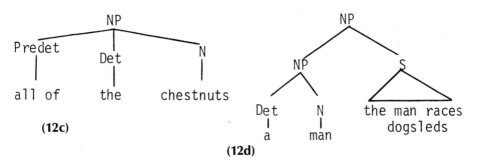

(Examples are the passive sentences "The people who drink Kickapoo Joy Juice were discovered by Veronica" and "All of the chestnuts were eaten by a man who races dogsleds.") In other words, the rule refers to noun phrase *constituents*.

Using our abbreviatory bracketing, the above changes can be represented as follows:

PASSIVE: Structural Description: $[_S$ PASSIVE – NP$_1$ – Aux – V –
NP$_2$$_S]$
Structural Change: $[_S$ PASSIVE – NP$_2$ – Aux – V – NP$_1$ $_S]$

(The indices 1 and 2 are used simply to keep track of the two *NP*'s.) The **structural description** (or SD) identifies the constituent structure necessary for application of the rule; the **structural change** (SC) specifies the manner in which the input constituents are changed by application of the rule. PASSIVE says that within a deep structure with a PASSIVE node, if two noun phrases are separated only by an *Aux* and a *V*, they are interchanged.

The rule, of course, is quite a bit more complex than this. If **(9a)** and **(9b)** are compared, it will be observed that not only is the position of the *NP*'s different, but that in **(9b)** the following are true:

1. A form of the verb *be* (in this case, "are") is present;
2. The word "by" precedes the second noun phrase;
3. The verb appears in the **past participle** form.

The past participle form of the verb is that form which appears in the perfect tense. It is usually represented by one of the endings "-en," "-ed," or "-n." Notice that sometimes the past participle form of the verb merges with the past tense form (as in "swallowed"); this can lead to confusion if pains are not taken to clarify which form is being exemplified. In other cases (e.g., "eat") the past participle ("eaten") is different from the past tense form ("ate").

The three additional characteristics of passives listed above, as well as the noun phrase transposition, are accounted for by the following rule:

$$\text{PASSIVE:}\quad \text{SD:}\quad [_S \text{ PASSIVE} - NP_1 - Aux - V - NP_2 {}_S]$$

$$\text{SC:}\quad [_S \text{ } NP_2 - Aux - be - V + \text{-}en - by - NP_1 {}_S]$$

The rule thus formulated indicates that in addition to the two *NP*'s being permuted, *be* is inserted between the *Aux* and the *V*, "by" is inserted before the final *NP*, and *-en* is inserted after the verb (as indicated by the "+"). Notice that *-en* is being used to abstractly represent the past participle marker, which may in any particular case be "-en," "-ed," "-n," or another irregular ending. Finally, the PASSIVE node is deleted. (Notice that the bracketing above displays order only, and not changes in hierarchical groupings. The details are highly complex, and will not concern us here.)

Our rule is still not quite complete, as evidenced by the following examples:

(13a)   The quarterback trains tadpoles daily.
(13b)   The quarterback trains tadpoles as a hobby.
(13c)   The quarterback trains tadpoles to be swimming stars.

PASSIVE as above formulated can apply only if the underlying object *NP* is last in the sentence, but "tadpoles" is not final in **(13a–c)**. It should be clear that there are many possible structures which can follow this second *NP*; however, this has absolutely nothing to do with the application of the PASSIVE rule. This type of situation is not restricted to the PASSIVE rule, but recurs often in the formulation of rules. The linguistic mechanism used in such cases is that of **variables**. Syntactic variables, normally represented by capital letters from the end of the alphabet, function as placeholders for indeterminate structures.

With a variable *Y* in final position, the PASSIVE Rule looks like this:

PASSIVE: SD: $[_S \text{PASSIVE} - NP_1 - Aux - V - NP_2 - Y_S]$
$\qquad\qquad\qquad 1 \qquad\quad 2 \quad\;\; 3 \quad 4 \quad\; 5 \quad\; 6$

$\qquad$ SC: $[_S NP_2 - Aux - be - V + \text{-en} - by - NP_1 - Y_S]$

The rule now allows for the object *NP* to be followed by additional material of any shape, as in sentences (13a–c). It is important to notice also that a variable like *Y* can stand for $\emptyset$ (the **null string**): that is, there may not be any following material, as in the case of (9a), but PASSIVE will nevertheless apply.

Now consider how PASSIVE will apply to the following sentences:

(14) The truck driver found a tiger in his tank.

(15) A bull killed the toreador last week at the bullfight in Barcelona.

There is another simple rule related to passives which we shall mention briefly here. It is known as AGENT DELETION. AGENT DELETION simply deletes the **agent** of a passive sentence; that is, the underlying subject, which in the passive appears in the "by" phrase. AGENT DELETION is optional, and it applies only when the agent is unknown or considered to be unimportant; thus,

(16) $\qquad$ Someone has murdered my pet rabbit.

PASSIVE $\quad$ My pet rabbit has been murdered by someone.

AGENT DEL. $\quad$ My pet rabbit has been murdered.

Further Comments on Passivization

The original motivation for considering PASSIVE to be optional, and for, at a historically later time, considering the deep structure of passives to differ from active sentences only in the existence of a meaningless "PASSIVE" node, was the assumption that active and passive sentences have the same meaning. This, however, is a somewhat questionable assumption. Even with sentences (9a) and (9b), we can see a difference in emphasis, if nothing else. The problem becomes more serious when we consider sentences like the following:

(17) Few people speak many languages.

(18) Many languages are spoken by few people.

It has been pointed out that, although dialects differ in their judgment of these two sentences, for many speakers they have very different meanings. For these speakers, (17) states that there are few people who speak many languages; (18) states that there are many languages which are spoken by only a few people. This is only one instance of many whereby difficulties arise with sentences involving **quantifiers**— words like "all," "none," "some," "each," "every," "many," "few," etc. Nevertheless, it is clear that although **(18)** appears at first glance to be the passive version of **(17)**, it cannot be, at least with the assumptions we have been making. There are several possible approaches to the problem: We could postulate entirely different deep structures for active and passive sentences, somehow capturing in the process the difference in meaning between **(17)** and **(18)**; we could retain similar deep structures for the two while allowing the PASSIVE transformation to radically change meaning in some cases, but not others; we could place certain restrictions on the PASSIVE transformation so that it will not apply to sentences like **(17)**. No attempt will be made here to argue for any one of these approaches; linguists themselves do not agree. It is sufficient for our purposes to point out that care must be taken in attempting to apply PASSIVE to certain types of structures to which it cannot apply, or, equivalently, in attempting to relate by the PASSIVE sentences which are actually not related in this manner.

Regardless of our formulation of the PASSIVE rule, it will necessarily apply to sentences **(19a)**, **(19b)**, and **(19c)** to produce **(20a)**, **(20b)**, and **(20c)**.

(19a) Mary wanted a zebra suit.
(19b) Mary's zebra suit cost $100.
(19c) Mary's outfit resembles a zebra suit.
(20a) *A zebra suit was wanted by Mary.
(20b) *$100 was cost by Mary's zebra suit.
(20c) *A zebra suit is resembled by Mary's outfit.

For most speakers, **(20a)**, **(20b)**, and **(20c)** are ungrammatical; the PASSIVE rule must be restricted so as to not apply to sentences like **(19a)**, **(19b)**, and **(19c)**. Actually, the influencing factor is the verbs of the sentences; PASSIVE is a **governed rule**—its application (or nonapplication) depends on the presence or absence of certain verbs. In addition to "want," "cost," and "resemble," PASSIVE does not normally apply to sentences with the verbs "last," "equal," "suit," "own," "measure," and "marry," and probably others. It is interesting to notice also that for some verbs PASSIVE must apply (i.e., it is obligatory); "rumor" is one such verb. This is shown by the following examples:

(21a) *Someone rumors that linguistics is damaging to the mind.
(21b) It is rumored that linguistics is damaging to the mind.

A final complication in the subject of passives deals with sentences like the following:

(22) Mary's boomerang got stolen.
(23) Someone is getting hoodwinked.
(24) Somehow this window got opened.

(Notice that AGENT DELETION has applied to each sentence.) It is clear that these sentences are quite similar to the following passive sentences:

(22a) Mary's boomerang was stolen.

(23a) Someone is being hoodwinked.

(24a) Somehow this window was opened.

Sentences like **(22)**, **(23)**, and **(24)** are commonly called "got passives." Although they are similar to the corresponding "be passives" **(22a)**, **(23a)**, and **(24a)**, there is a definite difference in meaning. It has been claimed by Robin Lakoff (1971) that "got" passives normally reflect the attitude of the speaker or the subject of the sentence toward the events described in the sentence, often in the sense that he perceives the events as being negative from his point of view. Consider the following two sentences from Lakoff:

(25a) Radicals must get arrested to prove their machismo.

(25b) Radicals must be arrested to keep the commies from overrunning the U.S.

In **(25a)** the obligation expressed in "must" rests on the radicals themselves (i.e., it is the radicals who must ensure that they are arrested); in **(25b)** the obligation is on some other unspecified person or persons. The following sentences, if not ungrammatical, are at least very strange (indicated by the question mark preceding each one).

(26a) ?Radicals must be arrested to prove their machismo.

(26b) ?Radicals must get arrested to keep the commies from overrunning the U.S.

That "got" passives and "be" passives are really quite different is also indicated by the type of adverbs they take, as shown by the following:

(27a) Mary was shot on purpose, the finks!

(27b) *Mary got shot on purpose, the finks!

It can be seen from the above that "be" passives and "got" passives, although they differ superficially only in one seemingly minor word, represent quite different semantic relationships between the words of the sentences, and thus must come from two quite different deep structures. Specific proposals have been made, but they will not be discussed here; it is sufficient for our purposes to be aware of the relevant similarities and differences between the two.

Relativization

Relativization is one of the recursive processes of language, exemplifying the process of embedding sentences in other sentences. The term **clause** has been traditionally used to refer to sentence parts which resemble sentences; that is, a clause has a subject and a verb. A **relative clause**, in traditional terms, is a clause which contains one of the **relative pronouns** "who," "whom," "which," or "that," as in the following examples, where the relative clauses are italicized and the relative pronouns underlined in addition.

(28)   The man <u>who</u> *is beating the drum* plays the bassoon.
(29)   The bassoon <u>that</u> *the man plays* is warped.
(30)   Axel rode the elephant *to* <u>which</u> *we gave peanuts.*

Generative grammar claims that relative clauses actually are, in deep structure, complete sentences. Traditionally, relative pronouns are said to "stand for" meaningful nouns; thus, in **(28)-(30)**, the relative pronouns represent "the man" (since it is the man who is beating the drum), "the bassoon" (since it is the bassoon that is played), and "the elephant" (since the elephant is what we gave the peanuts to), respectively. This intuition is formalized by transformational grammar, which postulates deep structures with these words as subjects.

In Chapter 3 the noun phrase expansion rule $NP \rightarrow NP + S$ was presented; it was noted there that constituents like "the dog that bit the mailman" and "people who water-ski" function as noun phrase constituents, and that relative clauses are properly analyzed as constituents of noun phrases. It was also shown that the relationship between relative clauses and sentences is captured in transformational grammar by representing relative clauses as sentences in deep structure (thus the S in the NP rule). The deep structures of sentences **(28)-(30)** are as follows:

(28a)

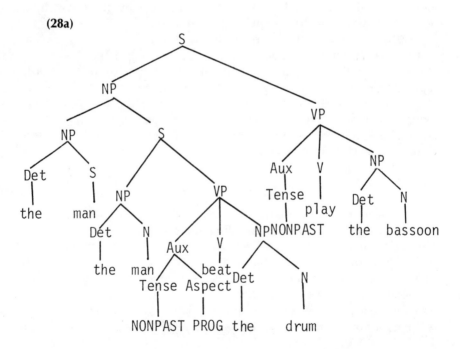

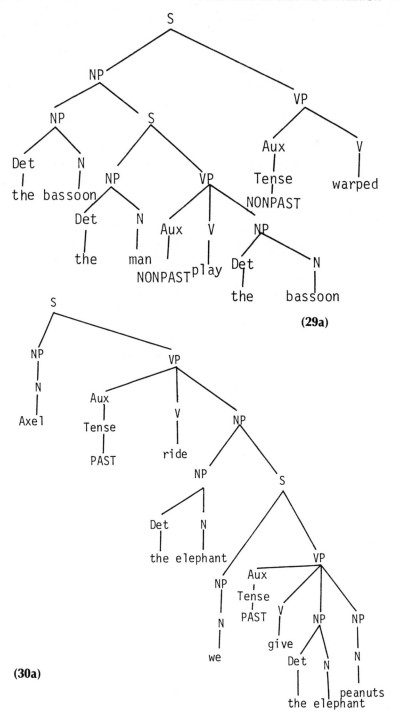

(29a)

(30a)

Notice that each *S* embedded in an *NP* is a sentence in its own right:
standing alone and with the usual transformations, they would appear
as:

(28b) The man is beating the drum.

(29b) The man plays the bassoon.

(30b) We gave the elephant peanuts.

It is only by virtue of their position inside the noun phrase that these
sentences appear, in **(28)-(30)**, as relative clauses.

One type of evidence for the claim that relative clauses are embedded sentences in deep structure is the fact that the embedded sentences themselves can undergo transformations for which they meet
the structural description. For example, an embedded sentence can undergo PASSIVE, as in the following:

(29c) The bassoon *that is played by the man* is warped.

In **(29c)**, the embedded sentence, "The man plays the bassoon," has
first been passivized and only then has RELATIVIZATION applied.

One additional crucial point must be noted here. Notice that in **(28)-
(30)** each relative word ("who," "that," and "which") refers to the
noun phrase immediately preceding. This noun phrase is known as the
head noun phrase. In order for a relative clause to be formed, one of
the noun phrases in the embedded sentence must be identical to the
head noun phrase. If this is not the case, RELATIVIZATION will not apply. Consider, for example, the following tree:

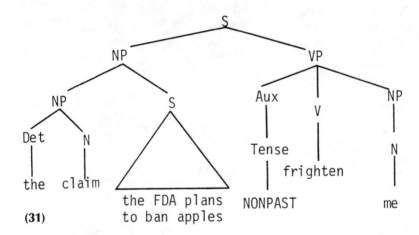

(31)

Application of the transformational component to **(31)** will not result in
RELATIVIZATION, since "the claim" does not appear in the embedded
S; in fact, the structure of the embedded sentence is preserved just as
it is, with the exception of the inserted morpheme "that" (not a relative
pronoun in this case!) as in **(31a)**:

(31a) The claim that the FDA plans to ban apples frightens me. Noun phrases like "the claim that the FDA plans to ban apples," "the fact that unicycles are dangerous," and "the idea that Jupiter controls our destiny" are known as complex noun phrases.

Let us return to RELATIVIZATION. We have seen that the crucial structure necessary for its application is **(32)**.

(32)

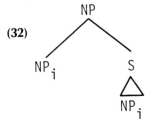

(The subscript *i* indicates identity of the two noun phrases.) Represented in bracketing form, the structure becomes **(32a)**.

(32a) $\left[_{NP} NP_i \left[_S NP_i S\right]_{NP}\right]$

It is clear that this is inadequate as a structural description, since an embedded sentence never consists of a noun phrase only. Trees **(28a)**-**(30a)** show that the identical noun phrase in the embedded sentence can be either preceded or followed by other material. If we represent this fact using variables, our structural description becomes **(32b)**.

(32b) $\left[_{NP} NP_i \left[_S X - NP_i - Y S\right]_{NP}\right]$

(Recall that variables may in some cases represent $\emptyset$). The variables X and Y will account for structures like the two following.

(33)

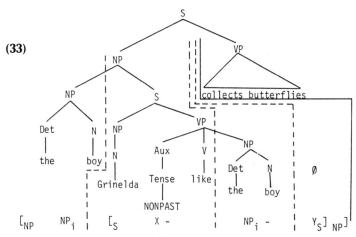

The boy who(m) Grinelda likes collects butterflies.

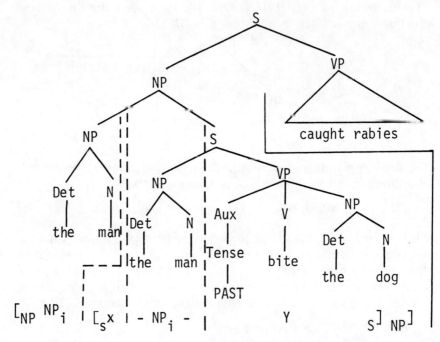

The man who bit the dog caught rabies.

(34)

The process of RELATIVIZATION consists of two steps. If the structural description is met (i.e., if the SD exactly matches some part of the tree),
   1. The identical noun in the embedded sentence is replaced by a relative pronoun ("who," "which," "whom," or "that").
   2. The relative pronoun is moved to the front of the embedded sentence.
(Actually these two steps may apply in the order 1-2, 2-1, or even simultaneously; we have arbitrarily chosen the above sequence for purposes of exposition.)
   Notice now how RELATIVIZATION applies to **(33)**:

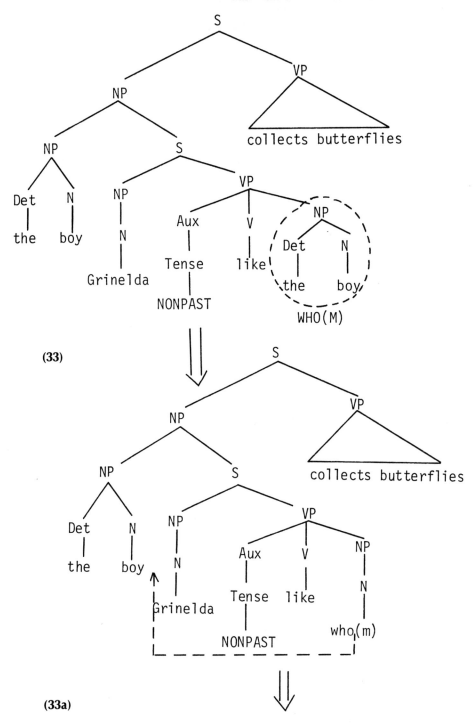

(33)

(33a)

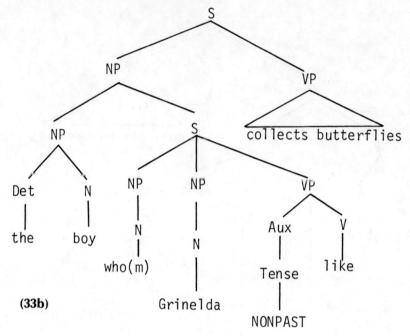

(33b)

Now notice what happens in the case of **(34)**:

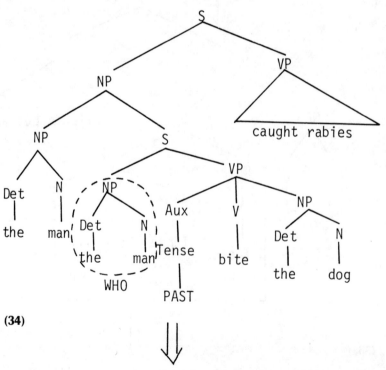

(34)

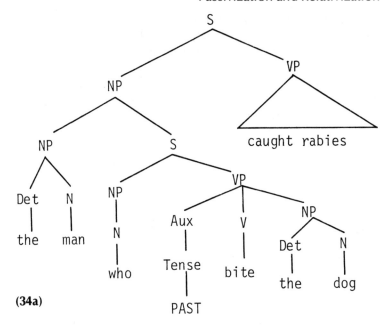

(34a)

Notice that "who" is already at the front of the sentence and need not be moved. We say that the movement part of the transformation does not apply, or that it applies **vacuously.** The RELATIVIZATION rule, then, is something like the following:

RELATIVIZATION: SD: $[_{NP} NP_i [_S X - NP_i - Y _S] _{NP}]$

SC: $[_{NP} NP_i [_S RELPRO_i - X - Y _S] _{NP}]$

The rule says that the noun phrase in the embedded sentence is moved to the front of the embedded sentence and becomes a relative pronoun. In cases like **(33)**, the variable X stands for real material; this is always the case when the second NP_i functions as the object of the embedded sentence, and relativization in such cases might be more completely specified as *Object Relativization*. In cases of *Subject Relativization* as in **(34)**, where the noun phrase to be relativized is the subject of the embedded sentence, X is normally $\emptyset$, and movement is vacuous.

In sentence **(33)** the relative pronoun was given as either "who" or "whom." This might be a good time to again point out the distinction between "prescriptivism" and "descriptivism." Although traditionally the use of "whom" in object position (as in **(33)**) is prescribed, most native speakers would use "who" in conversation. Written or highly formal English is another matter, and the distinction may still need to be brought out in the classroom to allow for these situations. Nevertheless, any child who is forced to use "whom" in spoken sentences like (33) is likely to have his language judged unnatural by listeners.

One more aspect concerning the relative pronoun should be mentioned here. The following sentences are clearly ungrammatical:

(35)   *People which eat uranium tablets are not too smart.

(36)   *The bear who Bill teased had a good breakfast.

Clearly the choice of relative pronoun is not free. The rule is simple: "who" replaces human ([+human]) noun phrases, and "which" replaces nonhuman ([−human]) ones. (Notice that (36) can be grammatical just in case the bear is considered to be [+human], as in a fairy tale.) The relative pronoun "that," however, has no such restrictions. It can replace either [+human] or [−human] noun phrases, as can be seen in the following.

(35a)   People that eat uranium tablets are not too smart.

(36a)   The dog that Bill kicked had a good breakfast.

Finally, there is one complication which we have ignored thus far. Notice that in sentence (30) (repeated below as (37)), the relative pronoun does not begin the relative clause, but rather is preceded by the preposition "to." The deep structure of (37) is (37a).

(37)   Axel rode the elephant to which we gave peanuts.

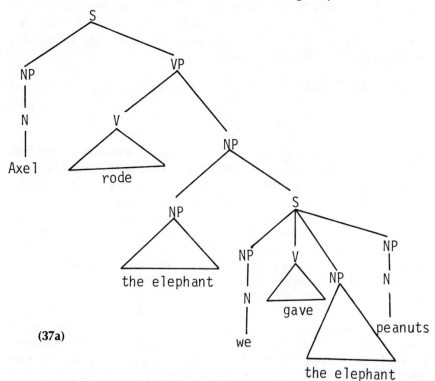

(37a)

Another rule we have not yet discussed will apply to the sentence embedded in **(37a)** to give **(37b)**.

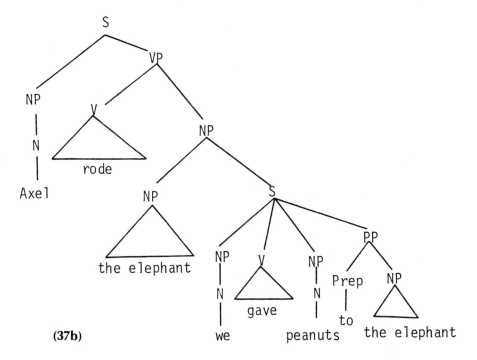

(37b)

Now, since "the elephant" in the embedded sentence is identical to "the elephant" higher in the tree, RELATIVIZATION will apply to give **(37c)**.

    (37c) Axel rode the elephant which we gave peanuts to.

Sentence **(37)** is thus not produced. It is necessary to add a condition on relativization in English, first proposed by Ross (1967) and known as PIED PIPING. PIED PIPING says that when the noun phrase is moved, a preceding preposition *may or may not* be moved with it. Thus, for most native English speakers, **(37)** and **(37c)** are equally grammatical, although **(37c)** may be more commonly used in spoken English. Notice that we again encounter a conflict with many prescriptivists who claim that sentences like **(37c)**, with "stranded" prepositions, are "bad English," or at least bad style. Again, this is an arbitrary law which has been enforced counter to the natural intuitions of most speakers.

    PIED PIPING is actually a more general phenomenon than this and often involves movement of a great deal of material to the front of the embedded sentence. The most famous example of PIED PIPING, provided by Ross (1967), involves the following deep structure (in simplified bracketed form).

(38)   [s Reports [s The government prescribes the height of the lettering on the covers of the reports s] are invariably boring. s]

RELATIVIZATION can apply to this sentence to give any of the following, where the material moved in each case is underlined. (While not all of the following sentences may be equally grammatical to a particular speaker, all are at least marginally acceptable to some speakers.)

(38a)   Reports *which* the government prescribes the height of the lettering on the covers of are invariably boring.

(38b)   Reports *of which* the government prescribes the height of the lettering on the covers are invariably boring.

(38c)   Reports *the covers of which* the government prescribes the height of the lettering on are invariably boring.

(38d)   Reports *on the covers of which* the government prescribes the height of the lettering are invariably boring.

(38e)   Reports *the lettering on the covers of which* the government prescribes the height of are invariably boring.

(38f)   Reports *of the lettering on the covers of which* the government prescribes the height are invariably boring.

(38g)   Reports *the height of the lettering on the covers of which* the government prescribes are invariably boring.

One other interesting fact dealing with PIED PIPING is the following. It seems that although most native speakers prefer "who" in relativized sentences without PIED PIPING, if a [+human] relative pronoun immediately follows a preposition, "who" is completely unacceptable. Examples are as follows:

(39a)   The man who we smuggled the hacksaw to escaped.

(39b)   The man whom we smuggled the hacksaw to escaped.

(39c)   The man to whom we smuggled the hacksaw escaped.

(39d)   *The man to who we smuggled the hacksaw escaped.

Thus if PIED PIPING applies (but only then) does the prescriptivists' "who/whom" distinction match actual usage.

Rules Which Apply to Relative Clauses

There are several rules of varying complexity which apply to relative clause structures to create new structures. First of all, consider the following sentences.

(40a)   The bassoon that the man plays is warped.

(40b)   The bassoon the man plays is warped.

(41a)   The boy who Grinelda likes collects butterflies.

(41b)   The boy Grinelda likes collects butterflies.

The relationship between **(40a)** and **(40b)**, and between **(41a)** and **(41b)**, is easy to see. In each case, the two sentences mean the same thing; and it is obvious that the object of "plays" is "the bassoon," and that that of "likes" is "the boy," whether or not relative pronouns are present. Relative pronouns are redundant in sentences like **(40a)** and **(41a)**, and can be deleted, with the result being sentences like **(40b)** and **(41b)**. This rule is known as RELATIVE PRONOUN DELETION (or WH-DELETION). Notice, however, that in each of these cases the relative pronoun which is deleted is one which has originated in object position in the embedded sentence. That is, the embedded sentences are "The man plays *the bassoon*" and "Grinelda likes *the boy*," respectively. Subject relatives cannot be deleted in this manner, as shown by the following sentence pairs:

(42a) The man who is beating the drum plays the bassoon. (=28)

(42b) *The man is beating the drum plays the bassoon.

(43a) The man who bit the dog caught rabies. (=34)

(43b) *The man bit the dog caught rabies.

As with most linguistic rules, there are dialectal exceptions, and to some speakers sentences like **(43b)** are acceptable, at least in informal speech.

One more restriction must be placed on the rule of Relative Pronoun Deletion. Not only can subject relatives not be deleted, but neither do object relatives qualify for deletion if PIED PIPING has previously applied. In this connection see the following examples:

(44a) Axel rode the elephant to which we gave peanuts. (=30)

(44b) *Axel rode the elephant to we gave peanuts.

(45a) The magnifying glass about which Sherlock boasts is excellent.

(45b) *The magnifying glass about Sherlock boasts is excellent.

In these cases with PIED PIPING applying, Relative Pronoun Deletion cannot apply because it leaves the preposition stranded. It might be noted, however, that for some speakers the relative pronoun can be deleted from sentences like **(44a)** *if* the preposition is deleted as well:

(44c) Axel rode the elephant we gave peanuts.

Now compare the following sentences which are derived from the same deep structures as the above examples, but without PIED PIPING.

(46a) Axel rode the elephant which we gave peanuts to.

(46b) Axel rode the elephant we gave peanuts to.

(47a) The magnifying glass which Sherlock boasts about is excellent.

(47b) The magnifying glass Sherlock boasts about is excellent.

Relative Pronoun Deletion, then, can apply only to object relatives which directly follow the head noun phrase.

Although subject relatives do not undergo Relative Pronoun Deletion, they do undergo a different rule, one which has been called

WH + *be* DELETION or WHIZ (=WH−is) DELETION. The **(b)** versions of the following sentences are derived from the **(a)** versions by WHIZ DELETION.

(48a)   The man who is beating the drum plays the bassoon. (=28)

(48b)   The man beating the drum plays the bassoon.

(49a)   The dog which was captured by the dogcatcher is mine.

(49b)   The dog captured by the dogcatcher is mine.

(50a)   The organ-grinder who is in the park plays "Swanee River."

(50b)   The organ-grinder in the park plays "Swanee River."

Whiz Deletion deletes any sequence of relative pronoun plus a form of the verb *be* ("is," "are," "was," etc.) directly following the head noun in a relative structure. Notice that this sequence may not exist in deep structure, but may result from the application of other rules such as PASSIVE, as shown by the passive sentence **(51a)**.

(51a)   The dog which was bitten by the man gave him rabies.

(51b)   The dog bitten by the man gave him rabies.

Observe what happens, however, when Whiz Deletion applies to a relative clause containing a predicate adjective.

(52a)   Cars which are purple are damaging to the eyes.

(52b)   *Cars purple are damaging to the eyes.

(53a)   A man who was tired played me his kazoo.

(53b)   *A man tired played me his kazoo.

In English (unlike some other languages), adjectives may not follow the nouns they "modify." A rule of ADJECTIVE PREPOSING will apply to structures like **(52b)** and **(53b)** to move the adjective to a position before the verb. Thus adjectives are considered by most generative grammarians to be derived from relative clauses in deep structure. You might recall that those adjectives which appear before nouns were not generated anywhere in the phrase structure component; the grammar is simplified by generating both relative clauses and adjectives in the same manner.

There are, as usual, some complications with the above. Notice the following examples:

(54a)   The man who was murdered belonged to the Mafia.

(54b)   The murdered man belonged to the Mafia.

(55a)   The man who was assassinated belonged to the Mafia.

(55b)   ?The assassinated man belonged to the Mafia.

(56a)   The man who was beaten belonged to the Mafia.

(56b)   *The beaten man belonged to the Mafia.

It seems as though some verbs in certain shapes (past participle in this case) can be proposed to become adjectives, but others cannot. The exact restrictions on Adjective Preposing have yet to be determined.

Hearing Children's Acquisition of the Passive Voice

A number of studies, both free and controlled, of hearing children's development of comprehension and production of the passive voice have been reported. Menyuk's analysis (1963; 1964) of a corpus of utterances which were freely produced in spoken form indicated that preschool children had considerable difficulty with production of the passive voice, but that it was "essentially acquired" by the time the children were in Grade 1.

Controlled studies of this structure have been numerous. Typical findings are those of Turner and Rommetveit (1967), who found that their 9-year-old subjects achieved "near perfect" scores on imitation, comprehension, and production tasks involving passive sentences. Below this age, however, errors were frequent, mainly involving inversion of the action of the sentence. For example, "The boy was pushed by the girl" would be interpreted to mean that it was the boy, rather than the girl, who did the pushing. Turner and Rommetveit also found that "got" passives were more frequent than "be" passives in the productions of pre-school children, and suggested that the few occurrences of the "be" form might be a result of formal school instruction. Similar results were reported by Hayhurst (1967) who also found that **non-reversibility** ("The car was washed by the boy") made intrepretation of such passive sentences easier than those in which the action was **reversible** ("The car was pushed by the tractor"). Fraser, Bellugi, and Brown (1963) asked children to identify pictures showing the action of passive sentences and to produce passive sentences in response to similarly pictured actions. None of their three-year-old subjects had yet mastered the use of the passive voice.

Thus it would appear that the use of the passive voice is relatively difficult for hearing children to learn and may not be mastered fully by many until they are 8 or 9 years of age. Most errors involve the reversal of the action of the sentence, and as Fraser, Bellugi, and Brown (1963) point out, "reverse responses seem to be made with high confidence." These same authors present an argument as to why this should be so. They point out that the rule for interpretation of active voice sentences (those presumably most frequently encountered by young children) involves straight left-to-right processing of word order:

> In active-voice sentences, subject and object appear in that order, whereas in passive voice sentences the order is object and subject. Suppose that the three-year-old processes each passive voice sentence as though it were in the active voice. "The girl is pushed by the boy" is not computed as: Object-Verb in passive-Subject, but rather as: Subject-Verb in active with odd appurtenances-Object. The odd appurtenances are *is*, *-ed*, and *by* which S may take to be

signs of some uncommon tense like "will have pushed." Processing the rule in this way would enable *S* to maintain the generality of the usual rule of English word order in which the subject precedes the object.

Deaf Children's Acquisition of the Passive Voice

Research on deaf children's acquisition of comprehension and production of passive voice indicates that they also process passive sentences in terms of the surface Subject-Verb-Object order, but continue to do so until a considerably later age than hearing children. Using a multiple-choice technique of matching sentences to pictures, Schmitt (1968) found that even at the age of 17 years, many deaf children had still not mastered the use of the passive voice. Power and Quigley (1973) used a comprehension task which involved children moving toys to demonstrate the action of passive sentences. They found consistent improvement with age, but even at age 17 and 18, nearly 40 percent of the subjects were still interpreting passive sentences using the "Surface SVO Order Strategy." Non-reversible sentences (e.g., "The soldier was killed") were somewhat easier than reversible ones, but AGENT DELETION made the task much more difficult (70 percent error rate), indicating that the verb morpheme markers mean little to most deaf students, who seem to recognize a passive only if "by" is present. The subjects did even more poorly in the production of passive sentences, only a little over 40 percent of them being able to correctly produce a full passive sentence at 17 or 18 years of age.

In a more extensive report of the same research, Power (1971) confirmed Turner and Rommetveit's (1967) finding about the possible suppression of "got" passives by formal instruction. At the 9-10 and 11-12 age levels none of his subjects accepted sentences with "got" passives as correct; by 13-14 years 30 percent did so, at 15-16 years the figure was 34 percent; but at 17-18 years the percentage accepting passive sentences containing "got" instead of a form of "be" dropped sharply to 4 percent. Power was able to trace this to formal teaching in the high school grades of the school in which the study was conducted, where it was taught that "got" was not "good English" and should be avoided in favor of "be."

In general, then, the process of acquisition of comprehension and production of passive voice sentences by deaf children seems to parallel that of hearing children, but is greatly delayed. Many deaf children appear not to have grasped the meaning implications of passive voice markers up to 10 years after the point at which virtually all hearing children have done so.

Hearing Children's Acquisition of Relative Clauses

In her study of the development of language use by hearing children between the ages of 3 and 7 years, Menyuk (1969) found that 87 percent of her 7-year-old subjects were using relative clauses. Her subjects used both medial clauses ("The man *who was sick* went home") and final clauses ("I met a man *who was sick*"), but clauses appeared earlier in final position than in medial and seemed to be easier for her children at all age levels: "Only 46 per cent of the children in the total population are using the second type of construction and 66 per cent of these are in the first grade." Hunt (1965) found that from Grade 4 to Grade 12 the "most important developmental trend" in the written language of his subjects involved relative clauses. Such structures more than doubled in frequency in those eight years of school life, with the increase being greater in the second half of the span. He also found that the number of relative clauses per "T-unit" (a syntactic unit measuring syntactic complexity and maturity) increased four-fold during this time. He concluded that the increased use of relative clauses was one of the most significant indicators of syntactic sophistication in written language. Similar results for both writing and speaking were found by Loban (1963), although O'Donnell, Griffin, and Norris (1967) report what they consider to be an "enigmatic feature" of their data: "kindergarten children used relative clauses more frequently than did children at any other stage, in either speech or writing."

Quigley, Smith, and Wilbur (1974) found that 83 percent of their oldest hearing subjects (10 years old) were able to respond correctly to the items of various tests concerned with RELATIVIZATION. Their findings also support Menyuk (1969) in showing that relative clauses were more difficult in medial than in final position in sentences, and further, that greater difficulty was found in understanding relative clauses when the pronoun had been in object position in deep structure (i.e., object relatives) than when it had been in subject position in deep structure (subject relatives). They found that the most difficult medial sentences were ones like "The girl who hit the boy went home," where even at 10 years of age, 41 percent of their hearing subjects interpreted this sentence to mean that it was the boy who went home. They point out that such misunderstandings seem to indicate that even hearing students might have "considerable difficulty in comprehending sentences with medially placed relatives at an age when they might be expected to encounter such sentences in their school reading materials."

Deaf Children's Acquisition of Relative Clauses

Quigley, Smith, and Wilbur (1974) further found that deaf students had significantly less understanding of all aspects of relative clauses than did hearing children of much younger ages. For instance, on a basic comprehension test the oldest hearing subjects (10 to 12 years) produced 83 percent correct responses, whereas the oldest deaf students (18 to 19 years) got only 76 percent correct. Overall results for each test used in the study showed similar retardation of the deaf subjects.

Detailed findings in this study are also of interest for one test whose items were of the form:

The girl who hit the boy went home.
What happened?

The girl hit the boy.	yes _____	no _____
The boy hit the girl.	yes _____	no _____
The boy went home.	yes _____	no _____
The girl went home.	yes _____	no _____

Items were provided with both subject and object relative clauses in final position and with both types of clause in medial position. There was found to be an interaction between clause and pronoun position, such that object relative clauses in final position ("I saw the boy *who(m) you helped*") were easiest, with subject relative clauses in final position ("I saw the boy *who kicked the girl*"), being next easiest. Next easiest were medially placed clauses with subject pronouns ("The girl *who hit the boy* went home"), which were easier than object pronouns ("The girl *whom you saw* went home").

The difficulty of medially placed relative clauses provides support for the conclusion of Power and Quigley (1973), based upon their study of the passive voice, that many deaf students, even at an advanced age, tend to interpret sentences only in terms of a "Surface Subject-Verb-Object Order" reading. They seem to adopt a strategy of looking for a "noun phrase-verb-noun phrase" sequence, and interpreting this as "subject-verb-object" irrespective of other markers in the sentence which indicate to a more sophisticated language user that such a reading is inappropriate. Thus a common interpretation by deaf students of "The boy who hit the girl went home" is that it was the girl who went home; similarly, "The boy was pushed by the girl" is interpreted to mean that the boy did the pushing. The presence of the relative pronoun and the passive markers are meaningless to many deaf students up to quite an advanced age, and the consequent misinterpretation of sentences must cause considerable confusion and frustration for deaf readers. Many other problems in the language learning of deaf students, such as their difficulties with auxiliary verbs and prepositions, may also be due to this sentence processing strategy.

In addition to illustrating the great retardation between deaf and hearing students in the use of relativized structures, and isolating the types of relative structures which presented most difficulty for their subjects, particularly those who were deaf, Quigley, Smith, and Wilbur (1974) identified several consistent deviancies from Standard English which deaf students found to be acceptable in comprehension tests and which they also used in their written productions. These deviancies from Standard English were labeled **Object-Subject Deletion, Object-Object Deletion,** "incorrect forms of the possessive," and **Relative Copying.** In Object-Subject Deletion the second occurrence of an *NP* in the embedded sentence is incorrectly deleted, apparently upon identity with an earlier occurrence in the matrix sentence. This produces such sentences as "The dog chased the girl had on a red dress," where "the girl" has been eliminated from the embedded sentence without being replaced by the relative pronoun "who" or "that." Object-Object Deletion is considered to have occurred when a deaf person, given the sentences "John chased the girl" and "He scared the girl" and asked to combine them, produces "John chased the girl and he scared." Deaf students in the study also continued to accept as correct such incorrect forms of the possessive as "I helped the boy's mother was sick" rather than "I helped the boy whose mother was sick." Thirty percent of responses were of this type even at almost 19 years of age. Confusion about the role of the relative pronoun is also evident in the occurrence of Relative Copying ("John saw the boy who the boy kicked the ball"). Even at almost 19 years of age, some 31 percent of the deaf subjects in the Quigley, Smith, and Wilbur study accepted such sentences as correct; such sentences also occurred frequently in the written language of the deaf subjects.

A major question which arises from these data is whether the consistent use by deaf persons of syntactic structures which deviate from Standard English indicates the presence of rules of grammar peculiar to the language of those deaf persons.

Quigley, Smith, and Wilbur concluded that the persistence of these deviancies along with correct forms of the same syntactic structures in the same subjects indicates that many deaf persons might have two or more parallel sets of rules for the generation of certain syntactic structures. These results and conclusions support those reported by Tervoort and Verberk (1967) in a study comparing the "esoteric" or private communication of deaf children with the "exoteric" language being taught to them in school. The Tervoort and Verberk study involved deaf students in four residential schools, two in the United States, one in the Netherlands, and one in Belgium. The investigators found that deaf students in the three countries apparently were operating with more than one rule for some syntactic structures, as indicated by the presence of consistent deviant forms along with correct forms of the same syntactic structures in the same students. There are important implications in these findings for teaching language to deaf students. If the teacher is armed with the appropriate techniques of linguistic analysis, and knowledge of the consistent syntactic deviancies in the language of deaf children, she can determine what rule of grammar underlies a number of specific deviancies in a deaf child's language and work for proper use of the appropriate rule of Standard English rather than attacking each of the deviancies separately. Such knowledge will also enable the teacher to evaluate and modify the syntactic structure of reading materials for deaf students, an area investigated by Power and Quigley (1973) and Quigley, Smith, and Wilbur (1974).

Analysis of Passivization and Relativization in the Reading Materials

The above-mentioned investigators analyzed the frequency of occurrence of syntactic structures in a typical series of readers used with both hearing and deaf students (McKee, et al., 1966) and consisting of three primers as well as eight books extending from the first to the sixth grade level. Results showed that the passive voice was used as early as the first-grade texts and that relativized structures first appeared in the second primer. Both structures increased in frequency of occurrence in successive books. It is obvious that for these two structures, passives and relatives, deaf students must be misunderstanding most of the reading materials they are expected to use, and in other chapters of this book it will be shown that this is true for other syntactic structures also. In fact, Power (1971), in analyzing the front page and the lead sports page of a newspaper for seven consecutive days, found a high incidence of sentences in the passive voice. Virtually every second sentence on the front page was written in the passive voice, and more than 25 percent of the sentences from both pages were passive voice sentences. Compare this, and the data from the reading series, with the findings of Power and Quigley (1973) that even 18-year-old deaf subjects had only 65 percent correct responses for non-reversible passive sentences, only 60 percent for reversible passives, and a mere 35 percent for agent-deleted passives, and the enormous importance of syntax in every phase of the deaf child's language development becomes apparent. It also becomes obvious that the deaf student's reading level is even lower than the very low level indicated by standard reading tests.

Furthermore, many of the *hearing* subjects in the Quigley, Smith, and Wilbur study had difficulty understanding some types of relativized sentences, indicating that control of syntactic structure might also be an important consideration in developing reading materials for hearing students. This is in agreement with the findings of Hatch (1969) and Labov (1967). Reading materials for young children generally are controlled for vocabulary and content, but not for syntax, except that sentence length usually is limited (Hatch, 1969). As Hatch points out, this lack of concern for syntactic structure in reading materials is probably related to the widely accepted notion that the child entering school already has internalized the structure of his language. As Quigley, Smith, and Wilbur have shown, this is not true for deaf children, and such studies as those of C. Chomsky (1969), Hatch (1969), Labov (1967), and Labov, Cohen, and Robins (1965) indicate that it is also not true for many other children.

CHAPTER 5

Transformations II: Question-Formation

The problem of Question-Formation in English is a rather involved one. Not only are there completely different classes of questions which are used, but there are often different ways of asking the same questions. One influencing factor is that of **intonation**. Intonation has to do with the relative pitch height of the voice throughout a sentence. Without going into detail here about pitch contours, we can distinguish between "falling intonation" and "rising intonation" on English sentences. Compare voice pitch, for example, on the **(a)** examples following as contrasted to the **(b)** examples.

(1a) John can visit Santa Claus.
(1b) John can visit Santa Claus?
(2a) Zorba has lost his Frisbee.
(2b) Zorba has lost his Frisbee?
(3a) Henrietta is the Ivory Soap Flakes girl.
(3b) Henrietta is the Ivory Soap Flakes girl?
(4a) Some intellectuals believe in poltergeists.
(4b) Some intellectuals believe in poltergeists?

In the **(a)** cases, all **declarative sentences** (or statements), the intonation can be described as falling; the **(b)** sentences, on the other hand, which are **interrogative sentences** (or questions), are characterized by rising intonation. Intonation is actually all that is necessary to distinguish between the two.

102

Yes-No Questions

English has another means of structuring questions with meanings like those of the **(b)** examples above: that class of questions known by linguists as (syntactic) **"Yes-No Questions."** Yes-No Questions can be answered by either "yes" or "no," in contrast to questions like "Who put the arsenic in the Dr. Pepper?" or "Where are the ostrich races being held?", where a "yes" or "no" answer would obviously bring nothing but stares. Sentences **(1b)-(4b)**, of course, are also Yes-No Questions, although they do not display the structural characteristics of those following.

The following examples are Yes-No counterparts to **(1b)-(4b)**, but with an obvious syntactic difference.

  (1c)   Can John visit Santa Claus?
  (2c)   Has Zorba lost his Frisbee?
  (3c)   Is Henrietta the Ivory Soap Flakes girl?
  (4c)   Do some intellectuals believe in poltergeists?

Sentences **(1c)-(4c)**, while displaying the characteristic rising intonation of Yes-No Questions, display in addition a structural difference from their counterparts in **(1b)-(4b)**. In the first three **(c)** examples, the difference is clearly one of order: the first two words of the sentence appear in a different order. Superficially the fourth example seems to be different, with the interrogative simply having the additional word "do," which does not appear in the declarative; it will be seen, however, that the same rule can account for all four examples.

Recall the following phrase structure rules:

  (5) $S \rightarrow NP + VP$
  (6) $VP \rightarrow Aux + V + (NP) + (NP) + (S) + (PP)$

The combination of these rules specifies the structure of any English sentence as **(7)**, where X may be $\emptyset$ or any of various combinations of *NP*'s, *S*'s, and *PP*'s.

  (7) $\left[_S NP \left[_{VP} Aux - V - X _{VP} \right] _S \right]$

Now let us consider more carefully the makeup of *Aux*, as summarized by the following phrase structure rules which were presented previously.

  (8) $Aux \rightarrow (Modal) + Tense + (Aspect)$
  (9) $Tense \rightarrow \left\{ \begin{array}{l} PAST \\ NONPAST \end{array} \right\}$
  (10) $Aspect \rightarrow (PROG|PERF)$

Tense can be either PAST or NONPAST; on the surface this distinction is incorporated into the verb, as in the following examples:

  (11a)   Grandfather *believed* Grandmother. (PAST)
  (11b)   Grandfather *believes* Grandmother. (NONPAST)

(12a) The wrestlers *fought* ferociously. (PAST)

(12b) The wrestlers *fight* ferociously. (NONPAST)

Regular verbs (those which form their past tense regularly) form the past tense by the addition of the suffix /d/ or /əd/ (as discussed more fully in Appendix A); **irregular verbs** may indicate the distinction in various idiosyncratic ways, as with the vowel difference in "fight:fought." The important point to remember is that in most cases past tense is manifest by the suffix. Nonpast tense, on the other hand, has no surface manifestation (the *s* on "believes" is the result of person-number agreement, not tense); nonpast tense is recognized only through the absence of a past tense indicator.

Notice now the relationship between the Tense morpheme and the verb at the level of deep structure. The auxiliary, including Tense, appears between the subject noun phrase and the verb. In order to arrive at the proper sequencing (considering that the Past Tense suffix must appear as part of the verb, and in most cases at its end), a rule is needed to move the PAST node. The rule which does this has been given the picturesque name of AFFIX HOPPING. The following example shows how it works:

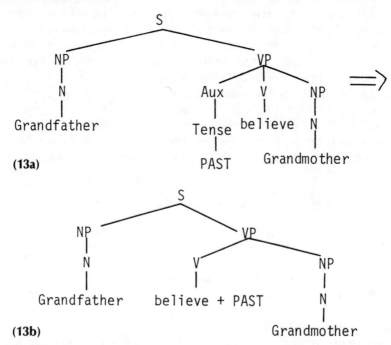

(13a)

(13b)

Notice that since everything has been moved out from under the *Aux* node, it no longer serves a purpose and can be deleted. Now morphological and phonological rules will specify *believe + PAST* as "believed." If the tense had been NONPAST, the morphological and phonological rules would eventually specify it as ∅, giving "believe."

Affix Hopping is an extremely complex phenomenon, and we shall not attempt to formalize it here. Let us consider, however, how it relates to Aspect. A sentence can be Perfective, Progressive, or both. For simplicity, we shall consider the two relevant lexical insertion rules to be as follows:

(14) PERF → have + -en

(15) PROG → be + -ing

(Remember, however, that -en represents the abstract Past Participle morpheme, and, depending on the verb, may appear as -en (has "eaten"), -ed ("has believed"), as a vowel change in the verb ("has fought"), and so forth.

Now consider the following tree:

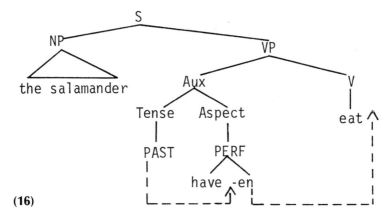

(16)

Notice that Affix Hopping must apply twice in this case: first to put "have" in the past tense, and second to produce the past participle form of "eat." The result is something like the following:

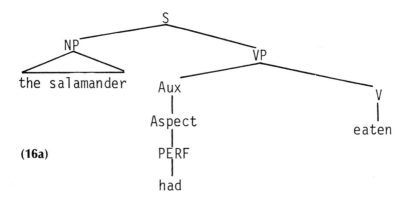

(16a)

The case is similar with the Progressive Aspect, as exemplified by the following:

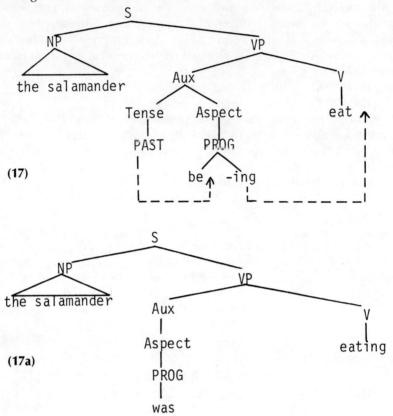

(17)

(17a)

Things become even more complicated in the case of a Perfect Progressive sentence, as can be seen by the following:

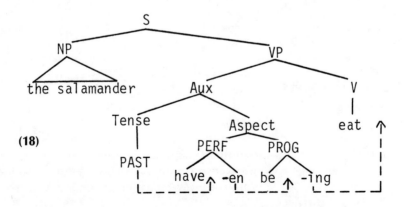

(18)

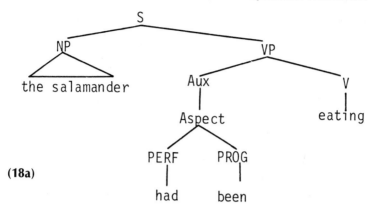

(18a)

In this case, Affix Hopping must apply three times: the PAST morpheme is attached to "have," the Past Participle morpheme *-en* is attached to "be," and the Progressive *-ing* morpheme is attached to the verb "eat."

Thus, in each case where an affix (suffixes in all of our examples) appears as a node by itself, Affix Hopping applies to attach it to the next morpheme to the right. There are many simplifications in our formulation, and many problems. In particular, notice that the "have" of the Perfective and the "be" of the Progressive take derivational suffixes such as the Perfective suffix and the Past Participle suffix, and in many other ways function just like verbs. Some linguists have proposed, therefore, that they be considered true verbs rather than auxiliaries.

Now that Affix Hopping has been presented, let us return to Yes-No Questions. Consider first **(1c)** ("Can John visit Santa Claus?") and **(2c)** ("Has Zorba lost his Frisbee?"). It is clear that "can" (a Modal) and "has" (a marker of the Perfective) are auxiliaries. We can say, then, that in these cases the auxiliary has been moved to a position before the subject noun phrase. This transformation has been called SUBJECT-AUX INVERSION.

Sentence **(3c)** ("Is Henrietta the Ivory Soap Flakes girl?") poses some difficulties, since "is" and other forms of *be* in predicate complement constructions such as this have traditionally been considered to be, and in fact look like, a special class of verb. If we were to consider Modals and Aspect markers to be verbs as well, we could avoid the problem, but we would then have to explain why Subject-Aux Inversion moves the verb in sentences like **(1c)-(3c)**, but not in sentences like **(4c)** ("Do some intellectuals believe in poltergeists?"), where "believe" does not move. Another possibility exists, however. Recall that with predicate adjectives it is possible to claim that *be* is not present in deep structure, (see page 61), but is inserted by a transformation; a similar claim could be made for predicate nominative constructions like **(3c)**.

It would be possible to claim, then, that the *be* is attached to the *Aux* node, when inserted, which will then make it eligible for Subject-Aux Inversion in questions.

It is interesting to consider the action of the verb *have* with respect to Subject-Aux Inversion. First of all, there appear to be two different words with the same shape: that which functions as the Perfective auxiliary, and that which has been considered traditionally to be a main verb, as in the following:

(19)   The Mafia *has* many informers.

In the case of Standard American English, Yes-No Question-Formation poses no problems; the question which is related to the above statement results from a rule called DO-SUPPORT (to be discussed in detail below), which inserts a form of the verb *do* in certain environments.

(19a)   *Does* the Mafia have many informers?

In some other dialects (especially British), however, the question is as follows:

(19b)   *Has* the Mafia many informers?

Here Subject-Aux Inversion has applied to what appears to be a main verb. It seems that in these dialects the verb *have* functions in some ways like an auxiliary; the problem is similar to that of *be*, but is a little more difficult to handle. This question is one which will have to remain unanswered here.

A noun phrase, of course, cannot take a Tense suffix ("dogged" is not the past tense of "dog"!), and as a result the Tense is stranded at the beginning of the sentence. However, because in English the Tense is an integral part of a sentence, the Tense is not lost. Instead, a rule called Do-Support applies. Do-Support inserts the morpheme *do* just in case the Tense marker is stranded! Thus the derivation of **(4c)** is something like the following (ignoring details of tree structure):

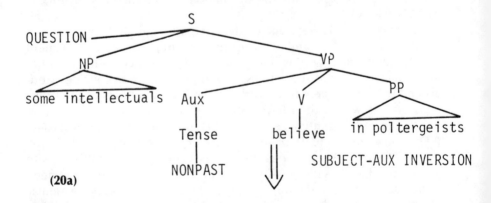

(20a)

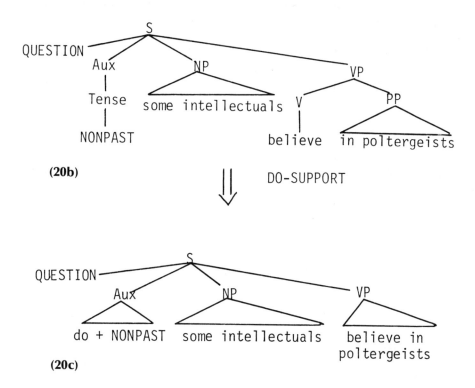

(20b)

⇓ DO-SUPPORT

(20c)

Finally, a morphological rule will specify *do + NONPAST* as "do" and the QUESTION node will be deleted.

Do-Support is not restricted to questions, but applies in certain other cases as well, as will be seen later.

One qualification must be stated with respect to application of Subject-Aux Inversion. Examples like the following show that it is not always the entire auxiliary that is moved in front of the subject.

(21) Might he have gone yesterday?
(22) Had he been going regularly?
(23) Will he have been going?

In **(21)**, the Modal has been moved, but the Perfective marker has remained behind; in **(22)**, on the other hand, the Perfective marker has moved but the Progressive marker has not. In **(23)** the Modal has moved and left both the Perfect and Progressive markers. Example **(22)** shows, however, that the *Tense* node must be moved to the front as well; this is further exemplified by the following:

(24) Did Hercules eat his spinach?
(25) Was Hosea weaving baskets?

Tense, then, is incorporated into the element which has moved, rather than the "main" verb. It seems, then, that what is moved in Subject-Aux Inversion is, first of all, the *Tense*, and second, the first "verb-like" element in the auxiliary.

It is clear that Subject-Aux Inversion, while seemingly a simple process, is actually very complex, and has thus far eluded attempts at full elucidation by linguists. The foregoing should at least suffice as a general description of the various aspects of its workings.

WH-Questions

Yes-No Questions, then, are characterized by Subject-Aux Inversion. The other major class of questions is known as **WH-Questions,** exemplified by the following examples:

(26)   Who ate the porridge?
(27)   What has Zelda done?
(28)   When did Columbus discover America?
(29)   Where can I find George Washington?

The reason for the name is apparent: each WH-Question begins with a WH-word: "who," "what," "when," or "where." Each such question is answered with either a noun phrase or a prepositional phrase: possible answers for **(26)–(29)** might be "Goldilocks," "Joined the Packers," "1492" (or "In 1492"), and "At the front." It has been claimed that WH-words are used to question **indefinite noun phrases** (those which do not specify unique items) in deep structure. Thus, the deep structure of **(26)–(29)** might be roughly as follows:

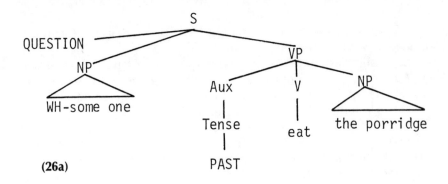

(26a)

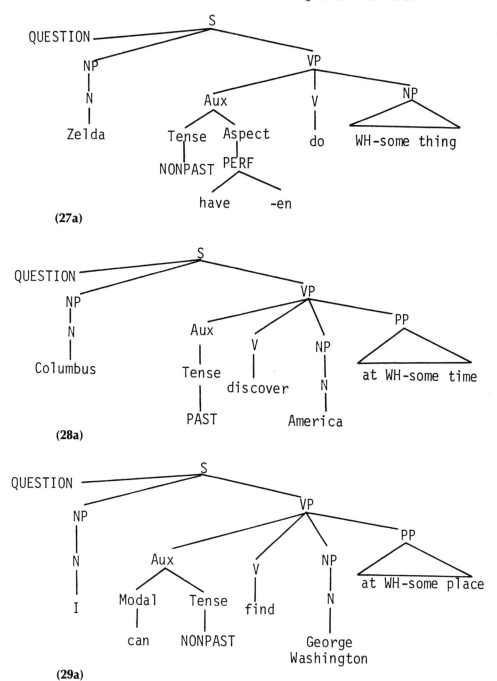

(27a)

(28a)

(29a)

Now notice an interesting thing about sentences **(27)–(29)**. It is clear that in each case Subject-Aux Inversion has applied to move elements of the auxiliary in front of the noun phrase. Although this does not seem to be the case in **(26)**, we shall see that Subject-Aux Inversion has applied here as well. Application of this rule to **(26a)–(29a)** gives the following:

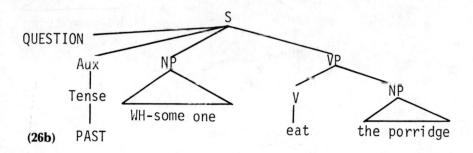

(26b)

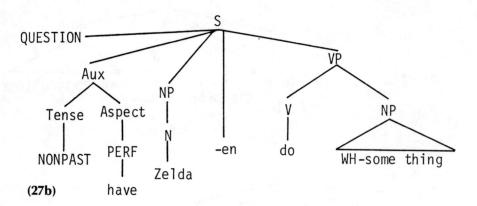

(27b)

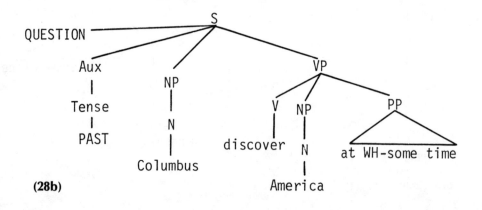

(28b)

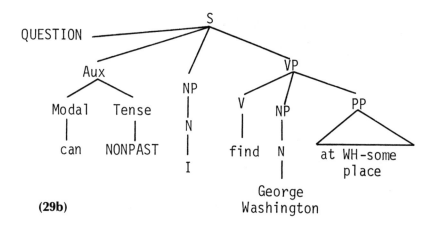

(29b)

(Recall that Subject-Aux Inversion does not always move the entire *Aux*, but the *Tense* and the first verb-like element; thus, in **(27b)** the *-en* is left behind. It is not clear what the tree should look like now in the vicinity of *-en*; the problem of derived tree structure is one which appears often in linguistic description.)

Now in order to produce the surface structure, the indefinite noun phrase must be moved into position at the beginning of the sentence. This movement transformation can be formulated as follows:

(30) SD: QUESTION – X – (Prep) – $[_{NP}$ WH – some N$_{NP}]$

SC: QUESTION – (Prep) – $[_{NP}$ WH – some N$_{NP}]$ – X

Condition: N = $\begin{Bmatrix} \text{one} \\ \text{thing} \\ \text{time} \\ \text{place} \end{Bmatrix}$

According to this rule, in any sentence with a question marker, if there is an indefinite noun phrase with *WH-some N*, where N is "one," "thing," "time," or "place," the noun phrase (with its preposition, if there is one) is moved across any intervening material to a position directly after the QUESTION node.

The result of application of the WH-Question Movement rule to **(26b)–(29b)** will be the following trees:

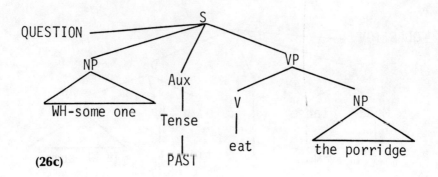

(26c)

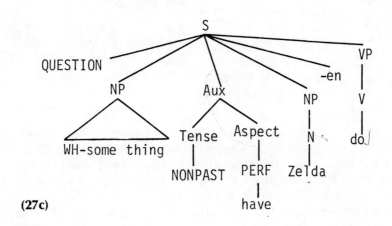

(27c)

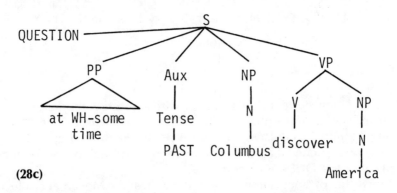

(28c)

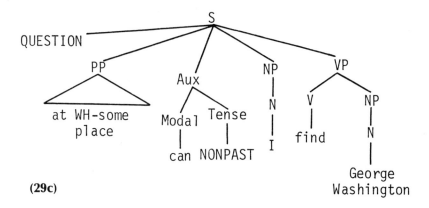

(29c)

Notice that in the case of **(26c)**, the *Aux* and the subject *NP* have changed places again (ignoring again the problem of the derived structure), essentially undoing the effect of Subject-Aux Inversion; this is the reason that its effect is not seen in **(26)**. Of course, this has been accomplished by applying Subject-Aux Inversion first, before the WH-Question Movement. If we were to apply the rules in the other order, we would somehow have to prevent Subject-Aux Inversion from applying. **Rule Ordering** has commonly been used in transformational grammar to avoid problems of this type.

Trees **(26c)** and **(27c)** now satisfy the environment for Affix Hopping (once in the case of **(26c)**, twice for **(27c)**). Sentence **(28c)** satisfies the environment for Do-Support (since there is no adjacent verb to attach the Tense to). Application of these rules gives the following:

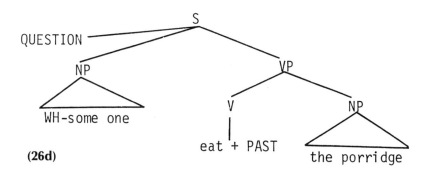

(26d)

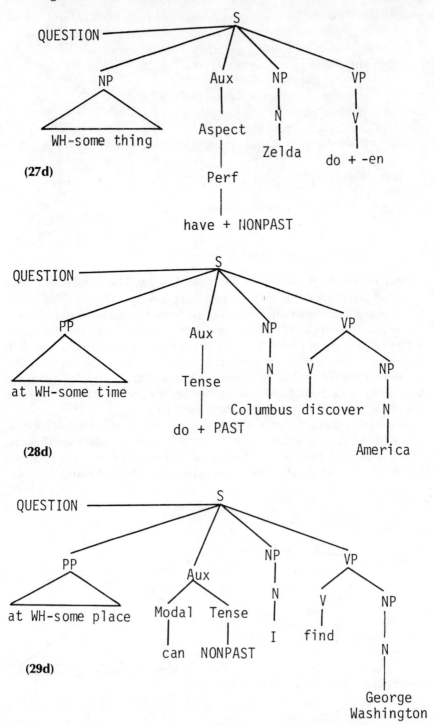

(27d)

(28d)

(29d)

Once rules have applied to incorporate PAST, NONPAST, and -*en* into the appropriate words, the only remaining steps are the following:

1. The indefinite *NP*'s are changed as follows:

   WH-some one $\Longrightarrow$ who
   WH-some thing $\Longrightarrow$ what
   at WH-some time $\Longrightarrow$ when
   at WH-some place $\Longrightarrow$ where

2. The QUESTION node is deleted.

Finally, the result is the questions **(26)–(29)**, repeated below as **(31)– (34)**.

(31) Who ate the porridge?
(32) What has Zelda done?
(33) When did Columbus discover America?
(34) Where can I find George Washington?

Tag Questions

Structures like the following are known as **Tag Questions.**

(35) Percival is a pickpocket, *isn't he?*
(36) Bridget brought balloons, *didn't she?*
(37) Willie will wind watches, *won't he?*
(38) Clarisse can count coins, *can't she?*
(39) Percival isn't a pickpocket, *is he?*
(40) Bridget didn't bring balloons, *did she?*
(41) Willie won't wind watches, *will he?*
(42) Clarisse can't count coins, *can she?*

In simplified terms, one can see that the tag of a Tag Question (*the italic portions above*) contains (1) the first auxiliary verb from the main sentence on which it is formed; and (2) a pronoun referring to the subject of the main sentence. The third feature, however, relates to whether the source sentence is positive or negative. Notice that in sentences **(35)–(38)**, each of which has a positive (or non-negative) source sentence, the tag is negative, containing the word "not" (or the contracted form "n't"); while in **(39)–(42)**, which have negative source sentences, the tag is positive. This is a general rule: positive sentences have negative tags, negative sentences have positive tags.

Some Additional Problems

It is plain that Question-Formation in English is a complex matter. Yes-No Questions involve Subject-Aux Inversion, Do-Support, and Affix Hopping, all of which are transformations difficult to define precisely. WH-Questions, in addition to the three transformations mentioned, also undergo WH-Question Movement.

There are still many question types which have not been discussed.

Although the field is much too complex for us to include all types here, we shall discuss two or three further complications.

Consider the following sentences:

(43) {Which / What} girl ate the porridge?

(44) What barbarism has Zelda done?

(45) In {which / what} year did Columbus discover America?

(46) At {which / what} front can I find George Washington?

Sentences **(43)**–**(46)** display obvious similarities to **(31)**–**(34)**. In these cases, however, the WH-word does not stand alone, but rather requests specification of a following noun which it modifies. It seems reasonable to assume that the deep structures of these sentences might be something like the following:

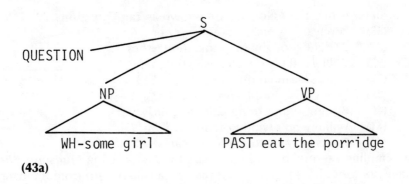

(43a)

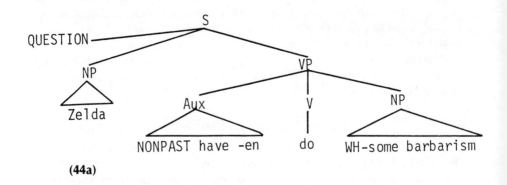

(44a)

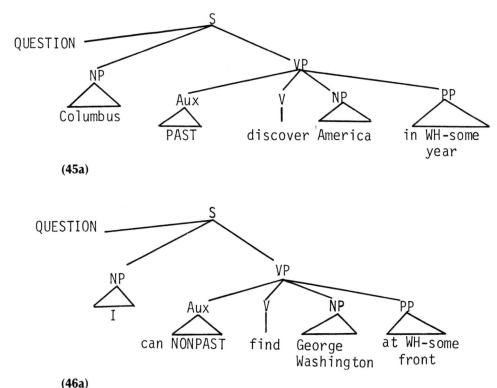

(45a)

(46a)

Trees **(43a)–(46a)** differ from **(26a)–(29a)** only in the noun of the indefinite noun phrase. It appears that sentences like **(43)–(46)** result from a rule which replaces only the *Determiner* in an indefinite Noun Phrase (rather than the entire Noun Phrase, as in regular WH-Questions) by a WH-word: that is, WH-some $\longrightarrow$ $\begin{Bmatrix} \text{which} \\ \text{what} \end{Bmatrix}$

As usual, there are complications. While "which" and "what" are usually interchangeable in such constructions, this is not always true (in **(44)**, for example, "which" cannot be used). In addition, sentences with "what" are not always exactly synonymous to those with "which," as pointed out in Borkin, et al. (1972). Sentence **(47)** exemplifies this difficulty.

    (47)   What student likes to take exams?

This sentence can be used to ask which student it is that likes to take exams, or it can be used rhetorically to claim that there is no such student. Sentence **(48)** cannot have the second, rhetorical meaning.

    (48)   Which student likes to take exams?

The last questions we shall discuss are those with "why" and "how," as in the following.

(49)   How does Clyde rob banks?

(50)   Why does Clyde rob banks?

These two sentences seem parallel to sentences **(31)–(34)**, and it is tempting to set up deep structures with indefinite prepositional phrases: we might use, for example, **(49a)** and **(50a)**.

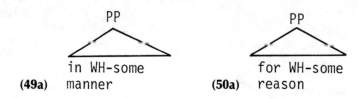

	PP		PP
	in WH-some		for WH-some
(49a)	manner	**(50a)**	reason

Borkin et al. have observed that sentences **(49)** and **(50)** are ambiguous, however. For example, **(49)** could be answered in either of the following two ways:

(49c)   By holding a gun on those present and ordering them to give him money.

(49d)   Very well.

Similarly, **(50)** could be answered in at least two ways:

(50c)   Because he enjoys it.

(50d)   So that he can support his family.

Only one of the meanings of each of the two sentences **(49)** and **(50)** will be produced by deep structures with indefinite prepositional phrases such as those proposed above. Whether two different deep structures must be provided to account for the ambiguity in each case, or whether the proposed deep structures are simply completely wrong, is not at all clear. "How" and "why" questions continue to be a problem.

Embedded Questions

The italicized portions of the following sentences appear to be semantically related to questions.

(51)   Bill wonders {if / whether (or not)} *John can visit Santa Claus.*

(52)   Bill wonders {if / whether (or not)} *Zorba has lost his Frisbee.*

(53)   Bill wonders {if / whether (or not)} *Henrietta is the Ivory Soap Flakes girl.*

(54) Bill wonders $\left\{\begin{array}{l} if \\ whether\ (or\ not) \end{array}\right\}$ *some intellectuals believe in poltergeists.*

(55) Bill wonders *who ate the porridge.*

(56) Bill wonders *what Zelda has done.*

(57) Bill wonders *when Columbus discovered America.*

(58) Bill wonders *where I can find George Washington.*

The italicized portions above are called **embedded questions.** It is clear that the embedded questions of **(51)-(54)** are related to the Yes-No Questions **(1c)-(4c)** (repeated below as **(51a)-(54a)**); similarly, the questions embedded in **(55)-(58)** are related to the WH-Questions **(26)-(29)** (repeated below as **(55a)-(58a)**).

(51a) Can John visit Santa Claus?

(52a) Has Zorba lost his Frisbee?

(53a) Is Henrietta the Ivory Soap Flakes girl?

(54a) Do some intellectuals believe in poltergeists?

(55a) Who ate the porridge?

(56a) What has Zelda done?

(57a) When did Columbus discover America?

(58a) Where can I find George Washington?

The first characteristic which stands out is the "if" or "whether" in the embedded Yes-No Questions, and the WH-word in each embedded WH-Question. There is a definite difference in structure between the original questions and their embedded counterparts: Subject-Aux Inversion has not applied to **(51)-(58)**! In other words, no question rules apply to embedded Yes-No Questions; instead, an "if" or "whether" is inserted at the beginning. In embedded WH-Questions, WH-Question Movement applies, but Subject-Aux Inversion does not.

Embedded questions function like noun phrases. Although we cannot apply the PASSIVE test, since "wonder" is a verb which does not passivize, we can demonstrate this by the PSEUDO-CLEFT transformation. The **(b)** version of each sentence following is related to the **(a)** version by PSEUDO-CLEFT.

(59a) Ben wants a horseless carriage.

(59b) What Ben wants is a horseless carriage.

(60a) A meteorite hit me.

(60b) What hit me was a meteorite.

The important thing to notice here is that in a pseudo-cleft sentence the element following the copula (i.e., the verb *be*) is a noun phrase. In this connection notice the following in comparison to **(51)**, **(52)**, **(55)**, and **(56)**.

(51a) What Bill wonders is $\left\{\begin{array}{l} if \\ whether\ (or\ not) \end{array}\right\}$ John can visit Santa Claus.

(52a) What Bill wonders is $\left\{\begin{array}{l} if \\ whether\ (or\ not) \end{array}\right\}$ Zorba has lost his Frisbee.

(55a)   What Bill wonders is who ate the porridge.
(56a)   What Bill wonders is what Zelda has done.

Not only are the embedded questions noun phrases, but they are also sentences, since they have a subject and an object. The deep structures, then, of **(51)**, **(52)**, **(55)**, and **(56)** look like this (ignoring irrelevant details):

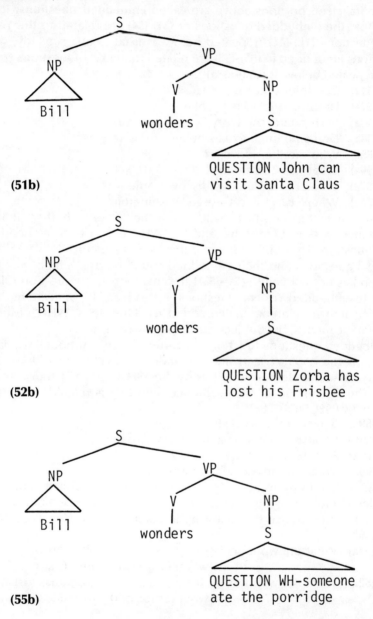

(51b)   QUESTION John can
                   visit Santa Claus

(52b)   QUESTION Zorba has
                   lost his Frisbee

(55b)   QUESTION WH-someone
                   ate the porridge

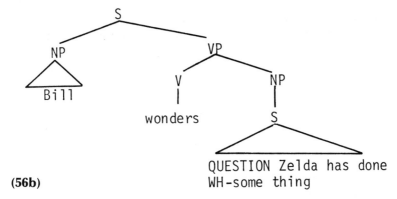

(56b)

Notice that in these trees the *NP* node admissibility condition is violated by those *NP*'s which dominate an *S* node only; it is necessary to add another rule to the base: *NP*→*S*.

The rules which have been discussed in connection with questions will all apply to the embedded *S* in each sentence, with the exception of Subject-Aux Inversion. In addition, a rule which applies only to embedded Yes-No Questions will insert "if" or "whether" into **(51b)** and **(52b)**. The final result will be the sentences **(51)**, **(52)**, **(55)**, and **(56)**.

A variety of constructions can take embedded questions; in addition to "wonder," there are verbs like "ask," negative structures like "don't know," and more complex structures like "wants to know." The reader can provide additional examples; we shall not go into any more detail here.

Some linguists have also claimed that sentences like the following are embedded question constructions (see A. Borkin, et al. for examples).

(61) What John admires in Martha is a mystery to me.

These will not be discussed further here.

Further WH-Question Types

In certain cases questions occur in which WH-words appear, but in which the WH-word remains in its deep structure position. Examples are the following:

(62) Zelda has done what?

(63) Columbus discovered America in what year?

Such questions differ not only in structure, but also in intonation, from regular WH-Questions with movement. Whereas normal WH-Questions have falling intonation, sentences like **(62)** and **(63)** show a rising intonation. They are used to repeat part of a statement made by someone else, and show surprise or a request for additional information. They are thus known as **Echo Questions.** Sentences **(1b)-(4b)** given earlier (repeated as **(64)-(67)**) are parallel examples of Yes-No Echo Questions.

   (64)   John can visit Santa Claus?
   (65)   Zorba has lost his Frisbee?
   (66)   Henrietta is the Ivory Soap Flakes girl?
   (67)   Some intellectuals believe in poltergeists?

Notice that in both cases, Echo Questions have the same basic structure as the corresponding statements, but are understood to be questions because of their rising intonation and, in the case of Echo WH-Questions, by the presence of a WH-word.

   One more complex type of WH-Question should be mentioned here, exemplified by **(68).**

   (68)   Who saw who throw what?

In sentence **(68),** three different elements are being questioned, but because only one WH-word can be moved in English, two of the WH-words remain in their original position. However, as A. Borkin, et al. (1972) point out, there is an additional problem with sentences like this: namely, the person asking the question may expect either to be told only who did the seeing, or to be given a specification of the different people involved in separate acts of throwing. It is also possible to use sentence **(68)** as an echo question.

Hearing Children's Acquisition of Questions

   As can be seen from the linguistic description in this chapter, the full set of Standard English question forms is highly complex, and research shows that its more difficult aspects (such as the use of embedded questions) may not be completely mastered until children are about 9 years of age (C. Chomsky, 1969). Nevertheless, most simpler aspects of asking questions seem to be mastered by most children by the time they start school. Klima and Bellugi-Klima (1966) found three broad stages in children's use of questions. In the first stage, Yes-No Questions consisted only of using the rising intonation contour without any re-arrangement of word order (i.e., with the "Echo Question" structure) ("I ride train?" "Ball go?"). Treatment of WH-Questions was similar. The WH-word was just placed before the **telegraphic sentence** nucleus without any other characteristics of question structure being present ("Where kitty?" "Who that?" "What cowboy doing?"). "Who that?" seemed to be the only "who" question used and the "what" and "where" questions were mostly restricted to narrow routines involving "doing" and "going." The authors also felt that children have little understanding at this stage of what constituent is actually being questioned. They reported such exchanges as the following:

Mother: What did you hit?
Child: Hit.
Mother: What did you do?
Child: Head.

As Klima and Bellugi-Klima conclude, "At this period . . . children are producing questions that only superficially resemble those questions in which the object of a verb has been questioned and preposed, and they do not understand this question when they hear it."

At Stage 2 of question development, little progress has been made toward the acquisition of standard forms. Major developments consist of increased use of pronouns, articles, and modifiers, and the appearance of Present Progressive verb inflections and plurals. It would appear that in this stage children are genuinely using questions to request information represented by a specific constituent of a sentence. There is still no Subject-Aux Inversion in Yes-No Questions, but appropriate answers are now being given to many questions:

Mother: What d'you need?
Child: Need some chocolate.
Mother: Who are you peeking at?
Child: Peeking at Ursula.
Mother: What d'you hear?
Child: Hear a duck.

It appears that the full development of question forms has to wait until the child has acquired the use of auxiliaries and modals, and it is the use of these at Stage 3 that signals the child's close proximity to an adult command of the simpler question forms. As can be seen from the following examples, there are still some problems with number agreement, but the system is almost complete.

Does lions walk?
Did I saw that in my book?
Are you going to make it with me?
Where I should put it when I make it up?
What I did yesterday?
Why kitty can't stand up?
Can't you work this thing?

The findings of Menyuk (1969) are essentially in agreement with those of Klima and Bellugi-Klima (1966). She found that question intonation superimposed on an otherwise unchanged sentence provided the earliest kind of question. According to Menyuk, "conjunction of an element to a sentence with no operations on the underlying sentence" appears next ("Where Daddy go?"). She also states that "Until the Auxiliary/Modal node of the Categorial component of the base structure of the grammar is acquired by the child, completely well-formed structures cannot be derived and the transformational rules that have been described for the generation of negative and question sentences cannot be applied. When one observes independent use of Auxiliary/Modal one also observes completely well-formed . . . questions."

Quigley, Wilbur, and Montanelli (1975) reported that the hearing children they tested demonstrated virtually 100 percent correct responses on tests involving the understanding of Yes-No, WH-, and Tag Questions, and Subject-Aux Inversion, by the age of 10 years.

Deaf Children's Acquisition of Questions

The findings of Quigley, Wilbur, and Montanelli (1974) indicated that there are developmental stages in the acquisition of Question-Formation by deaf students similar to those found for hearing children. They found that comprehension of Yes-No Questions was easier for their subjects than was comprehension of WH-Questions, which, in turn, was easier than comprehension of Tag Questions. It was also easier for the deaf subjects to make correct judgments of grammaticality on Yes-No Question stimuli than on WH-Question stimuli. This is the same order of difficulty predicted by transformational theory, and also the order of emergence recorded in young hearing children by Klima and Bellugi-Klima (1966) and Brown and Hanlon (1970). Further evidence of similarity in stages of development between deaf and hearing subjects was found in the results of tests of judgments of grammaticality of questions using WH-words. Ervin-Tripp (1970) reported that "who" as a subject was easier for young hearing children to understand than "when" or "who" as an object. Exactly the same results were found by Quigley, Wilbur, and Montanelli (1974) for deaf subjects. Thus, deaf children seem to differ from hearing children in the acquisition of Question-Formation primarily in rate rather than in sequence of acquisition. Deaf children studied by Quigley, et al. even at 18 years of age did not have the mastery of this structure common to their 10-year-old hearing subjects.

Despite the general similarity between deaf and hearing individuals in the development of question forms, Quigley, Wilbur, and Montanelli found some evidence of deviant rules in the language of deaf students co-existing with the rules of Standard English. Relative Copying, which was discussed in the chapter on Relativization, was found also in the study of Question-Formation. As the age of the deaf subjects increased, there was a significant tendency to reject questions in which Copying occurred (e.g., "Who did *the dog* chase the boy?"). However, even the oldest deaf subjects, at almost 19 years of age, still accepted such questions as correct 37 percent of the time. Since items containing Relative Copying were acceptable to large numbers of deaf students in tests of Questions and Relativization, and since Copying has been found frequently in the written language of deaf children (Quigley and Power, 1972; Taylor, 1969), it seems to reflect a stable grammatical rule in the language of many deaf people—a rule which is not found in Standard English.

Analysis of Question-Formation in the Reading Materials

The existence of deviant rules in question forms and the slower rate of development of these structures in deaf individuals has implications for the development of teaching materials. Quigley, Wilbur, and Montanelli (1974) compared the level of development of question forms in deaf students 10 through 18 years of age with the appearance of the same question forms in the reading series* discussed in Chapter 5. The series tested consists of 11 books including three primers and extending to the sixth-grade level of reading. Yes-No Questions were present in the first primer, and occurred approximately 8 times per 100 sentences in the third primer and first grade reader. WH-Questions first appeared in the second primer and occurred at the rate of 11 times per 100 sentences in the second and third primers. Yet, as Quigley, Wilbur, and Montanelli indicate, deaf students have difficulty comprehending printed questions. Since comprehension of questions is important, not only for reading, but in teacher-pupil interaction in the classroom, materials used with deaf students need to be controlled in syntax to the level of the deaf child's comprehension.

Reading for Meaning, 4th Edition, Houghton Mifflin Company, 1966

CHAPTER 6

Transformations III: Conjunction, Pronominalization, and Reflexivization

Conjunction

Conjunction (the joining of sentences by "and," "but," and "or") has been discussed briefly in earlier chapters as being generated by the base component through phrase structure rules like $S \rightarrow S$ and S, and $NP \rightarrow NP$ and NP.

Consider the following instances of conjunction with "and." In each case the conjoined constituents (**conjuncts**) are italicized.

(1)   *Henry fixes cars* and *Herman is a specialist on Afghanistan.*

(2)   *Myrtle* and *Murgatroyd* do fascinating artwork.

(3)   I especially like *Hopalong Cassidy* and *Roy Rogers.*

(4)   Zacharias *collects flies* and *races trains.*

(5)   We *caught* and *cleaned* 149 fish.

(6)   The guard was taken care of *quickly* and *silently.*

(7)   You will never grow up to be *big* and *strong.*

It is clear from the above that a wide variety of constituents can be conjoined. Sentences (1)-(7) exemplify, in order, conjoined sentences, conjoined noun phrases in subject and object position, conjoined verb phrases, conjoined verbs, conjoined abverbs, and conjoined adjectives. (In this chapter "and" conjunction only will be discussed; conjunction with "or" and "but" acts very similarly.) Also, although two constituents of the same type can be conjoined, two constituents of different types cannot; the following are clearly "word salad."

(8)   **Bill* and *quickly* rode through the town.

(9)   **Henrietta belives in *werewolves* and *stupid.*

Sentences like **(2)-(7)** are believed to be derived from underlying conjoined sentences through a process known as CONJUNCTION REDUCTION. Thus, the structures underlying these sentences will be the following (tree structures will be omitted, but it should be remembered that deep structures have a tree-like hierarchical structure):

(2a) Myrtle *does fascinating artwork* and Murgatroyd *does fascinating artwork.*

(3a) *I especially like* Hopalong Cassidy and *I especially like* Roy Rogers.

(4a) *Zacharias* collects flies and *Zacharias* races trains.

(5a) *We* caught *149 fish* and *we* cleaned *149 fish.*

(6a) *The guard was taken care of* quickly and *the guard was taken care of* silently.

(7a) *You will never grow up to be* big and *you will never grow up to be* strong.

In each of the structures **(2a)-(7a)**, at least one constituent of the first sentence conjunct is repeated in the second conjunct. These are italicized above for clarity. (Notice that in **(5a)** two constituents are repeated: "we" and "149 fish.") A comparison of these deep structure strings with sentences **(2)-(7)** reveals that in the latter, each of these constituents appears only once. In other words, when identical constituents appear in both conjuncts of an underlying conjoined sentence, Conjunction Reduction applies to delete one of the two identical parts. This is one of the processes of English which serves to reduce redundancy—the unnecessary repetition of words. Since any speaker of English understands from sentence **(2)** that Myrtle does fascinating artwork and that Murgatroyd also does fascinating artwork, it is unnecessary to repeat the verb phrase twice.

Again comparing **(2a)-(7a)** with **(2)-(7)**, it can be seen that sometimes it is the first of the two identical constituents that is deleted, and sometimes the second. For example, it is apparently the first instance of "do fascinating artwork" (the form of "do/does" is decided by later agreement rules) which is deleted in **(2a)**, since deletion of the second instance would result in the ungrammatical **(2b)**.

(2b)   *Myrtle {does} fascinating artwork and Murgatroyd.
           {do }

Similarly, in **(3a)** it appears as though the second "I especially like" is deleted, since deletion of the first would give **(3b)**.

(3b)   *Hopalong Cassidy and I especially like Roy Rogers.
(Sentence **(3b)** turns out by chance to be grammatical, but only with an entirely different meaning. In the sense of **(3a)**, **(3b)** is ungrammatical.)

As Wilbur, Quigley, and Montanelli (1975) have suggested, it may be that the reason that it is sometimes the first instance of an identical string which is deleted, and sometimes the second, is the existence of an additional constraint in English, which "specifies that the application of Conjunction Reduction must produce a sentence which has as its initial or final (but not medial) element, the word or phrase which was identical in both sentences before the sentences were reduced." That is, a constituent which is repeated in deep structure always ends up at either the beginning or the end of the sentence. Thus, in **(2a)**, correct application of deletion to the first instance of the identical constituents results in **(2)**, where the remaining instance of "do fascinating artwork" appears at the end of the sentence; incorrect deletion of the second instance gives **(2b)**, where the remaining instance of the verb phrase appears (contrary to the above constraint) medially in the sentence. In **(3a)**, on the other hand, if the first instance of "I especially like" is deleted, the result is **(3b)**, with the second "I especially like" appearing medially. In this case, the second instance must be deleted, which leaves the string at the beginning of the sentence **(3)**. In the same way, Conjunction Reduction applies to **(4a)**, **(6a)**, and **(7a)** to leave the remaining one of two identical strings in initial position in the corresponding surface sentences **(4)**, **(6)**, and **(7)**. It has already been seen that Conjunction Reduction must apply twice to **(5a)**: first to the identical subject noun phrases "we," and secondly, to the identical object noun phrases "149 fish." In the first case, the remaining string appears initially (in the final versions) and in the second case, the string remaining appears finally.

Another process similar to Conjunction Reduction is known as GAP-PING. Gapping applies to **(10a)** and **(11a)** to produce **(10b)** and **(11b)**, respectively.

> **(10a)**   Bill *caught* fish and Henry *caught* an old rubber tire.
> **(10b)**   Bill caught fish and Henry an old rubber tire.
> **(11a)**   Sally *believes* in witchcraft and Mortimer *believes* in ESP.
> **(11b)**   Sally believes in witchcraft and Mortimer in ESP.

Like Conjunction Reduction, Gapping depends on identity, in this case identity between the verbs of the two sentences (italicized above). With Gapping, deletion always applies forward in the sentence to delete the second of two identical verbs, and, in contrast to Conjunction Reduction, the result is not conjoined constituents, but rather a strange gap in the second conjunct of the sentence.

As a final comment, it might be noted that Conjunction Reduction and Gapping can apply not just once, but any number of times, depending on the number of conjuncts present in the deep structure. For example:

> **(12a)** Myrtle *does fascinating artwork* and Murgatroyd *does fascinating artwork* and Mabel *does fascinating artwork* and . . .

CONJ. RED.   (**12b**)   Myrtle and Murgatroyd and Mabel and . . . do fasci-
$\Longrightarrow$ nating artwork.

(**13a**)   Bill *caught* fish and Henry *caught* an old rubber tire
and Herman *caught* a pair of galoshes and . . . and
Zorko *caught* a salamander.

GAPPING   (**13b**)   Bill caught fish, Henry an old rubber tire, Herman a
$\Longrightarrow$ pair of galoshes, . . ., and Zorko a salamander.

Pronominalization

PRONOMINALIZATION is a term which refers to the process which produces **pronouns** (sometimes referred to as **personal pronouns** to distinguish them from relative pronouns), traditionally categorized as follows:

Singular

	Subject Pronouns	Object Pronouns	Possessive Pronouns	Possessive Adjectives
1st Person	I	me	mine	my
2nd Person	you	you	yours	your
3rd Person	he, she, it	him, her, it	his, hers, its	his, her, its

Plural

	Subject Pronouns	Object Pronouns	Possessive Pronouns	Possessive Adjectives
1st Person	we	us	ours	our
2nd Person	you	you	yours	your
3rd Person	they	them	theirs	their

The term **person** refers to the relationship between the speaker and the person being spoken about: if the speaker is speaking about himself, he uses a **first person** pronoun; if about the person (or persons) he is speaking to, **second person**; and if about some person or persons other than himself or the hearer, **third person**.

The difference in function between the four classes of personal pronouns is exemplified by the following (all in the first person singular):

(**14**)   *I* threw a rock. (SUBJECT)

(**15**)   A rock hit *me*. (OBJECT)

(**16**)   That is *my* rock. (POSSESSIVE ADJECTIVE)

(**17**)   That rock is *mine*. (POSSESSIVE PRONOUN)

In addition to function, person, and number (singular or plural), one additional factor in choice of pronoun is **gender**: that is, sex of the noun referred to. Gender is relevant only in the third person singular, where masculine ("he," "him," "his"), feminine ("she," "her," "hers"), and neuter ("it," "its") are distinguished.

Consider the following examples of Pronominalization (pronouns are italicized).

(18) Bill is my friend. *He* lost some money.
(19) Bill is my friend and *he* lost some money.
(20) Bill lost some money which *he* won in a lottery.
(21) Bill lost *his* winnings.
(22) The money Bill lost was *his*.

Each of the above is identical in meaning to an English utterance without Pronominalization, as follows.

(18a) Bill is my friend. Bill lost some money.
(19a) Bill is my friend and Bill lost some money.
(20a) Bill lost some money which Bill won in a lottery.
(21a) Bill lost Bill's winnings.
(22a) The money Bill lost was Bill's.

Because deep structure contains all that is necessary for the semantic interpretation of a sentence, it follows that sentences **(18a)–(22a)** are "closer" to deep structure than are **(18)–(22)**; that is, the deep structure of each sentence will contain a "Bill" in each of the positions where a pronoun appears in **(18)–(22)**. For example, the deep structure of **(19)** will be the following:

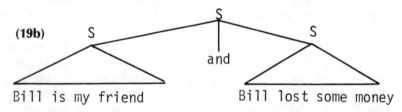

(19b)

A rule of Pronominalization will apply, changing the second "Bill" to "he." Pronominalization will also apply in the derivation of **(18)**, **(20)**, **(21)**, and **(22)**, replacing "Bill" by the appropriate pronoun in each case.

In each of the cases **(18)–(22)**, the pronoun has an **antecedent**. An antecedent is the noun phrase to which the pronoun refers; in each of the above cases the antecedent, "Bill," precedes the pronoun in the utterance (that is, the Pronominalization has applied in a forward direction). Thus Pronominalization, like Relativization and Conjunction Reduction, involves reference; one of two coreferential nouns is pronominalized.

Notice that the examples above all concern the third person. It is not quite as clear what the deep structures of sentences like **(14)–(17)** are like, or the corresponding ones in the second person:

(23) *You* threw a rock.
(24) A rock hit *you*.
(25) That is *your* rock.
(26) That rock is *yours*.

What makes these utterances different from **(18)–(22)** is that the sentences contain no antecedents corresponding to the pronouns. Also, while **(18a)–(22a)** are perfectly grammatical (albeit unnatural), pronouns are obligatory in **(14)–(17)** and in **(23)–(26)**. One cannot conceive of George Washington, speaking of himself, or of someone speaking to George Washington, saying:

    (27)   George Washington threw a dollar across the Potomac.

It seems, then, that first and second person pronouns are quite different from third person pronouns. It may well be that they are already present at the level of deep structure and have nothing to do with a Pronominalization transformation. Because this problem remains unresolved for linguistic theory, the remainder of this discussion will be restricted to the third person.

It is also necessary to make a distinction between Pronominalization within sentences and Pronominalization across sentences. Pronominalization across sentences is exemplified by **(18)**, where the antecedent of "he" occurs in a previous sentence. Pronominalization across sentences (or **textual Pronominalization**) always applies in a forward direction; that is, the pronoun always follows its antecedent. Usually, once the antecedent has appeared, Pronominalization in the following text can apply an indefinite number of times, as long as ambiguity can be avoided. One observation which might be made is that Pronominalization of this type is optional; **(18a)**, while not as natural as **(18)**, is grammatical, and both "Bill"'s are understood to refer to the same person.

Now consider again sentences **(19)–(22)**, repeated below as **(28)–(31)** for convenience.

    (28)   *Bill* is my friend and *he* lost some money.
    (29)   *Bill* lost some money which *he* won in a lottery.
    (30)   *Bill* lost *his* winnings.
    (31)   The money *Bill* lost was *his*.

In each of the above sentences, the italicized words have the same reference. Now consider the following slightly different sentences:

    (32)   *He* is my friend and *Bill* lost some money.
    (33)   *He* lost some money which *Bill* won in a lottery.
    (34)   *He* lost *Bill's* winnings.
    (35)   The money *he* lost was *Bill's*.

Each of the sentences **(32)-(35)** is grammatical, but only if the two italicized words refer to different people (i.e., have different reference)! For example, in **(32)**, my friend *cannot* be Bill! It is clear that, although the only difference between **(28)-(31)** and **(32)-(35)**, respectively, is that a different noun has been pronominalized, the meaning is entirely different.

Sentences **(28a)–(31a)** below were postulated earlier as relatively deep representations to which Pronominalization applies to give **(28)**–**(31)**.

(28a)   *Bill* is my friend and *Bill* lost some money.
(29a)   *Bill* lost some money which *Bill* won in a lottery.
(30a)   *Bill* lost *Bill's* winnings.
(31a)   The money *Bill* lost was *Bill's*.

Since in each of these structures there are two coreferent nouns, if no restrictions were placed on Pronominalization, either one of the two could be pronominalized. *Forward, or left-to-right*, Pronominalization would result in sentences **(28)**–**(31)**; *backward, or right-to-left*, Pronominalization would give **(32)**–**(35)**. But, as we have already seen, the latter sentences cannot have the meanings of **(28a)**–**(31a)**; they are ungrammatical in this sense. The conclusion forced upon us is that only forward, and not backward, Pronominalization may apply to structures like **(28a)**–**(31a)**.

It would be nice if Pronominalization could be explained this simply, but it cannot. There exist structural types for which backward Pronominalization is clearly possible, as in the following example:

(36)   The man who loved *her* murdered *Isabelle*.

While "her" in **(36)** might possibly refer to someone other than Isabelle, it might just as easily refer to "Isabelle." The sentence is ambiguous, and for its second meaning, the source is the following:

(36a)   The man who loved *Isabelle* murdered *Isabelle*.

Notice furthermore that while Pronominalization may apply right-to-left to produce **(36)**, left-to-right Pronominalization is also possible, as shown by sentence **(36b)**.

(36b)   The man who loved *Isabelle* murdered *her*.

Two differing classes of structures have been presented: (1) those where Pronominalization can apply forward only; and (2) those where it can apply in either direction. Forward Pronominalization is definitely preferred; if the environment is met for Pronominalization, forward Pronominalization can always apply. Backward Pronominalization is much more restricted, and the conditions for its application depend on embedding.

In cases of conjoined sentences where a coreferent noun appears in each conjunct, Pronominalization is always forward. When one of the coreferent nouns occurs in an embedded sentence, however, sometimes backward Pronominalization is possible (as for **(36a)**), and sometimes not (as for **(29a)**). The restriction was first stated by Langacker (1969), using the notions of **dominate** and **command**. Node A "dominates" node B if it appears above it in the tree and is connected to it by a path of branches; A **directly dominates** B if A dominates B and there are no intervening nodes.

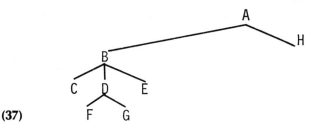

(37)

In tree 37:
A dominates B, C, D, E, F, G, and H;
B dominates C, D, E, F, and G;
D dominates F and G;
C, E, F, G, and H dominate no nodes;
A directly dominates B and H;
B directly dominates C, D, and E;
D directly dominates F and G;
C, E, F, G, and H directly dominate no nodes.
   A node A "commands" another node B if (1) neither A nor B dominates the other, and (2) the closest S-node dominating A also dominates B.

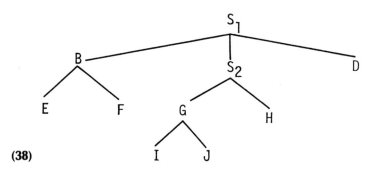

(38)

In the above diagram:
B commands S_2, G, H, I, J, and D;
S_2 commands B, E, F, and D;
D commands B, E, F, S_2, G, H, I, and J;
E commands S_2, G, H, I, J, D, and F;
F commands S_2, G, H, I, J, D, and E;
G commands H;
H commands G, I, and J;
I commands J and H;
J commands I and H.

The restriction on Pronominalization can now easily be stated as follows:

> When the two coreferent noun phrases are not elements of separate conjoined structures, backward Pronominalization can apply except when the leftmost noun phrase commands the rightmost noun phrase.

The simplified tree structures of **(36a)** and **(29a)** are **(39)** and **(40)**, respectively.

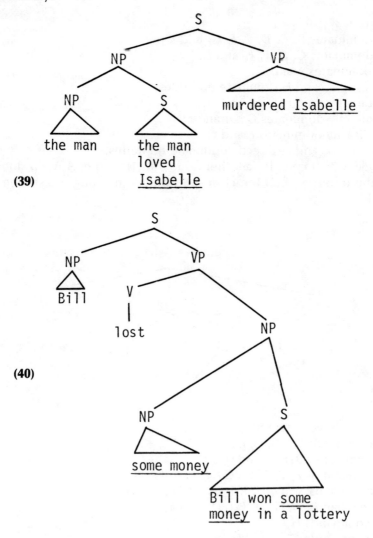

(39)

(40)

In **(39)** the leftmost instance of "Isabelle" is embedded in a lower sentence, and therefore does not command the rightmost instance of

Isabelle. Therefore backward Pronominalization can apply to give **(36)**. In **(40)**, however, the leftmost occurrence of "some money" is most immediately dominated by the highest *S*, which also dominates the rightmost occurrence; the "commands" relationship holds, and backward Pronominalization cannot apply.

Reflexivization

Consider the following examples:

 (41)   John loves *himself*.
 (42)   I think that the burglar shot *herself*.
 (43)   You should have faith in *yourself*.

The italicized words in the above sentences appear to be related to pronouns, but they are obviously not cases of Pronominalization, since the following are ungrammatical if the underlined words are considered to be coreferent:

 (41a)   **John* loves *him*.
 (42a)   *I think that *the burglar* shot *her*.
 (43a)   **You* should have faith in *you*.

The words "myself," "yourself," "himself," "herself," "itself," "ourselves," "yourselves," and "themselves" are known as **reflexive pronouns,** and the transformation producing them is REFLEXIVIZATION. The condition for Reflexivization applying is as follows: Reflexivization (and not Pronominalization) applies when two coreferent noun phrases occur in the same **simple sentence**; that is, when there is no *S* node separating them. Reflexivization, then, will apply to structures like the following:

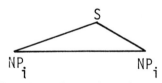

(44)

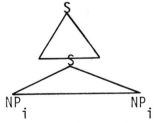

(45)   The woman <u>who</u> shot <u>herself</u> was a burglar.

Pronominalization will apply to structures like the following:

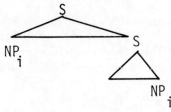

Bill lost some money which
he won in a lottery.

(46)

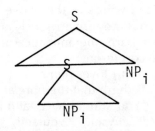

The man who loved <u>Isabelle</u>
murdered <u>her</u>.

(47) The man who loved <u>her</u> murdered
<u>Isabelle</u>.

Reflexivization was studied early by transformationalists, because of sentences like the following:

(48)   Wash yourself!

(49)   Don't talk to yourself!

(50)   Save yourself!

Sentences which express commands or orders, as do **(48)-(50)**, are known as **imperatives**. It is obvious that the subject of each of these sentences is "you," but there is no subject noun phrase present on the surface in imperatives. Each of the above has a surface structure like the following:

(48-50a)

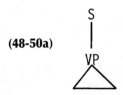

Since deep structure represents all meaningful aspects of a sentence, it was postulated by early linguists that deep structure imperatives contain a subject noun phrase, "you," and (for reasons which shall not be discussed here) also the modal "will," both of which are deleted by an Imperative transformation.

Now notice that this solution also solves another problem for sentences like **(48)-(50)**. In the absence of a subject noun phrase, Reflexivization could not apply. For example, if the deep structure of **(48)** were **(51)**, there would be no coreferent "you" to reflexivize the object *NP*.

(51)

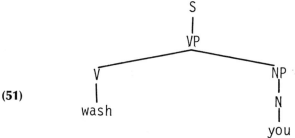

Now suppose the deep structure were, instead, **(52)**:

(52)

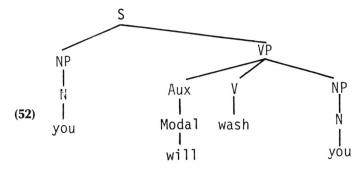

Reflexivization will first apply to give the following:

(52a)

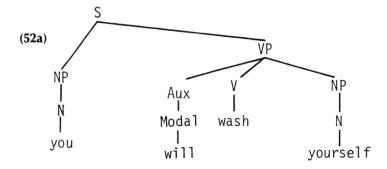

Finally, Imperative will delete the first *NP* node and the *Aux* node, giving the surface structure:

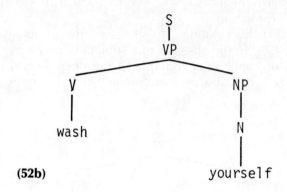

(52b)

Thus the inclusion of the subject "you" in deep structure not only accounts for the nonappearance of a meaningful element on the surface, but also for the occurrence of the reflexive pronoun "yourself."

This analysis was also used by early linguists to argue for ordering of transformational rules, since if Reflexivization and Imperative apply in the manner explained here, they must apply in that order to give the correct results. In other words, if Imperative were to apply first to **(52)**, **(53)** would be produced.

```
              S
              |
              VP
            /    \
          V        NP
          |        |
        wash       N
                   |
   (53)           you
```

Reflexivization could then not apply because the SD would no longer be met. And clearly, surface structure **(53)** is ungrammatical. Thus it seems as though either some transformational rules must apply in a certain order, or some other law of grammar is necessary to take care of cases like this. This question has not yet been resolved.

Non-Restrictive Relatives

Relative clauses of the following type have been discussed previously.

(54)　The Chinese who are industrious play ping-pong.

(55)　Beavers which have sharp teeth fell many trees.

(56)　I like people who are honest.

There is also another type of relative clause which has not been discussed. It can be exemplified by the following sentences.

(57)　The Chinese, who are industrious, play ping-pong.

(58)　Beavers, which have sharp teeth, fell many trees.

(59)　I like people, who are honest.

Relative clauses like those in **(54)-(56)** are known as **Restrictive Relatives**; those of the type displayed by **(57)-(59)**, which are identified by commas in the written form and by pauses when spoken, are called **Non-Restrictive Relatives**. The terms are descriptive. The speaker of **(57)-(59)** believes that all Chinese are industrious, all beavers have sharp teeth, and everyone is honest. In producing **(54)-(56)**, however, one claims that some Chinese are industrious and play ping-pong, while others are not industrious (and may or may not play ping-pong); that some beavers do not have sharp teeth; and that some people are dishonest.

Restrictive Relatives, as we have seen, are derived from deep structure sentences embedded in noun phrases:

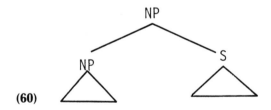

(60)

However, since the meanings of Non-Restrictive Relatives are so different from those of Restrictive Relatives, it is clear that their deep structure source must be quite different.

Consider sentence **(57)**. This sentence makes two assertions: (1) Chinese play ping-pong, and (2) Chinese are industrious. In addition, the relative clause can be deleted from the sentence without changing the essential meaning:

(61)　The Chinese play ping-pong.

Sentence **(54)**, on the other hand, makes only one assertion: that some Chinese, the restricted class of those that are industrious, play ping-pong. Deletion of the relative clause from this sentence results in **(61)**, which makes an assertion about all Chinese, and thus radically changes the meaning of **(54)**.

Since sentences with Non-Restrictive Relatives, in contrast to Restrictive Relatives, make two distinct assertions, one possibility is that there are two distinct and separate sentences which are conjoined in the deep structure; and, in fact, this is what has been proposed by transformationalists. Thus, the deep structure of **(57)** would be the following:

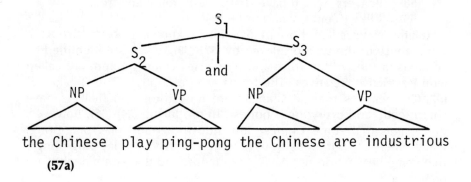

(57a)

In simplified form, we can say that a rule of NON-RESTRICTIVE RELATIVE FORMATION optionally moves the second conjunct in a conjoined sentence structure to a position following the noun phrase in the first conjunct. The result in the above case will be the following:

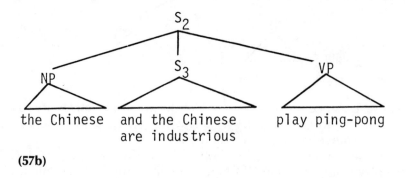

(57b)

A general law of transformations will delete the uppermost S (S_1) in this case. Although there remain some problems with the location of the "and," these will not concern us here.

Finally, Relativization can apply to **(57b)** to produce **(57c)**.

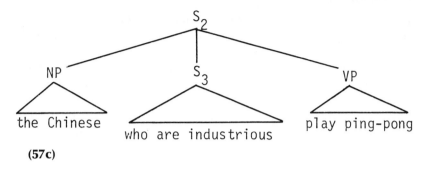

(57c)

The pronunciation of the clause, with intonation breaks before and after, is the reason that it hangs by itself from the S_2 node, rather than being integrated into the subject *NP* as with Restrictive Relatives.

Notice that both Non-Restrictive Relative Formation and Relativization are optional in cases like the above. If both fail to apply, **(57a)** remains basically the same on the surface, the final result being:

(57d) The Chinese play ping-pong and the Chinese are industrious.

Similarly, if Non-Restrictive Relative Formation applies but Relativization does not, **(57b)** remains basically the same to give sentence **(57e)**.

(57e) The Chinese, and the Chinese are industrious, play ping-pong.

Of course, Relativization cannot apply alone, since Non-Restrictive Relative Formation must first apply to create the proper structural description.

Finally, Pronominalization can optionally apply to either **(57d)** or **(57e)** to give **(57f)** and **(57g)**, respectively.

(57f) The Chinese play ping-pong and they are industrous.

(57g) The Chinese, and they are industrious, play ping-pong.

Sentences **(57c)**-**(57g)** all have basically the same meaning, the usual result of being derived from the same deep structure; this serves to justify the claim that Non-Restrictive Relative sentences like **(57c)** have deep structure conjoined sentences like **(57a)** as their source.

Constraints on Transformations

Transformations, if allowed to apply indiscriminately, will produce many ungrammatical structures. It is thus necessary to limit their power by placing on them various constraints. The best known constraints are termed **Ross Constraints**, since they were first proposed by John Robert Ross in his doctoral dissertation (1967).

The first constraint which will be discussed here has to do with the imposition of WH-Question Formation and Relativization on conjoined structures. Recall that both of these transformations move elements; WH-Question Formation moves an indefinite noun phrase (WH-some N) to the front of a sentence, while Relativization moves a noun phrase to the front of an embedded sentence (under the proper conditions) and changes it to a relative pronoun.

In WH-Question Formation, it is possible to question elements in various *NP* positions of a sentence. For example, consider the sentence below:

    (62)   Bill sent a letter bomb to the Maharaja.

The following WH-Questions are all related to **(62)**. In **(63)**, the subject is questioned; in **(64)**, it is the direct object that is questioned; and in **(65)**, the indirect object.

    (63)   Who sent a letter bomb to the Maharaja?

    (64)   What did Bill send to the Maharaja?

    (65)   Who did Bill send a letter bomb to?

The respective deep structures of **(63)**-**(65)** are of the following types: (for simplicity, we will eliminate the QUESTION node):

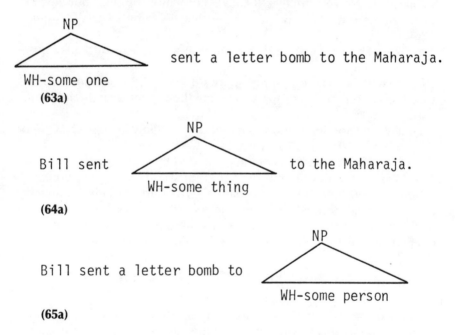

    NP

WH-some one   sent a letter bomb to the Maharaja.

    (63a)

         NP

Bill sent   to the Maharaja.

     WH-some thing

    (64a)

             NP

Bill sent a letter bomb to

          WH-some person

    (65a)

Now consider the following sentence:

    (66)   Bill put a chair between the table and the couch.

Related deep structures with an indefinite noun phrase in each *NP* position are as follows:

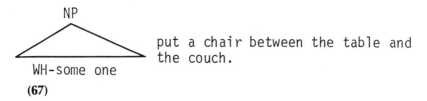

put a chair between the table and the couch.

(67)

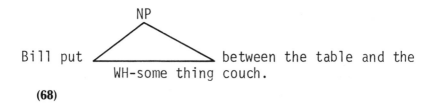

Bill put between the table and the couch.

(68)

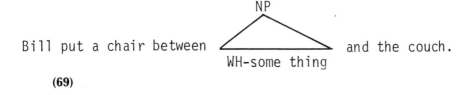

Bill put a chair between and the couch.

(69)

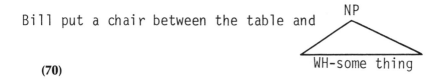

Bill put a chair between the table and

(70)

Applying WH-Question Formation to structures **(67)-(70)** results in the following:

(67a) Who put a chair between the table and the couch?
(68a) What did Bill put between the table and the couch?
(69a) *What did Bill put a chair between and the couch?
(70a) *What did Bill put a chair between the table and?

Most speakers of English would agree that **(69a)** and **(70a)** are so bad as to be almost incomprehensible! Obviously, however, **(69)** and **(70)** meet the conditions for application of WH-Question Formation as it has been formulated; somehow the rule must not be allowed to apply to structures like **(69)** and **(70)**. Ross proposed the following constraint: *No element contained in a conjoined structure may be moved out of that structure.* In other words, a structure like **(71)** cannot be broken up by moving any element out of it. Notice that the uppermost *NP* in **(71)**

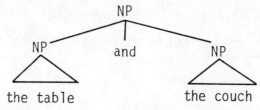

(71)

can be questioned, since the *NP* is moved as a whole:

    (72)   *What* did Bill put a chair between?

    That this constraint is a general one referring to conjoined structures as a whole, and is not confined to one transformation, is demonstrated by the workings of Relativization. As with WH-Question Formation, Relativization can apply to *NP*'s at various positions in a sentence (in this case, an embedded sentence). However, again, its operation is restricted by the constraint mentioned above. Consider the following deep structures:

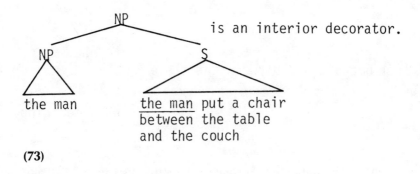

(73)

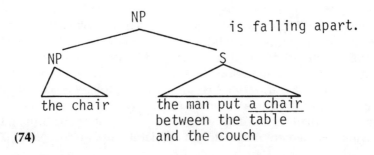

(74)

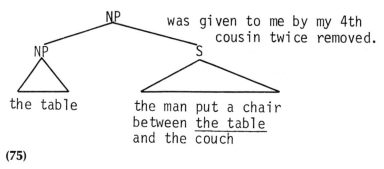

(75)

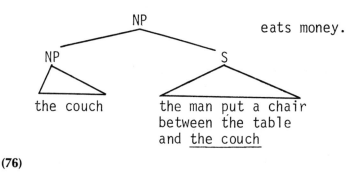

(76)

Application of Relativization to the above structures (each of which meets the conditions) will move the underlined word to the beginning of the embedded clause to give the following:

(73a) The man who put a chair between the table and the couch is an interior decorator.

(74a) The chair which the man put between the table and the couch is falling apart.

(75a) *The table which the man put a chair between and the couch was given to me by my 4th cousin twice removed.

(76a) *The couch which the man put a chair between the table and eats money.

While **(73a)** and **(74a)** are completely grammatical, **(75a)** and **(76a)**, which result from the movement of individual elements out of a conjoined structure ("the table and the couch") are even worse than the corresponding **(69a)** and **(70a)**. It is clear that any transformation which moves an element out of a conjoined structure will result in ungrammaticality.

That "movement" is an important feature of the above constraint is shown by the Echo Questions formed from **(69)** and **(70)**, where individual elements of conjoined structures are questioned, but with no movement.

(77)   Bill put a chair between what and the couch?

(78)   Bill put a chair between the table and what?

Sentences **(77)** and **(78)**, while somewhat unnatural to some speakers (and **(78)** seems to be better than **(77)**), are much better than **(69a)** and **(70a)**.

Similarly, many English speakers accept as grammatical the following relative sentences created from **(75)** and **(76)**, where the noun phrase is not moved; rather, a *copy* of it is placed at the beginning of the embedded sentence and the original *NP* is pronominalized.

(79)   The table *that* the man put a chair between *it* and the couch was given to me by my 4th cousin twice removed.

(80)   The couch *that* the man put a chair between the table and *it* eats money.

In some languages other than English, in which WH-Question Formation and Relativization do not involve movement, the constraint does not operate. Where movement does operate, it generally seems to hold true.

Ross proposed several other constraints on movement transformations, which shall not be considered here. Recently many seeming counter-examples to Ross's constraints have been brought forth, but it is clear that constraints of some type are necessary to rule out some of the horrible sentences presented above.

Hearing Children's Acquisition of Conjunction

Wilbur, Quigley, and Montanelli (1975) found that their hearing subjects had all of the tested aspects of the conjoining process well under control by the age of 8. Almost no errors were made in deleting constituents: sentences containing incorrect deletions were rejected about 90 percent of the time, and no deletion errors were found in a sample of written compositions elicited by a picture sequence stimulus. Tense sequencing in conjoined sentences was also well under control by age 8.

It would seem, further, that hearing children are competent in most aspects of the system at a much earlier age than this. The earliest forms of conjunction seem to occur merely by juxtaposing two words together. Bloom (1970), for example, reports the earliest evidence of conjoining for one of her subjects (Eric; age 19 months, 1 week) as "girl fish." This would seem to be the primal base upon which conjunction is built.

In an extensive study, Menyuk (1969) reported that the technique of conjunction and permissible deletions had been well accomplished for most children by 3 years of age. Her Nursery School-age group had 42 percent of its members correctly using all aspects of Conjunction, and this had grown to 81 percent by Grade 1, although some errors in tense sequencing were still made by 35 percent of Grade 1 children. Some tense sequencing problems were reported at the Nursery School level (as in "He eats the cake and he drank the milk"), as were some incorrect pronominalizations ("My baby brother has a gate and she could fall downstairs"). Some conjoining with "and" was produced by all members of the Nursery School group.

Menyuk reports some data from older hearing children whose speech and language were described as "deviant." She found that these children made many errors in verb tense sequencing and number agreement, as well as in observing restrictions upon the type of pronoun agreement required. Some of these errors seem to be typical of those made by deaf children up to a much more advanced age.

Deaf Children's Acquisition of Conjunction

Taylor (1969) found Conjunction to be the most frequently attempted transformation in the written language of deaf students between the ages of 10½ and 16½ years. Her deaf students generally did fairly well in approximating Standard English conjunction use, and improved steadily with age. However, many errors were still made, even at a relatively advanced age. Conjunctions were often omitted ("A ant see a tree a bird"), misplaced ("The dove got out of the tree and took a leaf threw it down"), or over-applied ("The ant ran to its home and get the scissors and hit a man's leg").

Taylor also first reported some deviant deletion rules in conjoining which have been confirmed by Wilbur, Quigley, and Montanelli (1975) and called Object-Subject Deletion. According to this rule, a subject of a second conjunct in a sentence is deleted on identity with the object noun phrase of the preceding conjunct, as, for example, in "The hunter scared the dove and flew away." Object-Object Deletion also occurred, although less frequently, in such sentences as "The ant threw a ball on the ground and put in his room," where the subject "ball" in the second conjunct has been deleted on identity with the object of the first conjunct. It would seem that for these deaf students, there is some confusion between Conjunction Deletion and Pronominalization rules of English; that is, they delete noun phrases where Standard English pronominalizes. Tense sequencing problems were also common in the writing of Taylor's deaf subjects.

Wilbur, Quigley, and Montanelli (1975), in an extensive study of the conjoining process, found that although deaf students, even at 18 years of age, still made numerous errors in conjoining various grammatical structures, the students found conjunction rules to be among the easiest of all English transformational rules to acquire, and continued to make steady improvement from age 10 through 18 years in the correct construction of sentences using the conjunction "and." Other forms of conjoining with "but" and "or" presented greater difficulty, and in many instances little improvement was indicated over the age range tested. The rules for conjoining were not quite as well established by 18 years of age as were the rules for Negation (Quigley, Montanelli, and Wilbur, 1974) to be discussed in another chapter, but were much better established than the rules for Relativization and for other syntactic structures that have been studied in the language of deaf individuals.

Menyuk (1963, 1964) reported that unreduced conjoined sentences emerged at an earlier age than did conjunction-reduced ones for young hearing children, and Wilbur, Quigley, and Montanelli (1975) found a similar developmental pattern for deaf children. When deaf students were requested to conjoin two sentences where the opportunity for Conjunction Reduction existed (e.g., "The girl chased the dog. The boy chased the dog") younger subjects usually simply inserted "and" between the two sentences; however, this immature practice decreased with age and was replaced by appropriate Conjunction Reduction (e.g., "The girl and the boy chased the dog"). Detailed study of Conjunction Reduction by the same investigators revealed that replacement of an unreduced conjoined sentence by a conjoined *subject* noun phrase where appropriate was easier than replacement by a conjoined *object* noun phrase, where appropriate, which in turn was easier than replacement by a conjoined verb phrase, where appropriate.

Wilbur, Quigley, and Montanelli also studied several deviant types of structures which were related to the conjoining process and which had been found in samples of written language obtained from a large number of deaf students. These were labeled *Object-Subject Deletion*, *Object-Object Deletion*, and *And-Deletion*. We have encountered Object-Subject and Object-Object Deletion in other syntactic structures such as Relativization and, like Relative Copying, they seem to be consistently recurring deviancies (in relation to Standard English) in the language of deaf persons. When presented with tests of Conjunction which provided opportunities for these two deviant forms to occur, deaf students produced both of them at all age levels studied, from 10 to almost 19 years. Object-Object Deletion decreased with age, indicating increasing replacement of this form by the appropriate forms from Standard English, but Object-Subject Deletion actually increased slightly over the age range. In Object-Subject Deletion the subject of the second sentence in a conjoined structure is deleted, resulting in a meaning different from that conveyed by the unconjoined sentences.

For example, "The girl hit the dog. The dog ran away" reduces by the deviant rule of Object-Subject Deletion to "The girl hit the dog and ran away," which would be derived by Standard English rules from, and for a speaker of Standard English would have the meaning of, "The girl hit the dog. The girl ran away."

And-Deletion refers to the deletion of "and" from conjoined structures, as in "The dog barked the cat ran away." When asked to make judgments of grammaticality of such sentences, deaf students accepted them as correct 56 percent of the time at age 10 with a decrease to 21 percent by age 18. The improvement in judgments of grammaticality took place for all types of conjoined structures studied: conjoined sentences, conjoined subjects and conjoined objects, and conjoined verb phrases, but the degree of improvement varied for each structure. Conjoined sentences were easiest, then conjoined subjects, followed by conjoined objects, with conjoined verb phrases being the most difficult.

In analyzing written language samples obtained from their subjects, Wilbur, Quigley, and Montanelli found many instances of And-Deletion in conjoined sentences and in conjunction reduced structures, thus confirming the data from their specific tests of the same structures. The analysis of written language revealed also that And-Deletion occurred much more frequently than did Object-Subject Deletion and Object-Object Deletion. And-Deletion was found in 30 percent of the deaf students' written samples, in approximately equal percentages at each age level. It occurred only very infrequently in the written language of the hearing subjects, but the fact that it did occur indicates that it is not entirely unique to the language of deaf individuals.

Again, in the acquisition of conjunction by deaf students, as in other syntactic structures we have examined, we have a pattern of retardation in comparison to hearing children, but also the persistent and consistent presence of structures not found in Standard English which indicate the existence of some rules of grammar peculiar to the language of deaf individuals.

Analysis of Conjunction in the Reading Materials

Again, as with other structures that have been discussed, conjoined structures are found in reading texts used by deaf children long before the children understand their use. In the series that was analyzed (McKee, et al., 1966), conjoined subject noun phrases, conjoined object noun phrases, and conjoined verb phrases appeared in the first primer and in all the succeeding books analyzed. Conjoined sentences appeared first in the first grade reader and with increasing frequency in the succeeding readers up to the sixth grade. Conjoined adjectives and adverbs also appeared early (first grade) and consistently in the readers. Given the difficulties deaf children have in understanding and using all of these conjoined structures, the possibilities for confusion in their reading of such books are great on the basis of syntactic structure alone.

Hearing Children's Acquisition of Pronouns

It can be seen from our linguistic analysis in this chapter that there are a number of aspects of the pronoun system which must be mastered for proficient use of English—number, case, and (for third person singular) gender. The child must, therefore, be able to correctly sub-categorize the referent noun before he can pronominalize. He also, of course, has to learn when pronouns may and may not be used.

A study by Huxley (1970) indicated that the speaker/listener (first/second person) distinction is made before third person reference appears. Also, pronouns unmarked as regards gender ("I," "it," "you") are learned before ones where the gender distinction must be made ("he," "she"). Singular pronouns are acquired before plural. The more complicated cases such as possessive pronouns and reflexives are acquired relatively late, and many children may not have completely mastered these before they begin school.

The findings of Menyuk (1969) substantially confirmed Huxley's. She found that "it" was the only pronoun which appeared regularly early in the second year of life ("Mommy try it"), and concluded that occurrence of pronouns other than "it" at this time appeared to be simply repetitions rather than generated uses. Late in the second year the other " simple" pronouns began to appear with increasing regularity and correctness, although even in Grade 1 incorrect usages such as "He's a big train," "She's a nice daddy," "It's a good boy," and so forth, were still quite common. Menyuk also reported the occurrence of a phenomenon which in Wilbur, Quigley, and Montanelli (1975) is called *Copying*—"I want it the brush." With the complex pronoun cases, she found that about 90 percent of her Grade 1 subjects used reflexives occasionally, but by no means always correctly.

Menyuk's general summary of her findings is probably a fair statement of the general level of correct use of pronouns by young hearing children: about one-third of her Nursery School subjects and about half of her Grade 1 subjects were using them properly. It would seem then that the intricacies of the pronoun system make it one of the most difficult aspects of English syntax.

The group of hearing children tested by Wilbur, Montanelli, and Quigley (1975) also provides some data about older children's continued acquisition of pronouns. Children aged 8-10 years were tested. It was found that subject and object cases were the most difficult for these children, followed by possessive adjectives and possessive pronouns which were about equally difficult, while reflexives were considerably more difficult than either of these groups. Singular pronouns were less difficult than plurals, and the order of difficulty with respect to person was first, second, third.

The results reported by Wilbur, Montanelli, and Quigley (1975) indicated that most hearing children have the pronoun system well under control by age 10, as virtually all the aspects of the pronoun system we have discussed were being correctly used at that age more than 90 percent of the time.

Deaf Children's Acquisition of Pronouns

Wilbur, Montanelli, and Quigley (1975), in an extensive study of Pronominalization in the language of deaf students, found that subject and object case pronouns (e.g., "he," "him") were better understood than possessive adjectives ("my," "your"), which in turn were easier than possessive pronouns ("mine," "yours") and reflexives ("myself," "yourself"). This approximates the theoretical order of difficulty predictable from transformational grammar and the order indicated in various psycholinguistic studies of hearing children (Huxley, 1970; Menyuk, 1969). Furthermore, singular pronouns were easier than plurals for all ages and cases, as predictable by the theory; first person pronouns were easier than third person, which were easier than second person; and masculine pronouns, with the exception of the reflexive, were somewhat easier than feminine pronouns, with neuter pronouns being more difficult. Comparison with studies of Pronominalization in hearing children's language indicated that the greatest difference for deaf students appeared to be a profound retardation in acquisition rather than consistent deviancies such as those found in other structures. The existence of an order of difficulty in the pronoun forms for deaf children should be taken into account in structuring materials and curricula for the teaching of those forms.

Analysis of Pronominalization in the Reading Materials

As would be expected, pronouns of all types appeared in all 11 books of the Houghton Mifflin *Reading for Meaning* series. They were so frequent, in fact, that no detailed analysis of them was made. It was obvious that, as with other structures, the great retardation in acquisition of the pronoun system of English by deaf children, and the particular difficulties they had with various pronoun forms, likely rendered much of the reading materials incomprehensible to them.

CHAPTER 7

Transformations IV: Negation

Another phenomenon in English shows many similarities to Question-Formation: that of Negation. Sentences can be negated (on the surface) in several ways, as the following examples show. (These are basically the same as the examples given by Klima (1964) in his early monumental work.)

The students did not believe that it had happened.

The students never believed that it had happened.

The students scarcely believed that it had happened.

No students believed that it had happened.

Few students believed that it had happened.

Little snow fell on Alabama.

Each of the above sentences denies the students' belief: the first three through the use of negative adverbs, and the last three through negative adjectives. Notice also that while "not," "never," and "no" have the form of negatives on the surface, "scarcely," "few," and "doubt" do not.

The negative element appears at various positions in the sentences. For example, in the first sentence it appears in the auxiliary (before the verb); in the second and third it is in initial position in the verb phrase; and in the last three it is part of the subject noun phrase. Since the negative element performs a similar semantic function regardless of its position, and, as will be seen later in this chapter, performs similarly with respect to other transformations, it seems reasonable to assume that the negative element always appears in the same position at the deep structure level. It can then be "moved" into the proper surface structure position by transformations. (Remember that transformations are not real time processes and that the word "moved" is used only for explanatory purposes!)

Sentence Negation

The above six examples are instances of **sentence negation**. Although there are other types of negation which negate only parts of the sentence rather than its whole, paraphrases of the above-mentioned sentences can be obtained by preceding their positive counterparts by "It is not the case that . . . ." (The idea of "positive counterpart" is a complex one which will not be considered here; the important thing is to realize that it is the entire thought which is negated.) For example:

(1a) It is not the case that *the students believed that it had happened.*

(2a) It is not the case that *the students ever believed that it had happened.*

The above test is a semantic one. However, as is the case for many linguistic phenomena, there are also syntactic tests available for sentence negation. Klima lists the following three:

1. Structures involving sentence negation permit the occurrence of an "either" clause. For example, sentence **(3a)** is a case of sentence negation and **(4a)** is not, according to the results of the test applied to give **(3b)** and **(4b)**, respectively.

(3a) Jonathan never goes to the dog races.

(3b) Jonathan never goes to the dog races and Johnny never goes *either.*

(4a) Jonathan often goes to the dog races.

(4b) *Jonathan often goes to the dog races, and Johnny often goes *either.*

2. Structures involving sentence negation permit tags (abbreviated structures appearing at the ends of sentences) with "not even." This test applied to **(3a)** and **(4a)** produces the following results.

(3c) Jonathan never goes to the dog races, *not even* high-stake ones.

(4c) *Jonathan often goes to the dog races, *not even* high-stake ones.

3. And finally, structures exemplifying sentence negation accept positive tag questions. The result of applying the "positive tag question" test to **(3a)** and **(4a)** is as follows:

(3d) Jonathan never goes to the dog races, *does he?*

(4d) *Jonathan often goes to the dog races, *does he?*

Sentence **(4d)** is ungrammatical as a sentence used merely to request information; in such a case, the tag "doesn't he?" would be necessary. Sentence **(4d)** could, of course, be uttered in a case in which the speaker did not require or desire information, but simply wanted to express sarcasm or anger. Such cases must be ignored in testing for negative sentences.

The above three tests may seem quite unnecessary with the black-and-white examples which have been presented. It appears obvious that use of "never" results in a negative sentence, while use of "often" does not. There are, however, other forms with negative connotations which display varying degrees of negation or non-negation, and semantic criteria are largely unsuccessful in classifying them. Examples of this type include adjectives ("few," "little"), verbs ("doubt," "hate"), and verbs and adjectives with negative affixes ("disobey," "impossible"), among others. Some of these will be discussed later in this chapter.

Positioning of NEG

Since it is the entire sentence which is negated, the negative element (NEG is commonly used to represent it) has traditionally been placed at the left of the deep structure tree, paralleling the deep structure representation of questions.

(4)

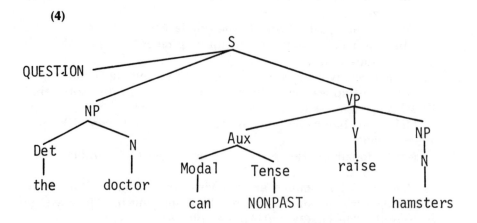

Can the doctor raise hamsters?

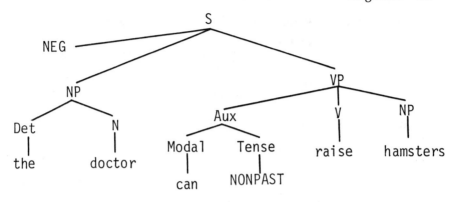

The doctor can't raise hamsters.

(5)

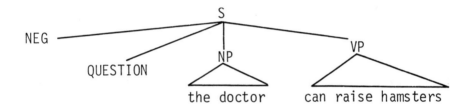

Can't the doctor raise hamsters?

(6)

Various transformations can apply to deep structures with NEG to position the negative element properly in the sentence. (Notice that, whereas the question node acts only as a trigger for transformations like Subject-Aux Inversion and WH-Question Formation, the NEG node is actually considered to have real semantic content. This is a notational inconsistency in the theory which can easily be taken care of, but which will not concern us.) The basic NEG Placement transformation moves (or inserts) NEG in a position following the first auxiliary. This is the most common means of formation of negative sentences, and is exemplified by the following derivations (with trees and higher nodes omitted).

(7)   NEG the doctor [$_{Aux}$ NONPAST can $_{Aux}$] raise hamsters

NEG PLACEMENT
$$\Longrightarrow$$ the doctor [$_{Aux}$ NONPAST can NEG $_{Aux}$] raise hamsters

AFFIX HOPPING
$$\Longrightarrow$$ the doctor [$_{Aux}$ can +NONPAST NEG $_{Aux}$] raise hamsters

(8)   NEG the doctor [$_{Aux}$ PAST have $_{Aux}$] raise hamsters

NEG PLACEMENT
$$\Longrightarrow$$ the doctor [$_{Aux}$ PAST have NEG $_{Aux}$] raise hamsters

AFFIX HOPPING
$$\Longrightarrow$$ the doctor [$_{Aux}$ have + PAST NEG $_{Aux}$] raise hamsters

(9)   NEG the doctor [$_{Aux}$ NONPAST must be -ing $_{Aux}$] raise hamsters

NEG PLACEMENT
$$\Longrightarrow$$ the doctor [$_{Aux}$ NONPAST must NEG be -ing $_{Aux}$] raise hamsters

AFFIX HOPPING (twice)
$$\Longrightarrow$$ the doctor [$_{Aux}$ must + NONPAST NEG be $_{Aux}$] raise + -ing hamsters

Morphological rules will specify the shape of the *Aux + Tense* sequences in each example above (e.g., *can + NONPAST* $\Longrightarrow$ *"can"*), and will also specify NEG as "not." The result (after application of one or two other minor rules) is the following surface structures:

(7a)   The doctor can not raise hamsters.

(8a)   The doctor had not raised hamsters.

(9a)   The doctor must not be raising hamsters.

In some cases, namely those for which there is no auxiliary verb, the above rule which places NEG "following the first auxiliary" is inoperable. Rather, the NEG is placed immediately preceding the verb, as in the following:

(10)   NEG the doctor NONPAST raise hamsters

NEG PLACEMENT
$$\Longrightarrow$$ the doctor NONPAST NEG raise hamsters

It has been mentioned previously that in some ways Sentence Negation closely parallels Question-Formation. One manner in which this is true involves the application of DO-SUPPORT. Recall that in Question-Formation, DO-SUPPORT applies when a tense node is stranded; that is, when there is no verb to the left of it to which it can be attached. Notice now that this is exactly the case in a negative structure like **(10)**. Because the Tense is stranded, DO-SUPPORT will apply to give **(10a)**.

(10a)   the doctor do + NONPAST NEG raise hamsters.

Morphological rules will then apply to specify *do + NONPAST* as "does," and NEG as "not," resulting in the surface structure **(10b)**.

(10b) The doctor does not raise hamsters.

For the sake of comparison, following is the positive deep structure counterpart to **(10)**.

(11) the doctor NONPAST raise hamsters

Obviously, NEG PLACEMENT cannot apply to **(11)** (since there is no NEG present). As a result, NONPAST remains contiguous to the verb and therefore will undergo AFFIX HOPPING to give **(11a)**.

(11a) the doctor raise +NONPAST hamsters

Application of DO-SUPPORT is now blocked, and morphological rules will produce the surface structure:

(11b) The doctor raises hamsters.

In Chapter 6 it was observed that *have* and *be* possess, at times, properties of both verbs and auxiliaries, and that these properties differ in strength from dialect to dialect. This is examplified not only by questions, but by negatives as well. Compare, for example, sentences **(12)** (Standard American) and **(13)** (Standard British).

(12) The doctor doesn't have a hamster.

(13) The doctor hasn't a hamster.

In Standard American English, *have* functions like a main verb when negated; **(12)** is derived as follows:

(12a) NEG the doctor NONPAST have a hamster

NEG PLACEMENT
$$\Longrightarrow$$ the doctor NONPAST NEG have a hamster

DO-SUPPORT
$$\Longrightarrow$$ the doctor do + NONPAST NEG have a hamster

MORPHOLOGICAL RULES
$$\Longrightarrow$$ The doctor does not have a hamster.

CONTRACTION
$$\Longrightarrow$$ The doctor doesn't have a hamster.

Sentence **(13)**, however, is produced only if *have* functions, not as a main verb, but as an auxiliary. (Recall that NEG PLACEMENT places NEG after the first auxiliary.)

(13a) NEG the doctor NONPAST have a hamster

NEG PLACEMENT
$$\Longrightarrow$$ the doctor NONPAST have NEG a hamster

AFFIX HOPPING
$$\Longrightarrow$$ the doctor have + NONPAST NEG a hamster

MORPHOLOGICAL RULES
$$\Longrightarrow$$ The doctor has not a hamster.

CONTRACTION
$$\Longrightarrow$$ The doctor hasn't a hamster.

In most dialects of English, the verb *be* seems to function like an auxiliary when negated (with NEG placed following rather than preceding *be*), as shown by the following examples:

(14)   The doctor is not a hamster.
(15)   *The doctor does not be a hamster.

Indefinite-Incorporation

Klima, in his important study of negation (1964), pointed out that certain words, known as **indefinites**, have a restricted distribution. Indefinites are words like "any," "anything," "anyone," "anybody," "anywhere," and "anyplace"; their restricted distribution is demonstrated by the following:

(16a)   Bagley doesn't have any money.
(16b)   Does Bagley have any money?
(16c)   If Bagley had any money, he'd buy a nose warmer.
(16d)   Only Bagley has any money.
(16e)   *Bagley has any money.
(17a)   Bagley doesn't know anybody.
(17b)   Does Bagley know anybody?
(17c)   If Bagley knew anybody, he'd follow them anywhere.
(17d)   Only Bagley knows anybody.
(17e)   *Bagley knows anybody.

(There is, of course, an "any" of a different type which can occur in sentences of the type starred above. This is the "any" which contrasts with "none" and has the meaning "any at all"; it will not be treated here.)

What makes this distribution so interesting is that so-called **quantifiers** like "some," "something," "someone," "somebody," "somewhere," and "someplace" exhibit a distribution which is completely complementary to that of the indefinites, as indicated by the following examples. (Some of the starred sentences following are grammatical for some speakers. They will be discussed shortly.)

(18a)   *Bagley doesn't have some money.
(18b)   *Does Bagley have some money?
(18c)   *If Bagley had some money, he'd buy a nose warmer.
(18d)   *Only Bagley has some money.
(18e)   Bagley has some money.
(19a)   *Bagley doesn't know somebody.
(19b)   *Does Bagley know somebody?
(19c)   *If Bagley knew somebody, he'd follow them anywhere.
            (i.e. "anywhere at all")
(19d)   *Only Bagley knows somebody.
(19e)   Bagley knows somebody.

The above facts were explained by Klima through the use of the following rule:

(20) INDEFINITE – INCORPORATION: [Affect] X-Quant-Y $\Longrightarrow$ Affect-X-Indef +Quant-Y

What is called [Affect] in the rule is actually a class of environments, including, among others, Sentence Negation, WH-Questions, conditionals (i.e., "if . . . then . . ." constructions), and "only." The rule states that following an affective element, all quantifiers are changed to indefinites. Robin Lakoff (1969) has summarized as follows:

> The facts, then, as stated by Klima and amended by other linguists later, were generally accepted: (1) There was a transformational rule that, in certain specific environments, changed the form that would eventually become "some" to a form which would ultimately appear as "any." (2) The application of this rule was dependent purely on syntactic factors within the sentence itself, identifiable in the superficial form of the sentence. (3) Since the occurrence of "some" and "any" was predicted by the application or non-application of a transformational rule, there could be no difference in meaning between sentences containing "some" and those containing "any" that was due solely to the appearance of one or the other of these quantifiers. (Of course, there might be differences in meaning caused by the presence of negatives, questions, etc., in one type and not in the other.)

With the rule of INDEFINITE-INCORPORATION, indefinites would be derived in the following manner. (Discussion will be restricted to negative environments only.)

(21) NEG Bagley NONPAST have [some] $_{Quant}$ money.

NEG PLACEMENT

$\Longrightarrow$ Bagley NONPAST NEG have [some] $_{Quant}$ money.

DO-SUPPORT

$\Longrightarrow$ Bagley do + NONPAST NEG have [some] $_{Quant}$ money.

INDEF-INCORP.

$\Longrightarrow$ Bagley do + NONPAST NEG have [Indef + some] $_{Quant}$ money.

MORPHOLOGICAL RULES

$\Longrightarrow$ Bagley does not have any money.

(22) NEG Bagley NONPAST know [[some] $_{Quant}$ body].

NEG PLACEMENT

$\Longrightarrow$ Bagley NONPAST NEG know [[some] $_{Quant}$ body].

DO-SUPPORT

$\Longrightarrow$ Bagley do + NONPAST NEG know [[some] $_{Quant}$ body].

INDEF-INCORP.

$$\Longrightarrow \text{Bagley do + NONPAST NEG know [[Indef}$$
$$+ \text{some]}_{\text{Quant}} \text{ body]}.$$

MORPHOLOGICAL RULES

$$\Longrightarrow \text{Bagley does not know anybody.}$$

NEG-Incorporation

Another rule stated by Klima was called NEG-INCORPORATION, which incorporates the NEG element into words of certain types, making them negative. For example, in sentences with indefinites, NEG will be incorporated into the first indefinite ("any") to give "no."

(23) $[\text{NEG}]_{\text{Pvp}} \text{ X [Indef + Y]}_{\text{Quant}} \Longrightarrow \text{X} - \text{NEG} +$
        $[\text{Indef + Y]}_{\text{Quant}}$
        (where Pvp = Preverbal Particle)

For example:

(24)   NEG Bagley NONPAST have [some] $_{\text{Quant}}$ money.
        NEG PLACEMENT

$$\Longrightarrow \text{Bagley NONPAST NEG have [some]}_{\text{Quant}}$$
$$\text{money.}$$

INDEF-INCORP.

$$\Longrightarrow \text{Bagley NONPAST NEG have [Indef +}$$
$$\text{some]}_{\text{Quant}} \text{ money.}$$

NEG-INCORP.

$$\Longrightarrow \text{Bagley NONPAST have NEG + Indef + some}$$
$$\text{money.}$$

AFFIX HOPPING

$$\Longrightarrow \text{Bagley have + NONPAST NEG + Indef +}$$
$$\text{some money.}$$

MORPHOLOGICAL RULES

$$\Longrightarrow \text{Bagley has no money.}$$

Notice that in the above sentence, Neg-Incorporation is optional. If it does not apply, the result will be:

(24a)   Bagley does not have any money.

In a similar way, Neg-Incorporation may or may not apply to the following "deep" structure:

(25)   NEG Bagley NONPAST know [[some] $_{\text{Quant}}$ body].

The two possible outputs demonstrating application and non-application of Neg-Incorporation are the following:

(25a)   Bagley knows nobody.

(25b)   Bagley does not know anybody.

While in cases like the above, Neg-Incorporation is optional, there are cases where it is obligatory: those for which an indefinite precedes Tense. This can be seen by examples like the following:

(26a)   Nothing is in Pandora's box.

(26b)   *Anything is not in Pandora's box.

(27a) Nowhere is there an honest man.

(27b) *Anywhere is there not an honest man.

Neg-Incorporation applies not only to initial indefinites, but also to "much" and "many" when they appear first in the sentence. For example:

(28) Not much shrapnel hit the soldier.

(29) Not many adults enjoy playing hide-and-seek.

For many dialects of English, Neg-Incorporation is obligatory with initial "much," and the following sentence, if acceptable at all, is not synonymous with **(28)**.

(30) Much shrapnel didn't hit the soldier.

For other speakers, Neg-Incorporation is optional in this environment, and **(28)** and **(30)** are alternative forms with identical meaning. With "much" and "many" in non-initial position, Neg-Incorporation does not apply.

(31a) The shrapnel did not hit many soldiers.

(31b) *The shrapnel hit not many soldiers.

There are two other common words which have positive counterparts: "never" and "neither" (compare "ever" and "either"). Both of these are also considered by Klima to undergo Neg-Incorporation. Again in this case, application is optional, as demonstrated by the following sentence pairs:

(32a) Ahab has*n't ever* been to Kalamazoo.

(32b) Ahab has *never* been to Kalamazoo.

(33a) Ahab has *not* been to Kalamazoo, and Mohammed has*n't, either*.

(33b) Ahab has not been to Kalamazoo, and *neither* has Mohammed.

Negative Prefixes

In addition to all of the above clearly negative elements, there are several prefixes in English which have traditionally been considered to be negative: "in," "im-," "un-," and so forth. That these are negative is indicated by their co-occurrence with "any," as in the following:

(34a) It is *not* possible for him to do *any* more.

(34b) It is *im*possible for him to do *any* more.

(34c) *It is possible for him to do *any* more.

(35a) It is *not* likely that he will do *any* more.

(35b) It is *un*likely that he will do *any* more.

(35c) *It is likely that he will do *any* more.

(36a) He did*n't* like doing *any* more than necessary.

(36b) He *dis*liked doing *any* more than necessary.

(36c) *He liked doing *any* more than necessary.

It is clear that the **(b)** sentences, with negative prefixes, are somehow like the **(a)** sentences, which are examples of sentence negation derived from deep structures containing NEG. However, close examination of the **(a)** and **(b)** pairs indicates that they do not have exactly the same meaning. This is borne out by syntactic evidence. For example, recall that one means of testing for Sentence Negation is with "either" clauses. If we apply this test to the two sentence types under discussion, we observe the following:

(37a)   Peter Rabbit isn't happy, and Bunny isn't happy, either.

(37b)   *Peter Rabbit is unhappy, and Bunny is unhappy, either.

(38a)   Winning isn't possible, and losing isn't possible, either.

(38b)   *Winning is impossible, and losing is impossible, either.

It seems, then, that although such affixes are negative, they do not negate the entire sentence, but only a portion of it. This fact can be captured if the deep structure of such a sentence does not contain a NEG in sentence-initial position, but rather a negative affix similar to the one which actually appears on the surface. Thus, for example, the deep structure of **(39a)** will be something like **(39b)**, but the deep structure of **(40a)** will be not **(39b)**, but **(40b)**.

(39a)   Peter Rabbit isn't happy.

(39b)   NEG Peter Rabbit NONPAST be happy.

(40a)   Peter Rabbit is unhappy.

(40b)   Peter Rabbit NONPAST be [[un] $_{NEG}$ happy].

Negative Words Without Negative Form

Finally, there are some words in English which display characteristics of Negation, yet do not superficially look negative. These are words like "little," "few," "seldom," and "scarcely." Some of these, like "little" and "few," can be considered to result from an optional fusing of NEG with positive counterparts. Thus, "little" would result from "NEG + much" and "few" from "NEG + many". The following sentence pairs are synonymous:

(41a)   *Not much* rain fell.

(41b)   *Little* rain fell.

(42b)   *Not many* vampires came to the meeting at the cemetery.

(42b)   *Few* vampires came to the meeting at the cemetery.

Negative Transportation

One final Negation rule which deserves mention here is one proposed by Fillmore (1963) called NEGATIVE TRANSPORTATION. Fillmore claimed that sentences **(43a)** and **(43b)** have the same meaning.

(43a)   John thinks that Bill doesn't like Harriet.

(43b)   John doesn't think that Bill likes Harriet.

In sentence **(43b)** the hearer is not supposed to understand that John doesn't think, but rather that he thinks Bill dislikes Harriet. Sentence **(43b)** is derived from a deep structure with an embedded sentence as object of the verb; that is, the verb phrase looks something like **(44)** in

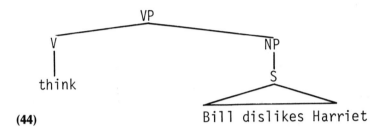

(44)

the deep structure. What is interesting, then, is that in **(43b)** the Negation applies not to the main sentence in which it occurs, but to a lower embedded sentence. This can be contrasted to the following sentence pair:

    (45a) John claims that Bill doesn't like Harriet.

    (45b) John doesn't claim that Bill likes Harriet.

In **(45b)**, the hearer is given to understand that Bill doesn't make a particular claim: namely, the claim that Bill likes Harriet. On the other hand, no information is provided as to whether or not Bill actually likes Harriet. In other words, the negative in **(45b)**, in contrast to that of **(43b)**, applies to its "own" sentence, and not to the embedded one.

In accordance with our previous assumptions about deep structure, the above facts can be explained only if **(43b)** and **(45b)** have very different deep structures. Also, since **(43a)** and **(43b)** have the same meaning, their deep structures must be similar; while since **(45a)** and **(45b)** are not synonymous, their deep structures must differ. Thus the deep structure underlying both **(43a)** and **(43b)** will be something like **(43c)**;

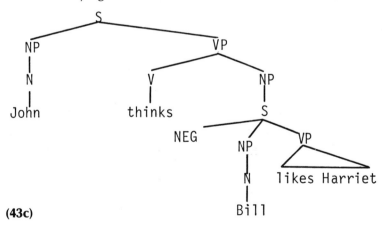

(43c)

(45c) underlies **(45a)**, and **(45d)** underlies **(45b)**.

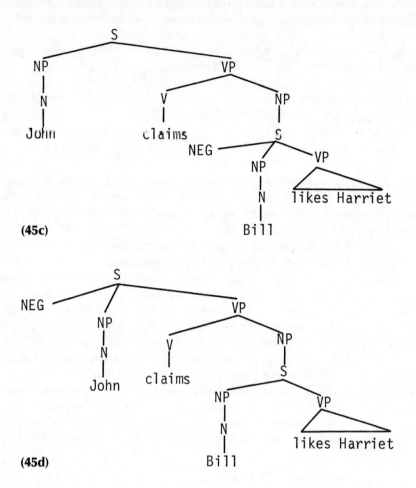

(45c)

(45d)

In **(45d)**, the main or matrix sentence is negated; in both **(43c)** and **(45c)** it is the embedded sentence which is negated. The negation rules discussed earlier will apply to **(43c)** to produce **(43a)**, to **(45c)** to produce **(45a)**, and to **(45d)** to produce **(45b)**. However, **(43b)** cannot be produced in this way. It can be produced, however, if the NEG can be *transported* from the lower (embedded) sentence into the upper (matrix) sentence. This is exactly what Fillmore proposed as Negative Transportation. We shall not attempt to strictly formalize the rule, but simply to point out a few of its features.

First of all, Negative Transportation is optional. Its application to **(43c)** results in **(43b)**; if it does not apply, the result is **(43a)**. As is usually the case with optional rules, there are no semantic differences resulting from application or non-application.

Second, Negative Transportation is restricted to only a small set of verbs dealing with mental state: for example, "think," "believe," "suppose," "guess," "want," "expect," "intend," "be likely," and "seem." Deep structures with verbs like "claim," "hope," "feel," "realize," "know," "say," etc., do not undergo Negative Transportation.

While this rule has been questioned by some linguists, there is also syntactic evidence which indicates that a rule something like this is necessary. One such argument, presented by Robin Lakoff (1969), is based on TAG-QUESTION-FORMATION. As discussed previously, negative tags occur with positive sentences, and vice versa. Thus, for example, the following sentence is grammatical:

(46)   I don't suppose the Yankees will win, will they?

The tag in this sentence is clearly formed on the embedded sentence, "The Yankees will win," rather than the main sentence. This is evident because: (1) the pronoun used is "they" (referring to "the Yankees"), and not "I"; (2) the verb "suppose" does not even take Tag Questions with first-person subjects, as seen in (47):

(47)   I don't suppose that's right, do I?

Now if (46) is examined carefully, it seems on the surface to form a counter-example to our rule of Tag-Question Formation; a positive tag ("will they") seems to appear with a positive sentence ("the Yankees will win"). But this seems unusual, since clearly (48a) is grammatical while (48b) is not (except with sarcastic overtones, as discussed previously).

(48a)   The Yankees won't win, will they?

(48b)   *The Yankees will win, will they?

However, if the deep structure of (46) is one which parallels that of (43c), the environment will be met for a positive tag question. That is, the embedded sentence will have the form [$_S$NEG the Yankees will win$_S$], and presence of the negative element will give the positive tag "will they." Negative Transportation will then move the NEG into the higher sentence.

Hearing Children's Acquisition of Negation

Because it has cognitive as well as linguistic implications, Negation has been one of the more thoroughly studied aspects of children's language acquisition. The pioneering work of Klima and Bellugi-Klima (1966) found that the syntactic expression of Negation in children's speech passed through three stages. In *Period 1* children mostly negated by simply placing "no" or "not" before a "nucleus sentence" (e.g., "No want stand head," or "No money"). At *Period 2* the negative element is usually included within the sentence, either as "no" or "not" or as one of a limited number of negated auxiliaries and modals, such as "can't" and "don't" (e.g., "You can't dance" or "He no bit you"). At *Period 3* the subjects typically had mastered most aspects of Verb Phrase Negation in English, although Indefinite Negation was still handled mainly by such forms as "I didn't see something." Klima and Bellugi-Klima did not report on the use of negative adjectives, presumably because they did not appear in the language of their three children (approximately 2 ½ years old). In her study of slightly older children, Menyuk (1969) found Negation developing in stages essentially similar to those found by Klima and Bellugi-Klima.

Bloom (1970) found that the apparent similarity of the syntactic expression of Negation at each stage may mask considerable differences in the semantics of Negation. She distinguished three aspects of negative meaning. *Nonexistence* refers to the case for which the object referred to no longer exists. Structures used to express this aspect include "Allgone" and "No more." In *Rejection* the child refuses some aspect of the environment: one of Bloom's subjects said "No dirty soap" as she refused to accept a worn piece of soap. The third aspect is *Denial*, in which a child denies that something asserted (usually by the mother) is the case. Bloom found that the three aspects emerged in child speech in the order given above: Nonexistence, Rejection, Denial. She found that even when a child was able to correctly express Nonexistence ("There's no more milk"), he usually reverted to an earlier syntactic stage when he arrived at later semantic stages ("No want supper"). This is a good example of the intricate interaction between syntax and semantics in language development.

Quigley, Montanelli, and Wilbur (1974) studied negation in the language of deaf and hearing children with tests constructed to parallel Klima and Bellugi-Klima's stages of acquisition of Negation. The youngest hearing subjects tested in the comparison group were 8 years old, and it would seem that the aspects of the Negation system tested were virtually completely under control by that age, with the errors which occurred being perhaps more attributable to unfamiliarity with the test format, or confusion about what is acceptable in speech versus writing, than in actual understanding of the syntax of the Negation system. By the age of 10 years, hearing students were making virtually no errors on the tests.

Deaf Children's Acquisition of Negation

The only detailed reports in the literature about deaf children's acquisition of the English Negation system deal with that part of it that we have called Sentence Negation. Two aspects have been studied.

Schmitt (1968) used a multiple choice set of pictures to test deaf students' *understanding* of such sentences as "The boy did not push the girl." He found that most of his subjects (aged between 8 and 17 years) performed quite well on this task, indicating that most of them understood well the implications of the negative marker for sentence interpretation. However, he also found that a number of his youngest subjects (aged 8 years) seemed to be operating with what he called the "No-Negative Rule," which specifies the ignoring of the marker "not" and the treatment of negative sentences as equivalent to affirmative sentences. It may well be that such a response is even more typical of children younger than those tested by Schmitt, and many deaf students may pass through a stage where they ignore the negative marker, with consequent misunderstanding of some of what is said to them.

Quigley, Montanelli, & Wilbur (1974) tested three features of the Negation system: NEG PLACEMENT, application of DO-SUPPORT, and CONTRACTION in hearing and deaf students. These features were considered for sentences in which the verb had a modal or an auxiliary, and for those in which it stood alone as a main verb. In general, their findings on the acquisition of the syntax of Sentence Negation support those of Schmitt: Negation is comparatively well established by most deaf students at a relatively early age.

In regard to Klima and Bellugi-Klima's *Period 1* for hearing children, it was found that at age 10 deaf students accepted NEG PLACEMENT sentence-initially ("No go home") about as frequently as they did finally ("Go home no"). By age 17 or 18 both these incorrect forms were being rejected by most deaf subjects. In *Period 2*, hearing children tended to place the negative element within the sentence, somewhere near the verb. This tendency was also apparent in the development of deaf students, with approximately 50 percent of them accepting sentences such as "Dogs not can build nests" at age 10, a percentage that gradually declined to about 20 percent at age 18, varying somewhat by verb type. As far as DO-SUPPORT is concerned, which, as we have seen, appears with hearing children at *Period 3*, deaf students were able to reject sentences where *do* was incorrectly inserted or not inserted at all, approximately 70 percent of the time by age 18, as compared to about 40 percent at age 10. It would seem that this rather complex aspect of the Negation system is not well acquired by a considerable number of deaf students. With CONTRACTION, the deaf subjects accepted correctly contracted modals, auxiliaries and *do* and rejected incorrectly contracted forms about 50 percent of the time at age 10, a success rate which steadily increased to over 90 percent at age 18. It appears that this aspect of Negation is rather well acquired by deaf students. Interestingly, it may be so well acquired that it is overgeneralized to apply to forms with which contraction is, in fact, not acceptable in English. About 70 percent of 10-year-old deaf students accepted "willn't" and amn't"; this declined to only just under 50 percent at age 18.

Quigley, Montanelli, and Wilbur feel overall, that the process of acquisition of Negation proceeds for deaf children fairly much the same as for hearing children, but at a considerably retarded rate.

Analysis of Negation in the Reading Materials

While the system of Negation in English is more readily acquired by deaf children than most other syntactic structures, problems are presented by reading materials such as the *Reading for Meaning* series because of the high frequency with which negatives occur very early in the readers. The negative internal to verb phrases is one of the most frequently occurring structures in the first primer, being exceeded only by modals and direct imperatives. Since deaf students usually have only a modest understanding of the role of some types of negatives until they are 15 or 16 years old, and some students still have difficulties at age 18, this structure, too, requires careful presentation and control in reading materials.

CHAPTER 8

Transformations V: Complementation

In previous chapters two different means of recursion in English have been discussed: Relativization and Conjunction. The topic of this chapter is the third such means: Complementation. The **complements** we shall discuss are embedded sentences which function as noun phrases, in subject or object position, as in the following examples, in which complements are italicized:

(1) Edsel demonstrated *that Santa Claus is an imposter*.
(2) Dreyfus wants *to fly to Katmandu*.
(3) Everyone was surprised at *Bertha's fitting in the car*.
(4) *That Santa Claus is an imposter* doesn't surprise Edsel.
(5) *To fly to Katmandu* is Dreyfus's only desire.
(6) *Bertha's fitting in the car* surprised everyone.

Sentences **(1)** - **(3)** are examples of Complementation in object position, the most common instance. Sentence **(3)** is different from the other two in exemplifying not a verbal object complement, but rather the complement of a preposition. Sentences **(4)** - **(6)**, in contrast to **(1)** - **(3)**, contain complements which function as subjects of their sentences. Simplified deep structure trees of the first three sentences follow:

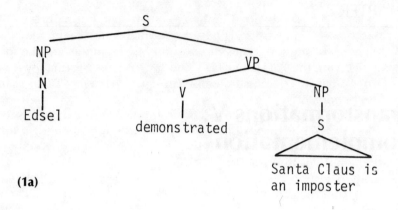

(1a)

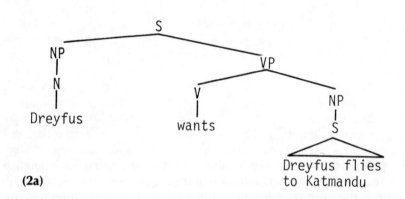

(2a)

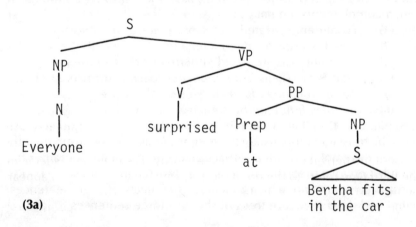

(3a)

(While the above deep structures, especially **(3a)**, are likely not exactly correct, they will be assumed to be so for our purposes.)

Evidence that the embedded sentences are, in fact, noun phrases, as indicated by the above trees, is based on syntactic tests which differentiate between different types of constituents. Examples are the following involving the PSEUDO-CLEFT and PASSIVE transformations:

(1b)   What was demonstrated by Edsel was *that Santa Claus is an imposter*.

(1c)   *That Santa Claus is an imposter* was demonstrated by Edsel.

Since these two transformations apply to move noun phrases, it follows that the italicized complements which have been moved (cp. **(1)**) are themselves noun phrases.

These two tests do not always work in a black-and-white fashion, however. The pseudo-cleft sentence **(2b)** corresponding to **(2)** is grammatical, but the corresponding passive **(2c)** is highly questionable to many speakers.

(2b)   What Dreyfus wants is *to fly to Katmandu*.

(2c)   *To fly to Katmandu* is wanted by Dreyfus.

In some instances, in fact, both tests give negative results when applied to complement structures. The procedure is complicated by the fact that some verbs fail to passivize at all (Chomsky provides the examples "John is *resembled* by Bill" and "Ten dollars is *cost* by this book"), and that other restrictions apply to the two transformations in question. In other words, the failure of one or even both transformations to apply to a complement structure is not conclusive evidence that the complement is not a noun phrase. However, because of such questionable cases, Peter Rosenbaum (in his 1967 dissertation which formed the basis for our present knowledge of complements) postulated that some complements are dominated by *NP*, while others which fail the above tests are not. The claim has been disputed, and we shall not discuss it further. Each of our examples will include an *NP*, although it should be remembered that some such instances may be proven at some future date to be erroneous formulations.

Three distinct classes of complements are represented by examples **(1)**–**(3)** above. Sentence **(1)** represents *That Complementation*; sentence **(2)** *For-To Complementation*; and sentence **(3)** *POSS-ing Complementation*. They are so named because of the form of the **complementizer**, the morpheme or group of morphemes introducing the complement. Notice that the morpheme "for" does not appear in the surface structure of sentence **(2)**; it is, however, present at an earlier stage of the derivation, as we shall see shortly. The POSS morpheme in the third type refers to the possessive *'s*, which may or may not appear on the surface in certain instances.

The three different complementizers have similar meanings, and are, in fact, more or less interchangeable in some cases, as evidenced by the following examples:

(7a)   The law requires that we testify.

(7b)   The law requires us to testify.

(7c)   The law requires our testifying.

For some speakers, at least, the above sentences are all grammatical and have the same meaning. There are, however, other cases for which the choice of complementizer is not so free, as in the following:

(8a)   John began walking when he was 9.

(8b)   John began to walk when he was 9.

(8c)   *John began that he walked when he was 9.

One factor which seems to have an influence on the choice of complementizer is the semantic class of the verb; that is, words with similar meaning (such as *ask*, *request*, *demand*) show similar restrictions. We shall not discuss this problem further here, but shall instead concentrate on transformations which apply once COMPLEMENTIZER PLACEMENT (the rule which inserts the appropriate complementizer into the complement sentence) has already applied.

Extraposition

Consider the following sentence pairs:

(9a)   *That Santa Claus is an imposter* doesn't surprise Edsel.

(9b)   It doesn't surprise Edsel *that Santa Claus is an imposter*.

(10a)   *That Santa is an imposter* was demonstrated by Edsel.

(10b)   It was demonstrated by Edsel *that Santa Claus is an imposter*.

(11a)   *For an elephant to fly* is unusual.

(11b)   It is unusual *for an elephant to fly*.

Sentences **(9a)**, **(10a)**, and **(11a)** have complements as their subjects. In such cases, the complement can be moved to the end of the sentence, as in **(9b)**, **(10b)**, and **(11b)**. Notice that the pronoun "it" is inserted as a placeholder; the following ungrammatical sentences are thereby avoided.

(9c)   *Doesn't surprise Edsel that Santa Claus is an imposter.

(10c)   *Was demonstrated by Edsel that Santa Claus is an imposter.

(11c)   *Is unusual for an elephant to fly.

This "it" holds no meaning, but simply preserves the structure of the sentence. (All sentences in English, with the exception of imperatives, must have a surface subject.) It was originally proposed by Rosenbaum that this "it" existed in the deep structure of all complement structures. Thus each of the above sentences would have the following deep structure:

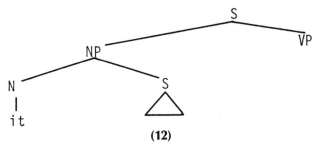

(12)

EXTRAPOSITION would move the embedded *S* to the right of the *VP*, leaving the "it" in its original position, as in **(9b)**, **(10b)**, and **(11b)**. If Extraposition did not apply, the pronoun "it" would be deleted, resulting in sentences like **(9a)**, **(10a)**, and **(11a)**. However, syntactically, it is no less reasonable to suppose that the pronoun does not occur in the deep structure, but is inserted only when necessary to preserve structure, as described above. Both formulations have been accepted and used by linguists in recent years. However, considering our definition of deep structure as the level of meaning, it seems as though an extraneous, meaningless element like the "it" of the above sentences would have no place here, and therefore is most likely inserted. This, in fact, is the analysis most commonly employed nowadays.

Notice that Extraposition can apply not only to deep structures, but also to intermediate structures resulting from the application of other transformations. Thus **(10b)** is produced as follows:

(13)   Edsel PAST demonstrate[ₛ Santa Claus NONPAST be an imposter ₛ]

COMP. PLACEMENT Edsel PAST demonstrate [ₛ that Santa Claus
================> NONPAST be an imposter ₛ]

PASSIVE   [ₛ that Santa Claus NONPAST be an imposter ₛ]
=====>   be + PAST demonstrate + ed by Edsel

EXTRAPOSITION   it be + PAST demonstrate + ed by Edsel [ₛ that
================> Santa Claus NONPAST be an imposter ₛ]

AFFIX
HOPPING   it be + PAST demonstrate + ed by Edsel [ₛ that
=====>   Santa Claus be + NONPAST an imposter ₛ]

MORPHOLOGICAL
RULES   It was demonstrated by Edsel that Santa Claus is
=====>   an imposter.

Our examples thus far have dealt only with extraposition of "that" and "for-to" complements. For some speakers, some "POSS-ing" complements may also be extraposed. For example:

(14a)   *Playing tiddlywinks* is fun.
(14b)   It's fun *playing tiddlywinks*.

(15a) *John's finishing so fast* amazed me.

(15b) It amazed me *John's finishing so fast*.

While in all cases discussed so far, Extraposition is optional (**(9a)** and **(9b)** are both grammatical, for example), there are other cases for which it is obligatory. One determining factor seems to be the choice of verb, with verbs like *happen*, *turn out*, *seem*, and *appear* triggering Extraposition when they are in final position. (In linguistic terminology, the rule is **governed** [by the class of verb, in this case].)

Observe, for example, the following sentence pairs; Extraposition must apply to the structure underlying **(a)** to give **(b)**, in each case.

(16a) *That John saw a flashing red light happened.

(16b) It happened that John saw a flashing red light.

(17a) *That John saw a flashing red light seems.

(17b) It seems that John saw a flashing red light.

Subject Raising

No cases similar to **(16a-b)** and **(17a-b)**, which involve "that" complements, seem to exist for "POSS-ing" complements. On superficial evidence, the same seems to be true for "for-to" complements. Consider the following:

(18a) *(For) John to be a used underwear salesman turned out.

(18b) *It turned out for John to be a used underwear salesman.

(19a) *(For)Samson to have discovered the missing link in Washington, D.C. appears.

(19b) *It appears for Samson to have discovered the missing link in Washington, D.C.

Whether Extraposition has applied or not, the sentences seem to be equally ungrammatical. Now notice, however, the following examples:

(18c) John turned out to be a used underwear salesman.

(19c) Samson appears to have discovered the missing link in Washington, D.C.

Sentences **(18c)** and **(19c)** differ from **(18b)** and **(19b)** only in the positioning of the subject of the complement ("John" and "Samson") and the absence of "it" (and also the deletion of "for," which results from a widely applying rule to be discussed shortly). Rosenbaum postulated a rule of SUBJECT-RAISING (he called it PRONOUN REPLACEMENT; others have used the term IT REPLACEMENT) which applies after Extraposition to replace the meaningless "it" and become the subject of the main verb. Notice that while Subject-Raising is obligatory for "for-to" complements which are extraposed, it never applies to extraposed "that" clauses, which seem to be impervious to division. The result is the following paradigm:

(20a) *That John saw a flashing red light happened.
(20b) *For John to see a flashing red light happened.
(21a) It happened that John saw a flashing red light.
(21b) *It happened for John to see a flashing red light.
(22a) *John happened that saw a flashing red light.
(22b) John happened to see a flashing red light.

Subject-Raising applies not only to subject complements, but also to those in object position. Consider the following:

(23) Grinelda imagines herself *to be beautiful*.

Obviously Reflexivization has applied to produce sentence **(23)**. Recall now that Reflexivization applies only when two coreferent noun phrases occur in the same simple sentence with no *S* node intervening. The deep structure of **(23)** is as follows:

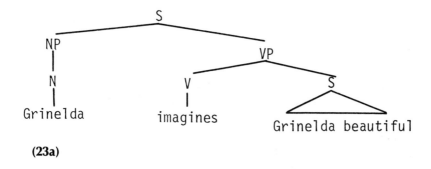

(23a)

Notice that the second occurrence of "Grinelda" occurs in a lower complement sentence and is separated from the first by an *S* node, thus failing to satisfy the environment for Reflexivization. Suppose now, however, that Subject-Raising were to apply (after *Be*-Insertion and Complementizer Placement) to move the subject of the complement sentence out to a position directly beneath the *VP* node, as follows:

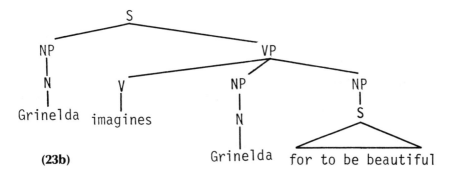

(23b)

"Grinelda" would now be in proper position to undergo Reflex-ivization as desired.

Additional evidence for this analysis is provided by sentences like the following:

(24)   Grinelda is believed by Henry to be beautiful.

A likely source for (24) is the following deep structure:

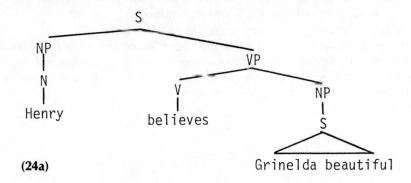

(24a)

Since the sentential object is the entire complement sentence, appli-cation of PASSIVE to (24a) will give (after be-Insertion and Com-plementizer Placement) (24b), where the entire complement is moved.

(24b) *That Grinelda is beautiful* is believed by Henry.

On the other hand, if Subject-Raising first applies to raise "Grinelda" to object position in the matrix sentence, PASSIVE can apply to move "Grinelda" alone, producing (24).

Notice that in the subject-raised sentence (24) the complementizer is "for-to"; in the non-subject-raised sentence (24b) it is "that." As men-tioned previously, Subject-Raising does not apply to "that" comple-ments. It does appear to apply to "POSS-ing" complements, as in the following examples.

(25a)   I prevented John from going.

(25b)   John was prevented by me from going.

Equi-Noun Phrase Deletion

EQUI-NOUN PHRASE DELETION, originally referred to by Rosen-baum as IDENTITY ERASURE, and now known familiarly as just EQUI, deletes the subject noun phrase in a lower complement sentence if it is coreferential (i.e., refers to the same person or object) to a noun phrase in the matrix sentence.

(26)   Thaddeus intends to play the bongos.

(27)   Thaddeus asked Thrim to play the bongos.

While the surface complement is identical in both of the above sentences ("to play the bongos"), it is clear that the subject of the complement is different in each case. In **(26)** it is Thaddeus who is to play the bongos; in **(27)** it is Thrim who (hopefully) will play. This can be seen by the semigrammatical paraphrases following:

(26a) ?Thaddeus intends for *Thaddeus* to play the bongos.

(27a) ?Thaddeus asked Thrim for *Thrim* to play the bongos.

This semantic information, of course, must be contained in the deep structures of the two sentences, which look approximately like the following:

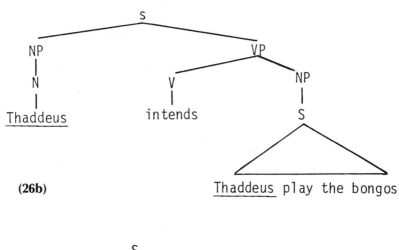

(26b)

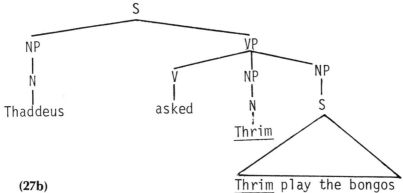

(27b)

Thus in the deep structure the subjects of the complements differ (paralleling the difference in meaning), but because of the identity of the underlined noun phrases, the subject is deleted from the complement in each case, resulting in a merger of form on the surface. Notice that in **(26b)** it is the subject of the matrix sentence which triggers the erasure, while in **(27b)** it is the object. (NOTE, however, that EQUI always deletes the subject of the complement sentence.) Observe also that in sentence **(27)** the word "Thrim" fills a double function: object of the matrix sentence but subject of the complement sentence.

EQUI can also apply backwards to delete the first, rather than the second, occurrence of a noun phrase if the first occurrence appears in a complement sentence.

> **(28)**   To play the bongos excites Thaddeus.

The above sentence can be paraphrased by:

> **(28a)**   ?For *Thaddeus* to play the bongos excites Thaddeus.

In addition to applying to "for-to" complements, EQUI also applies if the complement is of the "POSS-ing type," as demonstrated by the following:

> **(29)**   Thaddeus enjoys playing the bongos.
>
> **(30)**   Playing the bongos excites Thaddeus.

The following are semigrammatical counterparts of the above to which EQUI has not applied:

> **(29a)**   ?Thaddeus enjoys *Thaddeus's* playing the bongos.
>
> **(30a)**   ?*Thaddeus's* playing the bongos excites Thaddeus.

EQUI, on the other hand, does not apply to "that" complements; this is shown by the following pairs:

> **(31a)**   Thaddeus is pleased that *he* (Thaddeus) can play the bongos.
>
> **(31b)**   *Thaddeus is pleased that can play the bongos.
>
> **(32a)**   That Thaddeus can play the bongos excites *him* (Thaddeus).
>
> **(32b)**   *That can play the bongos excites Thaddeus.

Assuming that the sentences marked with ? in the preceding discussion are ungrammatical, we can say that application of EQUI is obligatory for those cases in which its application is indicated.

Other Complement Rules

A rule has been mentioned several times which deletes the preposition "for" in complement structures. Actually, there are two such rules, one which applies obligatorily and one which applies optionally. Let us consider the obligatory rule first.

When "for-to" Complementizer Placement applies, the "for" and "to" are inserted on either side of the subject of the complement sentence. This structure is sometimes preserved, as in the following:

> **(33)**   *For* Scrooge *to* give a gift is unheard of.
>
> **(34)**   Scrooge likes *for* his employees *to* suffer.

On the other hand, the complement structure is sometimes disrupted by other rules which move the subject of the embedded sentence. Two rules which do exactly this are EQUI and Subject-Raising. Consider the following deep structures:

(35)　Thurigold hopes [s Thurigold become an opera singer s].

(36)　[s Sebastian be a radiator salesman s] turned out.

Application of Complementizer Placement will give the following structures.

(35a)　Thurigold hopes [s*for* Thurigold *to* become an opera singer s]

(36a)　[s*for* Sebastian *to* be a radiator salesman s] turned out

Next Extraposition will apply to (36a) to give (36b).

(36b)　it turned out [s for Sebastian to be a radiator salesman s]

And finally, EQUI will apply to (35a) and Subject-Raising to (36b) (since the conditions are now met), giving the following:

(35c)　*Thurigold hopes for to become an opera singer.

(36c)　*Sebastian turned out for to be a radiator salesman.

The sentences (35c) and (36c) are obviously ungrammatical. It is necessary therefore to postulate a rule for English grammar of OBLIGATORY COMPLEMENTIZER DELETION which will delete "for" just in case it appears immediately before "to." (The rule is likely more general, having to do with a general English constraint against surface sequences of prepositions.) Additional examples of application of this rule are seen in the following:

(37a)　*I bribed Herman *for* to invite Clarabelle as my date.

(37b)　I bribed Herman to invite Clarabelle as my date.

(38a)　*I consider John's stupidity *for* to be beyond belief.

(38b)　I consider John's stupidity to be beyond belief.

Actually, the rule of Obligatory Complementizer Deletion is more far-reaching than this, however. It also applies when the POSS of the "POSS-ing" complementizer is stranded by a rule like EQUI, as seen by the following:

(39a)　*Lucretius enjoys 's driving like a madman.

(39b)　Lucretius enjoys driving like a madman.

The morphemes "for," "POSS," and "that" can all be optionally deleted from complement structures when following certain verbs (not the same verbs in the three instances). For example, each of the two members in each of the following pairs is equally grammatical to most speakers.

(40a)　I would hate *for* John to lose it.

(40b)　I would hate John to lose it.

(41a)　Everybody prefers you*r* driving slowly.

(41b)　Everybody prefers you driving slowly.

(42a)　Bill thinks *that* Mortimer Snerd is a genius.

(42b)　Bill thinks Mortimer Snerd is a genius.

The form or position of the verb is irrelevant in triggering this deletion, as shown by the following pair:

(43a) Preferring *for* John to leave is not nice.

(43b) Preferring John to leave is not nice.

On the other hand, it is necessary that the preceding element be the main verb of the sentence before "for" can be deleted. Notice the following examples from Rosenbaum.

(44a) I would hate very much *for* John to lose it.

(44b) *I would hate very much John to lose it.

(45a) *For* you to stay here would be impossible.

(45b) *You to stay here would be impossible.

(46a) It was important for you to do that.

(46b) *It was important you to do that.

In the first case, an adverb appears between the verb and the "for"; in the second case, the "for" is preceded by silence, and in the last case by an adjective. Notice that the restrictions are not the same for the deletion of "that" and "POSS," since the **(b)** examples that follow are grammatical.

(47a) It was important *that* you do that.

(47b) It was important you do that.

(48a) I dislike very much John's doing that.

(48b) I dislike very much John doing that.

For several verbs, the "to" of the complementizer is also deleted.

(49a) *Henrietta made Henry *to* beg on hands and knees.

(49b) Henrietta made Henry beg on hands and knees.

Compare the above paradigm to that of *force*, which does not cause deletion of the "to."

(50a) Henrietta forced Henry *to* beg on hands and knees.

(50b) *Henrietta forced Henry beg on hands and knees.

Some verbs having the characteristic of "to" deletion are *make*, *let*, and *have*.

EQUI vs. Subject-Raising

Certain verbs in English are restricted regarding coreference relationships in the sentences in which they occur. For illustration, consider the following:

(51a) I craned my neck.

(51b) John craned his neck.

(51c) *I craned John's neck.

(51d) *John craned my neck.

It seems as though the verb *crane* contains a selectional restriction requiring that the possessive adjective must be coreferential with the subject of the sentence. Compare now the following examples:

(52a) I attempted to solve the problem.

(52b) Harry attempted to solve the problem.

(52c) *I attempted for Harry to solve the problem.

(52d) *Harry attempted for me to solve the problem.

The verb *attempt*, when it takes an object complement, requires that the subject of the complement sentence be coreferential with the subject of *attempt*. Finally, consider the following:

(53a) I bribed Harry.

(53b) I bribed Harry to have a haircut.

(53c) *I bribed Harry for me to have a haircut.

Although there are no restrictions on the occurrence of subjects and objects with *bribe*, the object of the verb must be coreferential with the subject of the complement sentence, which will then be deleted by EQUI, as in **(53b)**.

Consider the following deep structure patterns:

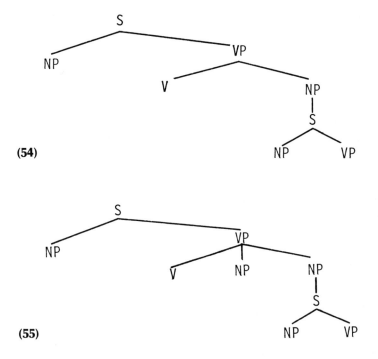

(54)

(55)

Structure **(54)** satisfies the environment for Subject-Raising (assuming an appropriate verb), while **(55)** meets the requirements for EQUI. Since both rules are obligatory, the results are the following.

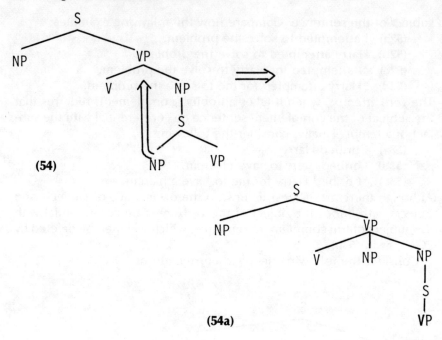

(54)

(54a)

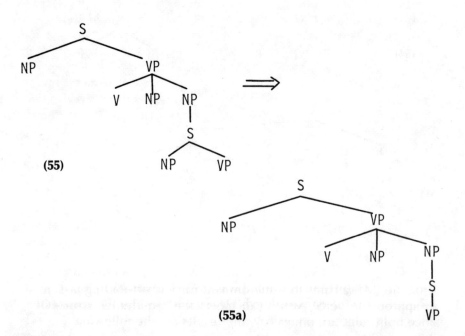

(55)

(55a)

A rule of **tree-pruning** which we shall not discuss in detail will then delete irrelevant nodes in each case, resulting in a structure something like the following:

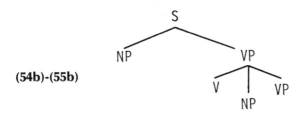

(54b)-(55b)

In other words, then, Subject-Raising and EQUI apply to contrasting deep structures to produce a merger on the surface. Why, then, are two rules necessary? Judging on the basis of surface structure only, our analysis so far seems redundant.

Consider the following sentences.

(56)   Herman asked Hermanella to leave.

(57)   Herman wanted Hermanella to leave.

Although sentences **(56)** and **(57)** have identical surface structures, any native speaker will acknowledge an intuitive difference between the two. Putting this intuition into words, the logical object of the verb in **(56)** is "Hermanella"; in **(57)** it is the entire complement "Hermanella to come." That is, in **(57)** Herman doesn't want Hermanella herself (at least the sentence doesn't tell us that!); he wants her visitation. In **(56)**, however, he is not directing his request at the visitation, but at Hermanella the person.

This intuitive distinction is borne out by several syntactic tests, two of which will be discussed here.

The first test has to do with the Pseudo-Cleft transformation. Recall that this transformation has the following effect:

(58)   X − NP − Y⟹What X − Y be NP.

The element which occurs to the right of the verb *be* must be a noun phrase dominated by an *NP* node. Consider the operation of Pseudo-Cleft on deep structures corresponding to sentences **(56)** and **(57)**.

(56a)   *What Herman asked was (for) Hermanella to leave.

(57a)   What Herman wanted was (for) Hermanella to leave.

The reason for the demarcation is clear if we consider the corresponding deep structures, which follow.

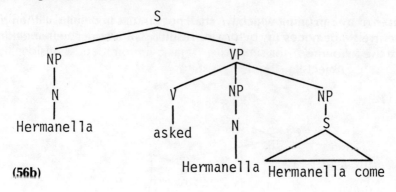

(56b)

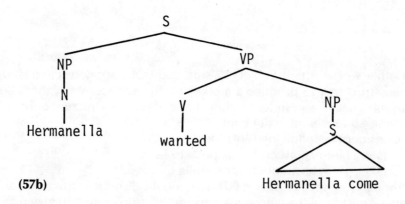

(57b)

The reason that **(56a)** is ungrammatical is that there is an extra *NP*, "Hermanella," in the deep structure **(56b)** which is not accounted for in the pseudo-cleft sentence. This is not the case with **(57b)**. We can say, then, that "EQUI deep structures" (i.e., those of the form of **(55)** which satisfy the structural description of EQUI) will not undergo pseudo-clefting *of this type*. The emphasis is necessary, because pseudo-clefts of other types may be possible, as can be seen by the following pair:

> **(58a)** Herman called the cat to come.

> **(58b)** What Herman called to come was the cat.

Thus it is possible to "pseudo-cleft out" the noun phrase "the cat," which, it will be recalled, serves as both the object of the matrix sentence and the subject of the complement sentence. Nevertheless, any attempt to pseudo-cleft out this noun phrase and the complement together will fail:

> **(58c)** *What Herman called was the cat to come.

The other rule which is useful in distinguishing EQUI and Subject-Raising structures is Passive. Since complements are embedded sentences, they can be passivized. (Strictly speaking, of course, a PASSIVE node would be necessary before Passive could apply, in the framework we have presented; for simplicity, it has been omitted.) Consider the following Subject-Raising deep structure.

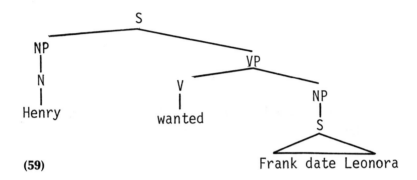

(59)

If Passive does not apply to the complement sentence, Subject-Raising and the various complementizer rules will result in the following structure (after tree-pruning).

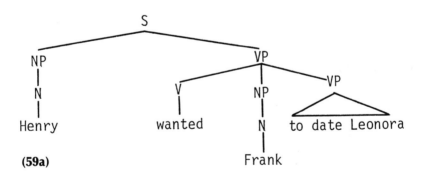

(59a)

Thus the surface sentence generated is:

    (59b) Henry wanted Frank to date Leonora.

Assume, however, that Passive applies first to **(59)**. The following intermediate structure will be produced:

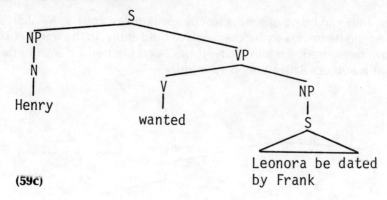

(59c)

Again, Subject-Raising and the complementizer rules will apply, giving in this case **(59d)**.

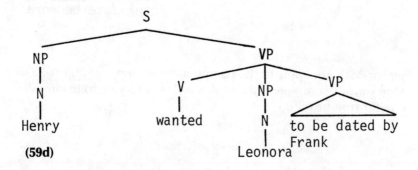

(59d)

The corresponding surface sentence is **(59e)**.

  (59e) Henry wanted Leonora to be dated by Frank.
Notice now that **(59b)** and **(59e)** are synonymous, just as the theory would predict, as they originate in the same deep structure.

  Now consider the parallel situation with EQUI deep structures. First, compare the two deep structures following:

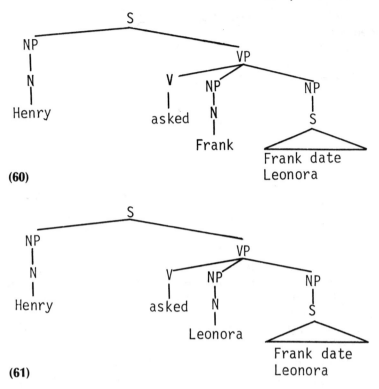

(60)

(61)

Both of the above deep structures are generated by the phrase structure rules of English, but the two are significantly different in meaning:
in **(60)** it is Frank who is asked, while in **(61)** it is Leonora. Notice now
that EQUI can apply to **(60)** to give **(60a)** (after tree-pruning and complementizer rules).

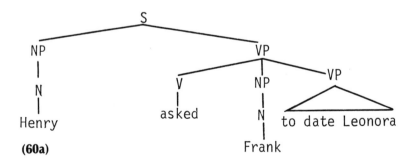

(60a)

The corresponding surface sentence, of course, is **(60b)**.

    (60b) Henry asked Frank to date Leonora.

However, if Passive is allowed to apply to the complement of **(60)**, **(60c)** is generated.

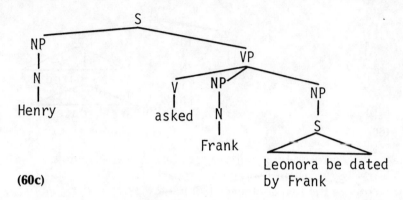

(60c)

Since the grammatical subject of the complement is now "Leonora" and there is no coreferential noun phrase in the matrix sentence, EQUI cannot apply (remember that EQUI always deletes the complement *subject*), and the derivation is blocked. No surface sentence is generated. Thus a deep structure like **(60)** does not allow passivization of the complement.

Now compare the deep structure **(61)**. The situation here is exactly opposite to that of **(60)**. EQUI *cannot* apply unless PASSIVE is applied to the complement first. On the other hand, the order PASSIVE-EQUI produces the following sequence of structures.

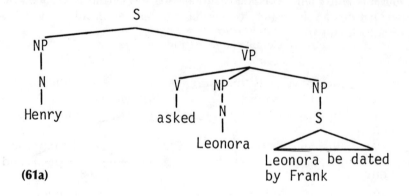

(61a)

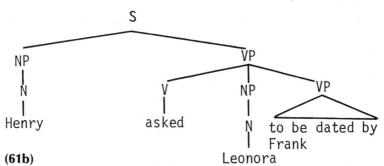

(61b)

Finally, the corresponding surface sentence is the following:

    (61c) Henry asked Leonora to be dated by Frank.

Now compare the two sentences **(60b)** and **(61c)**.

    (60b) Henry asked Frank to date Leonora.

    (61c) Henry asked Leonora to be dated by Frank.

The two sentences are clearly different semantically and, as expected, the difference parallels the differences in their deep structure (i.e., with respect to the logical object of "asked").

    If we contrast the meaning difference between the above two sentences to the synonymity in meaning between **(59b)** and **(59e),** we have another test for distinguishing EQUI and Subject-Raising structures. The two tests are summarized in the following table:

EQUI Structures	SUBJECT-RAISING Structures
Don't allow clefting out of complement	Do allow complement to be clefted
Sentences with Active/ Passive Complements differ in meaning	Sentences with Active/Passive Complements are same in meaning

Let us apply the above tests to a sentence with the verb *bribe.*

    (62) Snorkel bribed Beetle to clean the barracks.

First, we attempt to cleft or more properly, pseudo-cleft out the complement.

    (62a) *What Snorkel bribed was (for) Beetle to clean the barracks.

Second, we compare the corresponding sentence with a passivized complement.

    (62b) Snorkel bribed the barracks to be cleaned by Beetle.

Clearly this structure does not allow the complement to be clefted out, and even more obviously **(62)** and **(62b)** differ in meaning (if **(62b)** even has one!). The verb *bribe,* then, is one which occurs in EQUI structures, and **(62)** is a sentence produced through the operation of EQUI.

Contrast now the results of the tests applied to the following sentence.

(63)   The mailman resented the dog('s) nipping his pants.

Results of the two tests are as follows:

(63a)   What the mailman resented was the dog nipping his pants.

(63b)   The mailman resented his pants being nipped by the dog.

Sentences **(63a)** and **(63b)** show that *resent,* unlike *bribe,* occurs in Subject-Raising structures, and that **(63)** is the result of the application of this rule, rather than EQUI.

Although, as we might suspect, the Pseudo-Cleft and Passive tests will not always distinguish quite this clearly between EQUI and Subject-Raising structures (because of the influence of many other factors), they are a good guideline.

Hearing Children's Acquisition of Complements

It will be clear from this presentation that in learning the complement system of English, children have to master two major concepts: (a) the form of the three complement types—with their optional deletion and extraposition rules, and (b) the types of complements that can be taken by various classes of verbs. In addition, as C. Chomsky (1969) and Kessel (1970) have shown, certain exceptions to the general rules which are important for sentence interpretation must also be mastered.

C. Chomsky (1969) has pointed out that in sentence interpretation, it is generally correct to interpret the *NP* closest to the complement in surface order as being its subject. She has called this the "Minimal Distance Principle." Its operation is clear in such sentences as "John wanted *Bill* to leave," where the nearest *NP* ("Bill") is the subject of the complement sentence. However, with certain verbs (notably *promise*), this principle is violated, and the *NP* farthest away from the verb is the subject of the complement ("*John* promised Bill to leave"). Similarly, there are complex interactions of verb and complement type with verbs of commanding and requesting. In her research, Chomsky found that young children had considerable difficulty mastering these complexities. In fact, the correct use of *promise* was not mastered by some of her subjects until they were 9 years old, and for the *ask/tell* distinction, not all subjects had mastered its use at the oldest age she tested, 9 years. However, Kessel (1970) has disputed these findings. He considered that Chomsky's results may have been in part a function of the type of task she used. With a different task using pictures instead of dolls, he found that most of his subjects had mastered the *ask/tell* distinction by age 8, and some even at age 7.

In her analysis of samples of spoken language collected from children from Nursery School age up to Grade 1, Menyuk (1969) also looked at patterns of development of complement structures. She found that apparent infinitival complements in sentences like "I wanna (go)" and "I'm gonna (go)" were present very early, but felt that these were not rule-generated, but instead rote-learned and memorized fragments of routines. Somewhat later, however, true infinitive ("for-to") complements with a wide variety of main verbs began to appear. By the first grade, all the children were using infinitival complements—both with ("I told him to sit down") and without ("I used to fall off") pronoun objects. It seems that "POSSing" complements (called "participial" complements by Menyuk) are more difficult to acquire than are infinitival, or "for-to" complements, because by the time all of the children were using infinitives, only 43 percent were using participial complements, and half of these were in Grade 1. Menyuk also reports the presence of deviant structures like the following:

We've got to pasting.
Next year, I'd like to bowling.
I want to draw it.
We're going share.

These utterances are seemingly due to some confusion about the structure of complements. Menyuk likens them to the "redundant" use of rules which we have noted previously for the phrase structure rules. It should also be noted that these types of structures found in the spoken language of very young hearing children are strikingly similar to structures found in the written language of deaf adolescents.

Limber (1973) studied complements in children under 3 years of age, and his findings generally support those of Menyuk. His subjects were using marked and unmarked infinitives and "that" complements, but not "POSS-ing" complements. He also found a course of development in the types of verbs used with complements: first, **active verbs**, and second, **perception verbs** (*see*, *hear*, etc.); no **stative verbs** had been used with complements by his subjects up to the age of 3. Generally, Limber found that once a verb capable of taking a complement appeared in a child's speech, it was followed within a month by its actual use with a complement.

Quigley, Wilbur, and Montanelli (1975) studied the ability of deaf and hearing students from 10 through 19 years of age to judge the grammaticality of sentences containing correct and incorrect complement forms. They found that their hearing subjects had a response rate of 88 percent correct by 10 years of age. This was not a statistically significant improvement from the 83 percent correct response rate at age 8, so it can be concluded that most of these children had the comprehension of complements under control by that age.

In summary, it seems that complements of most types appear in the speech of hearing children before school age, and that the children have them well under control by age 8 or so, except that even up to age 10, some children might be having problems with certain of the variations on the standard rules for interpretation, such as the Minimal Distance Principle.

Deaf Children's Acquisition of Complements

The transformationally oriented study of the written language of deaf students produced by Taylor (1969) found a number of deviancies from Standard English complement forms. These included confused marking of tense in infinitives ("The ant like to played with insect," "The man began screamed"); confusion about the relationship between Infinitives ("for-to") and gerunds ("POSS-ing") ("He cannot know how to swimming," "The hunter missed to shoot the dove"). These errors appear to be of the same type as those reported by Menyuk for young hearing children, but in deaf students they persist to a much later age, appearing even in the writing of 16-year-olds, the oldest children surveyed by Taylor.

Quigley, Wilbur, and Montanelli (1975) found that of the three recursive processes in English, Complementation was the most difficult for deaf students, Relativization was next in difficulty, and Conjunction was least difficult. These investigators found that many types of Complementation could not even be attempted by deaf students, and that performance on those types that could be tested was only at the level of chance. The results from tests of comprehension of complements were compared with the use of complement structures in written language samples obtained from the same deaf students. In the written language samples there was a general increase of complement usage over the age range tested. No subject complements were produced by any of the students, but at least one object complement was used by 22 percent of the deaf students at age 10, increasing to 92 percent of the students at age 18. "For-to" complements were used most frequently, followed by "that" complements, and finally a few "POSS-ing" complements. Nearly all of the complements occurred with active verbs, fewer than one percent with verbs of perception, and none with stative verbs.

Some of the tests of complementation used by Quigley, Wilbur, and Montanelli examined the acceptability of deviant complement forms often found in the written language of deaf persons. Analysis revealed significant differences among the error possibilities. Deaf students were able to recognize sentences with an extra "for" ("For to play baseball is fun") as incorrect 58 percent of the time. When an extra "to" was present with "POSS-ing" complements ("John goes to fishing"), students made correct judgments only 39 percent of the time. When a "for-to" complement was used in place of "POSS-ing" ("John dislikes to fish") and when an infinitival complement was inappropriately inflected ("Bill liked to played baseball"), approximately 50 percent considered the sentences acceptable. Although performance improved with age, even at age 18 the sentences with an extra "for" were acceptable 21 percent of the time, those with an extra "to" were accepted 43 percent of the time, and where "for-to" was used in place of "POSS-ing" the 18-year-old deaf students found the sentence acceptable 50 percent of the time. It will be recalled that these deviant forms of complements used in the tests were not arbitrarily constructed but were forms that actually appear in the written language of deaf students. Thus, many deaf persons not only produce such deviant complement structures in writing, but when presented with them in a test situation find them to be quite acceptable. Another deviant form which was not included in the test battery was found by Quigley, Wilbur, and Montanelli in the writings of their deaf subjects. In 36 percent of "for-to" complements used at age 10, decreasing to 8 percent at age 18, the complement incorrectly appeared without the particle "to," as in "I wanted Bill go."

Analysis of Complements in the Reading Materials

Although these studies show that complement structures are poorly understood by deaf students even by 18 years of age, such structures occur very frequently in typical school reading materials. The analysis of school readers discussed in earlier chapters revealed that they occurred at the rate of approximately four per 100 sentences in the second primer and increased to a rate of approximately 62 per 100 sentences in the sixth grade reader. Analysis of the complement structures by type revealed that approximately half were "for-to" complements, which increased steadily in usage from the primers to the sixth grade text. "POSS-ing" complements appeared first at the second grade level and also increased steadily in subsequent grades. "That" complements did not appear until the fourth grade text, but then occurred at the rate of 21 or more per 100 sentences in the fourth, fifth, and sixth grade readers. Given the great difficulty experienced by deaf students, even at age 18, in understanding and using complement structures correctly, it is obvious that they would have limited success in understanding much of the material in this typical set of readers. When it is recalled that similar problems were experienced with other structures, as discussed in earlier chapters, it becomes obvious that "typical" reading materials cannot be used with deaf students without great modifications in the syntactic structure of the language in those materials. It is equally obvious that appropriate modifications can be made only on the basis of a thorough knowledge of language structure, the development of that structure in hearing children, its development in deaf children, and a detailed understanding of the deviant forms used by deaf children.

CHAPTER 9

Linguistics and the Language of Deaf Children

Much of what has been presented on transformational generative grammar probably seems technically specialized and highly abstract. The teacher will perhaps wonder what it all has to do with the language of deaf children. Some indication of the value of this linguistic approach has already been given in several chapters, in discussing its use for studying the dynamics of language acquisition in both deaf and hearing children; additional evidence will be presented in this chapter. Transformational generative grammar, during the past 15 years or so, has transformed the whole psychological approach to the study of language development from the tabulation and classification of units such as words and types of clauses to the investigation of the *processes* of language development and the study of the emergence of rules which generate language structures. The use of transformational generative grammar as a theoretical framework has produced techniques which have been used to accumulate a steadily increasing fund of knowledge about the processes and stages of language acquisition, particularly in very young children. This has led to the general realization that children internalize much of the grammar of their language by the age of 4 or 5 years and probably most or all of it by the age of 9 or 10, and that any severe disruption of the process of language development during the early years of life will produce language deficiencies that are probably irremediable except to a limited extent. Profound hearing impairment is, of course, just such a disruption, and the limited extent to which the language deficiencies it produces are corrected is painfully obvious to teachers of deaf children.

During the past eight to ten years the use of theoretical approaches and experimental techniques based on transformational generative grammar has also resulted in the accumulation of a body of knowledge about the acquisition of language by deaf children, much of which has been discussed in previous chapters. Different investigators have applied these approaches and techniques in studying various aspects of the language and communication process: the language of signs (Stokoe, 1960, 1972; Bellugi, 1972); esoteric and exoteric communication (Tervoort, 1961), morphology (Cooper and Rosenstein, 1966); syntax (Taylor, 1969, Quigley and a number of associates in a continuing series of studies at the University of Illinois), and the written language of deaf persons as a dialect of English (Charrow, 1974). Charrow's approach is of interest in that it views the written language of deaf persons in the manner that sociolinguists now generally view the spoken language of blacks and similar groups: that is, as a dialect of English rather than simply a distorted form of Standard English. This sociolinguistic view of dialects has much to contribute to an understanding of the language usage of deaf persons.

Sociolinguistics and Social Dialects

In recent years, sociolinguistics, the field of study which is concerned with language as it is used in society, has attracted several notable linguists to its ranks, such as William Labov (1965, 1971 a, b). Labov and other linguists have been more concerned with the "-linguistics" rather than the "socio-" of sociolinguistics, in contrast to the previous emphasis in the field. Concentration has been on the form taken by language in different contexts, both linguistic and social, and the indication is that variation is much more widespread, yet at the same time much more predictable, than had been believed. This concern of sociolinguistics for variation in language has achieved useful insights. First of all, sociolinguistics is interested, not in an idealized model of language (as is transformational generative grammar) or in an isolated speech situation, but in speech as it is used in real situations, by groups rather than individuals. And, while demonstrating that language is not by any means homogeneous, sociolinguistic research has shown even more clearly that it is systematic. Most variants do not have to do with individual, idiolectical differences, but occur with high probability in readily describable situations. Variation falls into several definable categories, as follows:

(1) Much linguistic variation is regional or geographic, and this is more widespread than is generally realized. This type of variation,

while minimized, is at least acknowledged by most linguists, and is likely one source of the recognized need for the notion of an "idealized" (i.e., free from dialect variation) speaker-hearer in theoretical formulations.

(2) Variation also occurs among speech classes, so that a person's background is often quite apparent just from listening to him speak. These differences are not haphazard, but quite regular, and may have a great deal to do with how a person is accepted among various groups in his community. This type of variation has been called **social dialect** by some sociolinguists.

(3) Variation in style is also a regularly occurring phenomenon. People speak very differently depending on their location, their subject matter, and those who are listening. Again, this has been considered by transformationalists to be a result of performance factors, or degenerate linguistic features, in casual situations. However, this type of variation has also been shown to be extremely systematic.

Of particular interest to us, because of its possible analogy to the written language of deaf persons, is the second type of variation: that is, **social dialect.** An excellent survey of this area of linguistics, including a philosophical perspective on social dialects, has been presented by Wolfram and Fasold (1974). These authors use the term dialect to indicate any combination of observable variable features of English; a social dialect can be considered to be a combination of features of English common to a particular social grouping of people. Sociolinguists have stressed, as have linguists in other fields, that no one dialect, either regional or social, is better than another. The dialect of a New Yorker serves as well as the dialect of a Californian; the dialect of a Southern lower-class black as well as a Northern upper-class black or a Midwestern middle-class white. Emphasis in the study of social dialects is on the linguistic features that the speakers of a particular dialect have in common that differentiate them from speakers of other dialects and on the features of the dialect which overlap with other dialects, typically with Standard English. Wolfram and Fasold state:

> Despite the philosophical validity of linguists' objections or their ethical preference to eliminate the notion of standard and nonstandard languages we must realistically concede that the establishment of prescriptive norms for "correct" speech usage is an inevitable by-product of the awareness of behavioral norms of all types.

Standard English, the spoken language of the educated middle-class white, is generally accepted as such a norm and Nonstandard Dialects can be described in terms of the linguistic features by which they differ from Standard English.

Because of social and educational programs initiated and pursued vigorously in the 1960's, **Vernacular Black English** is one of the most studied of American social dialects. It refers to the type of English spoken by working-class blacks. Sociolinguists have plotted the types and frequencies of particular linguistic features common to speakers of this dialect which serve to distinguish it from Standard English and from other forms of Black English; Charrow (1974) has advanced the thesis that the written language of deaf people, like Black English, has the characteristics of a nonstandard dialect of English, and has proposed the term Deaf English. She has attempted to list and describe those syntactic features which are common to the written language of many deaf people but which are not found in Standard English. She has also proposed linguistic rules which would account for the generation of some of the nonstandard structures.

Charrow's main argument for considering the written language of deaf people to be a nonstandard dialect of English is that many deaf writers display common features, particularly syntactic structures, that are not found in Standard English or in other social dialects of American English. This point has been made also by Quigley and a number of associates in a series of studies extending back to 1967, some of which have been discussed in various chapters of this book. The same point was made earlier by Tervoort (1961) in studies of the esoteric and exoteric language of deaf students in the Netherlands and the United States. None of these investigators, however, has referred to the written language of deaf people as a dialect of English. This is because, while there certainly are appealing similarities between characteristics of the written language of many deaf people and characteristics that define dialects, there are also some very important differences. First, dialects are generally based on spoken language, and any written form of them would be based on a spoken form. This is not the case with the written language of deaf people. Even if their writing were based on American Sign Language (ASL), which has yet to be proven, most students of ASL, such as Stokoe (1960, 1972) and Bellugi (1972), submit that ASL is a language completely distinct from English, rather than a dialect of it. Second, within a dialect, most language features are shared by most users of the dialect. While Quigley and his associates have shown that there is widespread use of certain syntactic structures by deaf people, none of the structures studied was common to all and most were used by fewer than 50 percent of the subjects. Third, dialects are acquired by individuals as the result of exposure to those dialects in their childhood environments. But what deaf child was ever exposed to such structures as "John like to Alice but John will can't play with Alice," or "Yesterday Jack go to home because Jack sore his toe" (Charrow, 1974)? If we attempt to relate the distinctive structures of the written language of deaf people to the structure of American Sign Language, we face the problem that most deaf children are born to hearing parents who have no knowledge of the language of signs, and also that casual inspection by persons fluent in both ASL and English indicates that the differences between ASL structure and the structure of deaf persons' written language are at least as great as the similarities. Finally, a dialect serves as a stable means of communication among speakers of that dialect. It is highly unlikely that the written language of most deaf people serves such a purpose. In fact, most deaf people probably rely on writing as a means of communication only as a last resort.

It would seem, then, that the language problem of deaf children is much more complex than a simple dialectical one. Social dialects are culturally imposed; they are the products of particular environments, and the speakers of such dialects form a relatively homogeneous social group. Deaf children, however, come from varying social backgrounds. What they have in common is not a homogeneous social environment, but instead, a severe impairment of hearing, the normal channel for acquiring language. The result is a forced reliance on the visual channel as the primary means for acquiring language and communication. To put it another way, a black child will acquire a particular dialect not because his skin is black, but because he is exposed to that particular dialect in his formative years; a black raised among speakers of Standard English will, of course, acquire that dialect the same as will a white child. A deaf child, on the other hand, has language problems (far too deviant from Standard English to be called a dialect) not for social and cultural reasons but because he is deaf—the causative factor is organismic rather than cultural.

While treatment of the written language of deaf people as simply a nonstandard dialect of English seems to oversimplify a complex problem, there are, as stated earlier, some appealing similarities between characteristics of the written language of deaf people and characteristics that define dialects. The problems encountered by the child who speaks a nonstandard dialect of English, in acquiring Standard English and in learning to read and write, are similar enough to the problems of deaf children to make the problems and approaches as defined by sociolinguists worthy of careful consideration by teachers of deaf children. We will consider some of these problems and approaches regarding the teaching of reading.

Reading

While there is heated controversy concerning methods of communication to be used by and with deaf children, there likely is near-unanimous agreement that deaf children need to learn to read and write Standard English. Nevertheless, very few of them ever come close to achieving that goal. As discussed in previous chapters, standard reading tests show that deaf children rarely exceed the fifth-grade reading level by the time they leave school, and studies using "cloze procedures" which require students to fill in blank grammatical frames (Moores, 1967) have shown that the standard reading tests give spuriously high estimates of the reading ability of deaf children. It is obvious that written language ability can be no better than the reading level. Thus, if the reading and writing of Standard English can be considered a sort of common denominator in the education of deaf children, we have failed dismally in our efforts to attain it. A somewhat similar situation prevails in teaching the reading and writing of Standard English to children who speak nonstandard dialects, and some of the approaches suggested in that area by sociolinguists might apply to teaching deaf children.

Wolfram and Fasold describe the problem of the child with a nonstandard dialect learning to read as follows:

> The child who speaks a nonstandard dialect faces two problems when he is being taught to read, while the Standard English-speaking child primarily needs to learn the process and mechanics of reading: of deriving meaning from the printed page. The child who speaks a nonstandard variety must learn the reading process, but must also learn the language of the reading materials at the same time—and this is a language variety which matches his spoken variety very poorly. The match between spoken and written language is very important, because spoken language is primary and writing derived from it. Speaking is not an attempt to approximate written forms, but written forms are basically attempts to reflect speech. Therefore any mismatch between speech and writing, whether at the level of spelling, vocabulary, or grammar, reflects a failure of the writing system, not of spoken language. In learning to read, a student is really learning to see his speech on the printed page. To the degree that his speech is not represented on the pages of the material being used to teach him to read, an obstacle is being raised for him.

Reading materials, especially those used in the beginning stages of teaching reading, are based on the spoken form of Standard English. For the child raised with this as his primary dialect, no great problem is presented, although even for this child, learning to read is not always a simple matter. For the child who speaks a nonstandard dialect such as Vernacular Black English, the problem can be great. And for the deaf child, who may come to the reading process with any type of language ranging from Standard English in manual communication form through Ameslan (American Sign Language) through a variety of crude visual gestural systems and varying degrees of oral communication to almost nothing, the problem is horrendous. As stated in the quote from Wolfram and Fasold, any substantial mismatch between the language of the reading materials and the dialect the child brings to the reading process will create reading problems, and the greater the degree of mismatch the greater the reading problem is likely to be. In the case of most deaf children, the mismatch is great indeed.

We have presented information throughout this book from studies by Quigley and others indicating the grade level at which particular syntactic structures appear in a series of typical reading books and also the age and rate at which deaf children attain various levels of understanding of the structures. Power (1971) performed a similar type of linguistic analysis of the front pages and sports pages of a newspaper and found a similar great mismatch between the language of the newspaper and the language of deaf students. The value of studies like these is not simply in their demonstration of a great mismatch between the language of the child and the language of reading materials, but in the detailed identification of the ways in which the mismatch occurs. Teachers should be able to use linguistic information to compare the syntactic structures known to deaf students, and to modify the language of the materials to better match the knowledge of the students. Because the mismatch is so great, it is likely that mere modification of existing materials will not suffice, and new materials will have to be constructed. Teachers of deaf children do much of this anyway, and the linguistic studies we have cited will provide the information to enable them to do it with more precision. Again, however, we hasten to emphasize that a knowledge of the techniques and methods of analysis of transformational generative grammar will enable the teacher to perform her own analysis of the language of reading materials and of individual pupils, rather than relying on curricula and materials constructed by others. The language variation among deaf children is great enough to make desirable the individualization of materials for the child, or at least for small groups of children.

Sociolinguists, in approaching the problem of teaching reading to children with nonstandard dialects, have proposed two main types of alternatives. One type involves the construction of entirely new materials specifically designed for the nonstandard dialect child; the other group of alternatives involves the use of extant materials. Stated another way, some approaches attempt to change the language of the materials to match the language of the child, while others attempt to change the language of the child to match the language of existing materials.

Modification of the Materials

Two main methods have been proposed and experimented with in this approach: (1) the use of dialect readers; and (2) the neutralization of dialect differences in the readers. Dialect readers involve the writing of materials in the dialect of the children. A number of such materials have been written using Vernacular Black English (see, for example, Davis, Gladney, and Leaverton [1969]). Wolfram and Fasold explain the reasoning behind this approach.

> The alternative that advocates the use of dialect readers seems to be based on three assumptions: (1) that there is sufficient mismatch between the child's system and the Standard English textbook to warrant distinct materials, (2) the psychological benefit from reading success will be stronger in the dialect than it might be if Standard English materials were used, and (3) the success of vernacular teaching in bilingual situations recommends a similar principle for bidialectal situations.

Proponents of this approach believe that after the child has successfully learned to read materials in his own vernacular, he can then be taught to read materials written in Standard English.

If we accept Charrow's concept of the written language of deaf persons as a dialect of English, then we can apply this approach to writing materials for deaf children in their dialect. As we have discussed previously, however, the view of deaf children's written language as a dialect of English is hardly tenable, at least in the formal concept of dialect. Specifically, although many consistencies exist in the written language of deaf people, it is doubtful whether their language is homogeneous enough to make it possible to write readers in a dialect mutually understandable to all or most of them. Also, the use of dialect readers has usually been rejected by teachers and parents of black children for reasons we need not detail here. It is highly probable that such an approach to teaching reading to deaf children would also be rejected by their teachers and parents. However, before going on to discuss other possible sociolinguistic approaches to the reading problems, we should point out that the dialect reader approach might have some limited applications to deaf children. The studies of Charrow, Taylor, and Quigley and his associates have identified a number of specific syntactic structures which are different from any structures of Standard English and which are consistent in use among substantial numbers of students and persistent in use by individuals over time. While these structures do not seem to result from early exposure to them by deaf children, as is the case in true dialect acquisition, they are similar in function to dialect structures and might be amenable to change through the use of reading techniques associated with dialect readers. A more promising approach to reading for deaf children, however, seems to be the neutralization of dialect differences in reading materials.

In this approach, extant materials are used but language features that are not part of the language system of the child are eliminated from them. As Wolfram and Fasold point out, this assumes that there is enough of a common core between the dialect of the child and the Standard English of the reading materials to make such an approach practical. In the case of deaf children, the mismatch between the Standard English of common reading materials and the child's language system is so great that the approach probably has limited practicality. Nevertheless, it has possibilities and, of course, teachers of deaf children have commonly constructed and modified reading materials for their students. What linguistics has to offer are techniques and methods of analysis such as those described in this book, which will enable the teacher to perform these tasks with increased effectiveness. These techniques provide the means for analyzing the linguistic system of the child and of reading materials, and modifying the materials to more closely match the child's language.

Some of the research on the language of deaf children which has been based on transformational generative grammar, such as the studies of Charrow, Quigley, Taylor, and others we have cited, is beginning to provide a fund of knowledge about the written language of deaf children which might eventually serve as the basis for development of curricula, reading materials, and diagnostic tests to aid the teacher in her task. The studies cited by Quigley and his associates have used a Test of Syntactic Ability (TSA) to study the development of specific syntactic structures in the written language of deaf children. While it is cumbersome in its present form, it could likely be developed into a standardized instrument which would enable the teacher to assess the level of development of syntactic structures in deaf children, and knowledge of a child's level of development should precede any attempt to use materials to further his development. Likewise, reading materials could be developed to take into account the knowledge provided by these studies about the linguistic system of deaf children and the linguistic system of extant reading materials. We remain convinced, however, that the greatest value of recent developments in linguistics will be realized by those teachers who learn the basic methods of linguistics and its techniques of analysis so they can themselves develop the applications to teaching.

Modification of the Child

By modification of the child we mean, of course, modification of his language system to match the Standard English of the reading materials he uses. This approach, also, has been used with children speaking nonstandard dialects, the objective being to teach them Standard English before teaching them reading. This seems on the surface to be a reasonable approach, but many sociolinguists feel that attempts which have been made to apply it have met with very limited success. When a child has acquired a particular dialect during early childhood because of environmental influences and has acquired a group reference orientation to it, changing him to another dialect is extremely difficult. In fact, in the absence of strong motivation on the part of the child to learn the new dialect, all efforts to teach it are likely to fail. Again, however, we must view the language of the deaf children approaching the learning-to-read process not as a dialect of English but rather as a variety of systems ranging from relatively good Standard English in oral or manual form to almost no language at all. Only a very few deaf children will have the command of Standard English required for the reading process, and so the teacher must either teach the necessary Standard English In some form or start by teaching reading as the initial form of language.

Early language teaching for deaf children in the classroom almost always involves use of the printed word or, in other words, reading. So, rather than developing a language base on which reading can be superimposed, as is the case with hearing children, reading itself is being used as at least part of the means of teaching reading. The extremely limited success that has resulted from these methods seems to indicate that other approaches are needed. One such approach would be to develop Standard English in the deaf child during infancy and early childhood, and only later develop reading on that language base.

Psycholinguistic studies of the development of language in infancy and early childhood in hearing children have begun to describe how the important early stages of language development take place. Some of these studies have been cited in earlier chapters and Brown, Cazden, and Bellugi (1969) have summarized the essence of the interactive conversation between child and parent which seems to be a factor of major importance in the process.

> It seems likely that the many kinds of grammatical exchange in discourse will prove to be the richest data available to the child in his search for a grammar. It may be as difficult to derive a grammar from hearing unconnected static sentences as it would be to derive the invariance of quantity and number from simply looking at liquids in containers and objects in space. The changes produced by pouring back and forth and by gathering together and spreading apart are the data that most strongly suggest the conservation of quantity and number. *We suspect that the changes sentences undergo as they shuttle between persons in conversation are, similarly, the data that most clearly expose the underlying structure of language.* (emphasis added)

Conversational interaction, then, between the child and adults in his environment forms the basis of language development. And the type and quality of that development will depend on the type and quality of the input and the child's ability to react to it. For a hearing child, early exposure to Vernacular Black English will develop in him that dialect, while exposure to Standard English will develop Standard English. The deaf child not only has problems with the type and quality of input, but also with interpreting it and reacting to it. The great importance of the early years of life in language development for hearing children holds for deaf children also. And the basic procedure of interactive conversation—with adults reflecting back to children their speech productions in a way that provides them with information about language structure that will enable them to develop their understanding still further— needs to be adapted to developing language in deaf children during the early years of life.

Van Uden in his work, *A World of Language for Deaf Children. Part 1: Basic Principles* (1968), terms this the **Reflective Method** and illustrates how it can be applied to the early language development of deaf children. One of the major tenets of modern linguistics is that language is generative; that is, any natural language has a potentially infinite number of allowable sentences, produced by a limited, albeit large number of rules. Van Uden points out that the use of the Fitzgerald Key and similar structured methods leads to children being forced to use "recipes" to put words into "baked sentences"—fixed complexes of ideas and words which lead to the oft-noted lack of flexibility in the language of deaf children. In Van Uden's phrase, language is not "transparent" for most deaf children. They cannot break through the difficulty of the construction of correct syntactic forms in order to express their meaning fluently. Their English sentences never become "their own"; they are not assimilated in their innate language system. English structures remain foreign to their personal "esoteric language" systems as described by Tervoort, and hence they never achieve fluency in their use. The best way for deaf children to achieve fluency in the English language seems to be the conversational interaction used by hearing children and adults, or the **Reflective Method** as Van Uden terms it.

Although the term "conversational" has been used above, useful interaction between deaf children and adults proficient in English might actually take several forms; the question of the relative merits of these varying forms of early communication is a topic still being debated by educators of deaf students. Nevertheless, research has shown that despite the intensity and type of early language interaction, the performance of deaf children is still below what would be expected of hearing children of comparable age, intelligence, and socioeconomic background. This means a mismatch of some degree between the child's language system and that of extant reading materials. Teaching language and its read and written forms will still remain the teacher's chief task, at least through the elementary years. But if the deaf child reaches the stages of beginning reading with some reasonable command of Standard English, the teacher's task is simplified. She can then use the same procedures used in teaching reading to children with non-standard dialects, of neutralizing dialect differences in the reading materials or in some other manner adjusting the reading materials to the language level of the child. While the increasing number of linguistic studies of deaf children will eventually supply a fund of information which will undoubtedly be used as the basis for developing specialized language materials and curricula for deaf students, successful application of those materials and curricula will depend on the teacher's understanding of the linguistic principles on which they are based.

Morphology

A morpheme can be defined as the "minimal unit of grammatical structure." Since morphemes sometimes, but not always, correspond to words in the language, it is necessary first of all to make this distinction clear.

Since this is not a theoretical text, there will be no attempt here to arrive at a formally exact definition of a "word." Since words are separated by spaces in written English, of course anyone who can read English knows what the words of the language are. Even an illiterate speaker of the language would have an intuitive sense of where the word breaks occur in a sentence. However, notice that this is not a real physical distinction, but rather a psychological one. Although in slow, precise reading it is possible to pause briefly after each word (and this is where the breaks would naturally occur), ordinary speech is not so subdivided. This should be evident to anyone who has listened to an unfamiliar foreign language and attempted to pick out the words; pauses there are, but they tend to coincide with syntactic phrases rather than single words.

Words, of course, are sequences of sounds and can be segmented (broken up) into their parts. These individual speech sounds, however, have nothing to do with meaning, and are simply the physical manifestation of the abstract grammatical units produced by the grammar. These abstract ("deep") units are called morphemes. A traditional view of the morpheme considers it to be a "minimal unit of meaning." Although this definition is not completely satisfactory, it provides us with a fairly good informal criterion for determining which units of language are morphemes and which are not.

For example, words like "Bill," "cat," "pelican," and "history" are morphemes, and also cannot be divided into smaller meaningful units. The words "blueberry," "blackboard," and "cowboy," on the other hand, would be considered in most analyses to consist of two morphemes in each case ("blue" and "berry," for example). "Rasp" in "raspberry," however, would not be considered by most linguists to be a morpheme, because it is meaningless in Modern Standard English, and even more important, it is restricted in its occurrence to the one word "raspberry."

Types of Morphemes

There are several linguistically significant classes of morphemes. One distinction that is often made by linguists is that of **free morphemes** vs. **bound morphemes**. A free morpheme is simply one which can stand by itself; in other words, it is used as a word in the language. For instance, some free morphemes from the above examples are "blue," "berry," "black," "board," "cow," and "boy." Bound morphemes, however, can never occur in isolation, but always appear combined with other morphemes to form words. An example is what is known as the plural morpheme in English, which can be represented as /z/. (We shall follow the standard practice of using slashes (/) to designate abstract phonological entities before all phonological rules have applied. Brackets ([ ]) will represent the sound (or sequence of sounds) as actually spoken.) If we consider the words "books," "hens," "bones," and "calendars," it is clear that each can be separated into two parts. The units "book," "hen," "bone," and "calendar" are each free morphemes (and words as well) which can be used just as they are. The plural unit spelled with an "s," however, although it has meaning and is widely used in many different environments in English, is never used alone; there is no word "s" with the meaning "more than one."

In words consisting of a combination of two or more morphemes such as "bones," the basic part of the word (often a free morpheme) is known as a **root**; the morpheme which is added (often bound) is called an **affix**. Affixes are further specified as **prefixes** or **suffixes**, depending on whether they are added at the beginning or the end of the root, respectively. For example, "de-" in "deemphasize" and "im-" in "impossible" are prefixes (and affixes by definition); the roots to which they are added are "emphasize" and "possible." Similarly, the suffixes

"-ment" and "-ing," when added to the root "achieve," give "achieve-ment" and "achieving," respectively.

Affixes often have varying shapes. (Often, in fact, it is impossible to extract a bound affix from the root, as is the case with the plurals of "goose" ("geese") and "woman" ("women"). What is the form of the plural morpheme in these words? Certainly not "s.") Such bound mor-phemes are represented in the surface structure (i.e., after all transfor-mational rules, but no morphological or phonological rules, have ap-plied) in abstract form. This is true not only for the plural morpheme, but also for other bound morphemes such as those indicating tense. Consider the following surface structure tree, for example. (Don't wor-ry about some of the details you may not yet have encountered.)

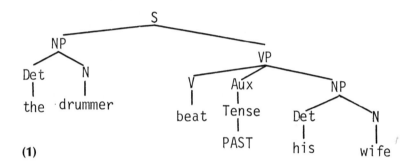

(1)

Notice that, although lexical insertion has already applied to the output of the phrase structure rules to insert lexical items into the tree (trans-formations have applied after lexical insertion, of course), and the words "the," "drummer," "beat," "his," and "wife" have been pro-duced, there still remains the abstract morpheme PAST. (**Abstract mor-phemes** are spelled in capital letters in this book to distinguish them from **concrete morphemes**.) This abstract marker has the effect of in-structing the morphological component of the grammar to put the verb in the past tense, so that:

hop + PAST = hopped,
send + PAST = sent,
go + PAST = went,
beat + PAST = beat, etc.

It perhaps should be noted here that the surface structure distinction between abstract morphemes like "PAST" and concrete morphemes like "wife" is not nearly so great as it may seem. The reason is that what is abbreviated "wife" in the above tree is actually a semi-abstract *lexical item* which must be acted upon by the morphological and phonologi-cal rules before it can become a pronounceable word.

The Place of Morphology in a Generative Grammar

The role which morphology is to play in a transformational grammar is a question which has not really been decided yet. Whereas in traditional and structural grammars the morphological component was a distinct level kept separate from the syntactic and phonological components, this was not the case in the writings of Chomsky and other early transformationalists. Transformationalists have tended to implicitly deny the existence of a separate morphological level. Since only three grammatical components are recognized (semantic, syntactic, and phonological), some of what earlier grammarians called morphological rules are placed in the syntactic component and others in the phonological component.

Without entering into the theoretical arguments, we will assume here for practical purposes that there is a distinct morphological component. In the words of Wilbur (1973), the function of the morphological rules is to apply to the output of the syntax "to spell out in full the representation to which the phonological rules apply." So, for example, the abstract morpheme PLURAL will be specified as /z/ by a morphological rule. Then, depending on whether it is combined with the word "hog," "elephant," or "ostrich" (for example), the phonological rules will give the pronunciation [z], [s], or [əz]. (These three different pronunciations of the plural morpheme are called its **allomorphs.**)

Some Common English Morphological Processes

There are two basic types of morphological rules which function in English (as well as in other languages). They are known as inflectional rules and derivational rules.

Inflectional Rules

Inflectional rules are those which determine the syntactic function and relationships of various elements of the sentence: for example, rules of tense, number, gender, etc. Following are some examples:

1. *Plurals.* Plurals in English are formed in several different ways. The majority of nouns, however, are pluralized by adding the morpheme /z/. The phonological rules then specify whether the plural morpheme is to be pronounced [z] as in "hogs," [s] as in "elephants," or [əz] as in "ostriches."

That these three different plural shapes do, in fact, comprise a single morpheme is evidenced by the fact that many speakers of English interpret them as the same sound, not realizing the significant differences in pronunciation. One factor which contributes to this situation is the regularity of the phonological rules involved. (Notice the close interrelationship between the level of morphology and those of phonology and syntax.)

Consider the following three classes of words, each of which exhibits a different pronunciation of the plural morpheme.

[z]	[s]	[əz]
gangways	telescopes	damages
reeds	watts	diseases
standards	fifes	mantises
emus	cooks	sashes
unions	births	wrenches
hammers	mites	rouges

It is clear that the *last sound* of the root is what determines the form of the suffix. The distribution is as follows:

[əz] after /s z š ž č ǰ /;

[s] after /p t k f θ /;

[z] after all other sounds.

If we consider /z/ to be the basic shape of the plural, we can account for its variants by two general phonological rules of English:

/ə/-INSERTION: *Insert /ə/ before the suffix when the root ends with a sound which is phonologically similar to the first sound of the suffix.*

DEVOICING: *Devoice a consonant if it is preceded by another voiceless consonant.* (A **voiced** sound is one which is pronounced with vibration of the vocal cords; a **voiceless** sound is one pronounced without such vocal cord vibration.) This devoicing rule will produce the following changes:

Voiced		Voiceless
b	⟶	p
d	⟶	t
g	⟶	k
v	⟶	f
z	⟶	s
ǰ	⟶	č
ž	⟶	š

(Other analyses of the plural have been proposed; the above is probably the most common and logical.)

One test of any rule of grammar, be it semantic, syntactic, morphological, or phonological, is whether it can account for more than one single isolated phenomenon. If the /ə/-INSERTION rule applied only in the case of plurals, it would simply be a description of the facts, rather than a useful general rule. Notice, however, that there is additional evidence for its validity. Consider the Possessive morpheme, which also has /z/ as its basic form, as exemplified by "Zelda's," "Hector's," and "Fred's." The same rule of /ə/-INSERTION that we discovered with plurals will account for cases such as "Butch's" and "Liz's." In other words, the underlying phonological forms of these words (i.e., their shape after the syntactic and morphological rules have applied) are /bɨč+z/ and /liz+z/. (The symbol + represents a morpheme boundary, deleted by later rules.) Because the last sound of the root and the first sound of the suffix are phonologically similar, /ə/ is inserted, and these become [bɨčəz] and [lizəz], and not the (to English speakers) "strange" forms [bɨč-z] or [liz-z]. The /ə/-INSERTION rule is even more general than this. It accounts not only for certain cases of the possessive, but also for the third person singular verb ending of certain verbs. The basic abstract shape of this ending is again /z/, as indicated by forms such as "nags" and "goes." However, the /ə/-INSERTION rule is needed to account for "crashes," "crunches," etc.

Finally, consider the different shapes of the Past Tense morpheme, which is basically /d/, as indicated by forms like "begged" [bɛgd] and "lived" [livd]. If we add this ending to words like "sound" or "rot," the result is /sawnd + d/ and /rat + d/, but the result of application of the /ə/-INSERTION Rule is the normal surface pronunciation, [sawndəd] and [ratəd].

The DEVOICING rule similarly can be extended to cover cases other than the plural. Again, crucial examples are the Possessive, the Third Person Singular, and the Past Tense morphemes. For example:

Possessive	"Pop's" /pap+z/	⟶	[paps]
	"Pete's" /piyt+z/	⟶	[piyts]
Past Tense	"popped" /pap+d/	⟶	[papt]
	"faked" /feyk+d/	⟶	[feykt]
Plural or Third	"pops" /pap+z/	⟶	[paps]
Person Singular	"fakes" /feyk+z/	⟶	[feyks]

In fact, this rule corresponds to a general principle of English which requires that in a *consonant cluster* (a sequence of consonants without intervening vowels), the consonants must be either all voiced or all voiceless. Examples of both types of sequences occur in the following words, where voiceless sequences are underlined once, and voiced sequences twice: "exact" [ɛgzakt], "egzist" [ɛgzist], "insect" [insɛkt], "spin" [spin], etc. (Notice that while some speakers pronounce "exit" as [ɛksit] and others as [ɛgzit], it is *never* pronounced [ɛkzit] or [ɛgsit].)

Thus, we have two very general rules of English, /ə/-INSERTION and DEVOICING, which enable us to account for the variant pronunciations [əz] and [s] of the basic plural (as well as the possessive and third person singular) morpheme /z/, as well as various other phenomena of English which we have not considered here.

As mentioned previously, a minority of English words are exceptional with respect to the plural, as for example "women," "children," "geese," "fish," "knives," etc. Each speaker, in learning these words, has to learn each form individually. This is contrasted to the case of the **regular forms,** which need not be memorized individually. Thus, a child in learning English may hear only a few cases of words with the regular plural ending /z/ (and its pronounced variants [z], [s], and [əz]), from which he "internalizes" the general rules we have discussed which he can then apply to new forms. That a rule has been internalized can be demonstrated by presenting a nonsense word such as "wug" to a native speaker and asking him to pluralize it. Almost without exception, the response will be "wugs" [wʌgz] (Berko, 1958).

2. *Past Tense.* Certain facets of the Past Tense morpheme have been discussed in the section on plurals. The regular Past Tense morpheme in English has the underlying form /d/, with the following two rules applying:

/ə/-INSERTION: *Insert /ə/ before the suffix if the root ends in /t/ or /d/.*

DEVOICING: *Devoice the /d/ of the suffix if the last phonological segment of the root is voiceless.*

For example:

Basic

"begged" /bɛg+d/ ⟶ [bɛgd]
"lived" /liv+d/ ⟶ [livd]

/ə/-*INSERTION*

"sounded" /sawnd+d/ ⟶ [sawndəd]
"rotted" /rat+d/ ⟶ [ratəd]

DEVOICING

"popped" /pap+d/ ⟶ [papt]
"faked" /feyk+d/ ⟶ [feykt]

The past tense, like the plural, exhibits many exceptional cases. Some of these (for example, "went" as the past tense of "go") are unique to specific verbs. Others, however, cover several verbs of similar phonological shape. For example, in many verbs with the vowel /i/, the past tense is formed by changing this vowel into /æ/, as in "sit:sat," "sing:sang," "drink:drank," "begin:began," etc. This type of rule is sometimes called a **minor rule** (see Lakoff, 1970), as contrasted to the **major rule** of English past tense formation which uses the morpheme /d/. (Verbs which form the past tense in the irregular way, as in "sat," are traditionally called **strong verbs,** as contrasted with regular or **weak verbs.**) A child, in learning the language, must abstract from specific instances of past tenses he hears and generalize, in order to form the past tenses of new verbs which he learns. Since there are several minor rules for past tense in English, generalization of major and minor rules often produces anomalies in the child's speech, such as "goed" or "wented."

3. *Third Person Singular and Possessive.* The basic morpheme shape for both the possessive of nouns and the third person singular of verbs is /z/, with the /ə/-INSERTION rule and the DEVOICING rule accounting for variants, as discussed previously.

Possessive Nouns

Basic:	"Zelda's" /zɛldə+z/	⟶	[zɛldəz]
	"Hector's" /hɛktər+z/	⟶	[hɛktərz]
/ə/-INSERTION:	"Butch's" /bɪč+z/	⟶	[bɪčəz]
	"Liz's" /liz+z/	⟶	[lizəz]
DEVOICING:	"Pop's" /pap+z/	⟶	[paps]
	"Pete's" /piyt+z/	⟶	[piyts]

Third Person Present Verbs

Basic:	"nags" /næg+z/	⟶	[nægz]
	"goes" /gow+z/	⟶	[gowz]
/ə/-INSERTION:	"crashes" /kraeš+z/	⟶	[kraešəz]
	"crunches" /krʌnč+z/	⟶	[krʌnčəz]
DEVOICING:	"pops" /pap+z/	⟶	[paps]
	"fakes" /feyk+z/	⟶	[feyks]

4. *Progressive.* The progressive tense of the verb in English is comprised simply (ignoring the relevant syntactic processes) of some form of the verb *be* ("is," "are," "were," etc.) plus the stem of the main verb (i.e., the basic unchanging part) and the suffixal ending "-ing." For example: *"is going," "were lying," "will be stamping,"* etc.

5. *Comparative and Superlative.* The **comparative** and **superlative** forms of most English adjectives are created in one of two ways. One way involves the use of the words "more" and "most" before the adjective as in "more friendly," "most friendly." The other method utilizes the suffixes "-er" and "-est," as in "friendlier" and "friendliest." Both rules are widely used and, as the examples show, can often apply to the same forms equally well. This is not always the case, however; "more fantastic" and "most fantastic" are fine, but "fantasticer" and "fantasticest" would be to most people absolutely unacceptable. (We shall not enter into the reasons for this discrepancy.) And, as with most rules of English morphology, there are exceptional cases like "good:better:best" or "bad:worse:worst."

Derivational Rules

Derivational rules, in contrast to inflectional rules, are concerned with "the formation of a new word from an existing word, root, or stem by the addition of a prefix or suffix or by other means." (Pei and Gaynor, 1967). For example, the words "transformation," "transformational," and "transformationally" are all derivative forms of the verb "transform," with one, two, and three suffixes, respectively. The word "derivation" itself is derived from the verb "derive." In general, derivational forms belong to different grammatical classes than the word from which they were derived. For example, while "transform" is a verb, "transformation" is a noun, "transformational" an adjective, and "transformationally" an adverb. This is not always the case, however. For example, "unlikely" is derived from "likely," yet both are adjectives.

Following are a few of the more common derivational processes which have been considered in language acquisition studies:

1. **Agentive (-er/-or).** The ending "-er" (sometimes spelled "or" but pronounced the same as "er") is added to many verbs in English to produce a meaning something like "one who does." For example, "-er" added to "teach" results in "teacher," or one who teaches. Other examples are "believer," "skydiver," "executioner," "educator," etc. (Notice that in Modern English some "-er" words must be considered to be a single morpheme. "Carpenter" is one example; "carpent" has no meaning.)

2. **Adjective (-y).** The suffix "-y" can be added to many words (usually nouns) to produce adjectives. Notice, for example, "craze:crazy," "risk:risky," "breeze:breezy." All adjectives ending in "-y," however, are not derived from other morphemes by adding "-y": "tidy," for example.

3. **Diminutive (-y/-ie).** The sound [iy], spelled "y" or "ie," can be added to a noun to signify a small object or animal of that type. This is used often, for example, when speaking to small children. Examples are "fishie" and "doggie." (Notice the doubling of the consonant. This is simply a spelling convention, with no bearing on the form of the suffix itself or the relevant phonological rules, or, accordingly, on the pronunciation of the word.)

4. **Compound Words.** Two or more words in combination often form a new word with a new meaning. Sometimes the meaning can be easily constructed from the elements of the compound, as in "airplane" or "football." Sometimes this is not possible, as in "holiday," for example. (Many English speakers are not aware that the origin of this word is "holy" + "day.") An interesting case is that of "blackboard," which at one time simply meant "a board which is black," but can now refer to similar boards which are green or other colors. (Notice that many speakers' knowledge of the source of the compound is indicated by the fact that the new word "chalkboard" has been coined and is used by many people.)

5. **Adverbial (-ly).** The ending "-ly" is added to adjectives to form ad-

verbs. For example: "strong:strongly," "slow:slowly," or "magnanimous:magnanimously."

Summary

The morphemes generated by the syntactic component of the grammar must be combined in the necessary manner before being acted upon by the phonological rules. Although these combinatory functions could be performed by special syntactic or phonological rules, we have chosen to isolate the processes and to consider them to be morphological. One reason we have done so is because of some interesting psychological studies in the area, which will be discussed in Appendix B. Some of the previous discussion may seem quite "traditional," since we have largely ignored the complex syntactic operations which produce the input to the morphological component.

We have discussed several of the specific morphological processes of English, both inflectional and derivational, and referred to the manner in which a child generalizes from specific instances which he hears to formulate (internally) general morphological rules which he can apply to new forms. Some of the major processes we have discussed depend heavily on such generalizations (plural formation, for example); others, especially those of the derivational type, probably rely less on generalization and more on memorization (compound words like "merry-go-round" and "handkerchief," for example). At any rate, these are all processes necessary for fluency in English, and thus a necessary part of the knowledge of anyone who intends to teach English.

Hearing Children's Acquisition of Morphology

Cooper and Rosenstein (1966) make a distinction between "free" and "controlled" studies of language acquisition. **Free studies** are those in which the investigator collects a sample of written or spoken language from children and examines those of its characteristics that he is interested in. In **controlled studies** the researcher uses carefully chosen tests and other techniques (memory recall, for example) to elicit language performance from his subjects.

Typical of early controlled studies was the now classic one of Berko (1958), who looked at acquisition of several aspects of morphology. She reasoned that it was possible to argue that children's acquisition of (for example) plurals consisted of memorizing that the correct plural form of "witch" was "witches," but that if a child could supply the correct plural form to a word he had never heard before, then he was using a general pluralization rule, not just memory. She conducted studies using nonsense words ("wug," "gutch") to ensure that children could not know by rote recall what the correct plurals were. She then constructed tests with pictures of mythical animals. For plurals, for example, she presented the subject with a picture of a "gutch" and said:

> This is a gutch. Now there is another one. There are two of them.
> There are two_____.

The child was expected to complete the sentence with a plural form. With this and similar techniques Berko examined the ability of pre-schoolers and first graders to supply noun plurals and possessives, past tenses of verbs, simple present third person singular marking, present progressive, and regular comparison of adjectives—all inflectional morphemes; as well as such derived forms as diminutives, adjectives, agentive nouns, and some compound nouns.

In general, she considered that her evidence supported the hypothesis that children were operating not on rote recall, but on the basis of generative rules. For pluralization, she concluded the following (it should be noted that Berko uses / / in many cases where we would use [ ]):

> Children were able to form the plurals requiring /-s/ or /-z/, and they did best on items where general English phonology determined which of these allomorphs is required. Although they have in their vocabularies real words that form their plural in / əz/, in the age range that was interviewed (4–7 years), they did not generalize to form new words in /-əz/. Their rule seems to be to add /-s/ or /-z/, unless the word ends in /szšžčj/. To words ending in these sounds they add nothing to make the plural—and when asked to form a plural, repeat the stem as if it were already in the plural.

For verbs,

> The children's handling of the past tense parallels their treatment of the plurals, except that they did better on the whole with the plurals. Again, they could not extend the contingent rule. Although they have forms like *melted* in their vocabulary, they were unable to extend the /- əd/ form to new verbs ending in /t d/. They treated these forms as if they were already in the past.

In general, forming plurals of nouns was easier than forming possessives and verb inflections. Within the verb system, children did best in supplying the "-ing" ending for the present progressive, and were able to do somewhat better with past tense forms than with correctly inflecting the verb for the third person singular present tense. At this age, very few children provided correct irregular past forms like "glung" or "glang" for "gling" (i.e., most said "glinged"). Interestingly, only one child of the 80 tested could give "quirkier" as the comparative of "quirky" but, when supplied with "quirkier" as a prompt, 35 percent were then able to supply "quirkiest" as the superlative. Very few of the children could give any kind of correct response when faced with the need to construct an agentive noun. Instead of "zibber" for "a man who zibs," 11 percent supplied "zibbingman," and 5 percent "zibman"—the rest could not at all cope with the task. They also tended to reply with things like "baby wug" or "little wug," where most adults gave "wuglet" or "wuggie" as a diminutive. They also tended to have private and idiosyncratic explanations for compound words ("Friday is a day when you have fried fish.").

Overall, Berko concluded:

> The answers were not always correct so far as English is concerned; but they were consistent and orderly answers, and they demonstrated that there could be no doubt that children in this age range operate with clearly delimited morphological rules.
>
> The picture that emerged was one of consistency, regularity, and simplicity. The children did not treat the new words according to idiosyncratic pattern. They did not model new words on patterns that appear infrequently. Where they provided inflectional endings, their best performance was with those forms that are the most regular and have the fewest variants. With the morphemes that have several allomorphs, they could handle forms calling for the most common of these allomorphs long before they could deal with allomorphs that appear in a limited distributional range.

A "free" study by Cazden (1968) of the data obtained from "the Harvard children" (Adam, Eve and Sarah) complements and supplements Berko's findings. Like Berko, Cazden found that plurals generally were mastered before possessives, and verb inflections were correctly used somewhat later than noun derivatives. She further observed that all three of the children supplied plurals correctly within an *NP* ("some crayons") before their correct use across *NP* boundaries ("Those my crayons"), and possessives occurred in ellipsis ("That's Daddy's") before they did with a noun ("Daddy's hat"). As far as verbs were concerned, she found, like Berko, that the present progressive seemed to be easiest (in terms of its correct use emerging earlier), but found the present indicative third person singular marking ("He *goes*") and simple past tense to be of equal difficulty. She clarifies a point that could not be seen in Berko's data because of Berko's always supplying the child with the "is" for the progressive. Cazden found that the progressive was at first marked only by "-ing" and that it was not until relatively late that an appropriate part of the verb *to be* was supplied. *Be* as an auxiliary verb was the last to emerge of the verb phenomena she studied.

Cazden found instances of "overgeneralization" of rules—mainly the extension of plurals to pronouns (e.g., "somes"), to **mass nouns** (e.g., "sugars") as well as to irregular forms ("mans"). There was also "overapplication" of tense markers ("I didn't spilled it"), and incorrect selection of allomorphs ("knife-es," "pants-es"). There were infrequent violations of the transitive-intransitive distinction ("I falled that down'') and the process-status distinction ("I'm having a dress on'') with verbs.

Cazden felt she was able to distinguish four periods in the acquisition of inflections:

a. Absence of inflection.

b. Occasional production of inflections with no errors or overgeneralizations.

c. Frequent production with regular occurrence of errors and overgeneralizations.

d. Virtually completely correct use (Cazden used 90 percent correct as a criterion of "correct use'').

Deaf Children's Acquisition of Morphology

Studies of deaf children's acquisition of morphology indicate that, in general, the sequence of its acquisition is the same as that for hearing children, but grossly delayed. In a "free'' study of the written language of deaf children, Taylor (1969) found a steady decline with age in the frequency of occurrence of the omission of verb and noun inflection, although the frequency of occurrence of overgeneralization did not decline. Taylor also found that verb problems were more severe than noun problems, and that with nouns there were more errors with plurals than possessives. Plural errors were similar to hearing children's—application of plural inflection to mass nouns ("sheeps''), and failure to inflect when necessary ("six boy''). She did report one type of error that has not been noted for hearing children—incorrect use of an irregular plural stem as singular ("A leave fell from the tree'').

Taylor did not report on the difficulty of different verb tenses, but a controlled study by Cooper (1967) using a similar approach to Berko indicated that, like hearing children of a much younger age, the progressive tense marker "-ing'' was somewhat easier than the past tense, and that the third person singular present tense marker was the most difficult of the three. Plurals were generally easier than verb inflection markers. Like Berko's hearing children, Cooper's deaf subjects also did better on superlative adjective forms than on comparatives (if first given the comparative form). Somewhat surprisingly, in view of Taylor's findings about continued use of overgeneralization of the major rule to strong verb forms, Cooper found that his subjects did better on irregular forms than regular ones. Cooper's subjects were all from one school, and he himself warns that they may not be typical. The school was strongly influenced by the "natural'' methods of Mildred Groht (1958) and it may well be that these differences between the two studies are due to differences in instructional methods used in the schools studied.

Like Berko, Cooper also examined performance on derived forms. Almost every inflectional form was easier than the derived forms. Generally speaking, derived adjectives ("-y") were easier than derived adverbs ("-ly," "-wards") and verbs ("-ate") and all these were much easier than derived nouns ("-ness," "-ing"). In accord with much other research, these deaf children found comprehension easier than production. The severity of the delay of deaf children's acquisition of the morphological structure of English is dramatized by the fact that Cooper's 19-year-old deaf subjects still did not perform as well on the test as his 9–10-year-old hearing comparison group.

It can be seen from the above that the general outline of development of morphological structures in the language of deaf children appears to be similar to that reported for hearing children, but considerably delayed. Noun plurals and possessives are generally learned earlier than verb tense markers. For verbs, the progressive marking (with "-ing" only) occurs before the past, which in turn is learned before the third person singular simple present; superlative adjective forms were easier than comparatives; and inflected morpheme forms were easier than derived ones.

A certain degree of caution should be displayed in describing any order of acquisition of language structures in deaf children as the "natural" one. Such an ascription may be in order for the sequence displayed by non-deaf preschool children, since they have usually learned language by "natural" methods from their mothers, siblings, and others around them, and it is only in rare cases that "artificial" intervention in their language development occurs. This is not so for most deaf children, certainly of school age, and usually even for preschool-age youngsters. Direct intervention in their language acquisition process has usually occurred—from teachers and parents and often other professionals. Hence, we can never be sure that any observed sequence of emergence of language structure phenomena is a "natural" one. It will possibly have been considerably influenced by the language intervention process, and to say that the observed phenomena are "due to deafness" is to go beyond the presently available data.

Recent Research in Linguistics and Related Areas

Linguistics has changed a great deal since the early days of transformational grammar. Because more recent viewpoints have not been fully developed and because their efficient applications in teaching have not been largely researched, the main text of the book has been restricted to discussion of the more completely researched means of analysis. We have tried to stress the idea that many of these concepts have been questioned in recent years, and that for purposes of simplicity of exposition it has been necessary to mention only briefly some of the relevant facts, to postpone discussion of some others, and to completely ignore still others. The goal has not been to teach formal structures and rules, but to develop an appreciation of, and, at the same time, a limited understanding of, some of the more important phenomena of generative theory and English syntax. More important to the teacher than memorization is development of the ability to analyze in transformational terms structures appearing in reading materials or in the productions of the students.

Nevertheless, recent innovations both in linguistics and in related fields have profound implications for linguistic theory. A few of these are discussed below for the sake of completeness, and so the reader will know what he can expect of linguistics in the future. The innovations to be discussed in the following pages have come about through work in several areas: linguistics itself, psycholinguistics, sociolinguistics, and others. Work in each of these areas has led to essentially the same conclusion: linguistic interactions are much more complex and are influenced by many more factors, both internal and external to language proper, than had formerly been considered. Factors such as geographic and social dialect, social situation, status of speaker and hearer and their interrelationships, perceptual strategies, and pragmatic decisions all influence choice and use of language. Because of the volume of research sources available, the following references will not be exhaustive, but simply exemplary of the changes developing in linguistics.

Linguistic Refinements—Pragmatics

The new field of **pragmatics** has recently developed within the bounds of linguistics proper, although it has been strongly influenced by the ideas of philosophers and logicians. Pragmatics departs from the traditional generative approach, which is restricted to the consideration of form and structure and, sometimes, a restricted view of meaning, with external and social influences being related to extralinguistic performance factors. Pragmatics, in contrast, has been defined by Weiser (1974) as "language in relation to the real-world situation of its use and the people who use it." This concept of "real world" is crucial for recent linguistic theory. It involves the attitudes of both the speaker and hearer toward their worlds and the present situation, the presuppositions of the speaker (that is, those things which he assumes to be true), as well as sociolinguistic considerations of appropriateness and politeness, among other things.

One idea which foresaw the later development of pragmatic theory was the postulation of **performatives.** As early as 1962, the philosopher John L. Austin, in a book called *How To Do Things With Words* (1965) (as well as in much earlier lectures) pointed out some interesting differences between what he called **(1) constative sentences,** and **(2) performative sentences,** as exemplified by the following:

(1)   The hen laid a golden egg.
(2)   I pronounce you man and wife.

Sentence **(1)** can be either true or false; it is nonsense, however, to speak of **(2)** as being either true or false. On the other hand, sentences like **(2)** are bound by pragmatic conditions on appropriateness of use; only a person with certain authorities and powers can appropriately produce **(2).** And, simply by uttering **(2),** the speaker performs the act of binding the couple in matrimony. (This is seen even more clearly if we insert "hereby" into the sentence.) Austin, however, also looked at sentence pairs of the following type:

(3a)   Go play in the traffic.
(3b)   I order you to go play in the traffic.

Consider the following statement by Austin: ". . . any utterance which is in fact a performative should be reducible, or expandable, or analysable into a form with a verb in the first person singular present indicative active (grammatical)." In modern terms, we might say that Austin was arguing that in fact the deep structures of **(3a)** and **(3b)** are identical; we might postulate one something like the following:

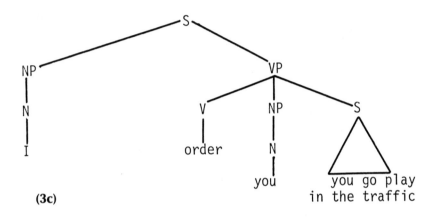

(3c)

Sentence **(3b)** is produced by the normal rules for Complementation, plus the rule which deletes the subject of an imperative sentence. Sentence **(3b)**, on the other hand, also requires the application of a rule deleting "I," "order," and "you," leaving only the complement sentence. Syntactic evidence is available for such an analysis, but because of its complexity it will not be discussed here.

John Robert Ross, in an article titled "On Declarative Sentences" (1970), made the surprising claim that performative verbs occur in the deep structure of not only imperatives like **(3a)**, but also declarative sentences like **(1)**. According to his analysis, the approximate deep structure of **(1)** would be:

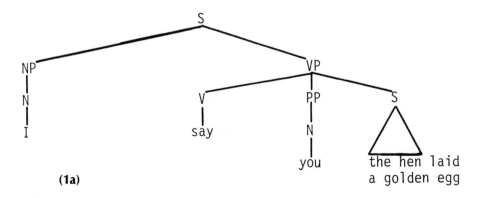

(1a)

The argument can be expanded to claim that every sentence of English has in its deep structure a performative verb with a first person subject ("I") and second person object ("you"). An optional rule deletes these three elements, resulting in sentences like **(1)**, with no surface performative. If the optional rule does not apply, the result is a sentence like **(2)**.

Although the above performative analysis (which includes concrete performatives in the deep structure trees of sentences) has been widely accepted, Ross in the same article proposed an alternative *pragmatic* analysis. In such an analysis, the deep structure of **(1)** would be not **(1a)**, but the expected **(1b)**.

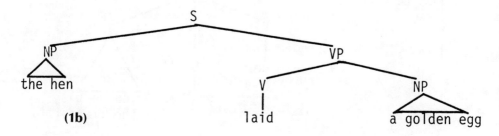

(1b)

The same complex facts discussed in Ross's article and accounted for there by deep structures like **(1a)** could also be accounted for in a pragmatic analysis by a consideration of certain elements "present in the context of a speech act." Thus, for example, the context provides an "I" which is "in the air" and which can be referred to by syntactic rules which apply to **(1b)**. Possibly Ross's most significant statement is the following: "Therefore, while I would urge that the performative analysis be adopted now, giving the vanishingly small amount of precise present knowledge about the interrelationship between context and language, I consider open the question as to whether the theory of language can be distinguished from the theory of language use."

Another recent addition to the theory is the related considerations of **presupposition** and **conversational implication.** This has resulted from the realization that sentences often "mean more than what they say." As with performatives, the idea of presupposition has been around for some time; only recently, however, has it been made explicit in linguistic theory. Consider, for example, the following sentences.

(4) Serpico discovered that the world is round.

(5) Serpico pretended that the world is flat.

(6) Even Serpico believes that the world is round.

The speaker of each of the above sentences presupposes, or assumes, certain things. In both **(4)** and **(5)**, for example, he assumes that the world is, in actual fact, round. In **(6)**, this is not presupposed; whether the world is round, flat, or shaped like a pelican does not affect the appropriateness of **(6)**. The speaker of **(6)** does, however, presuppose two other things: that others besides Serpico believe in the roundness of the earth, and that one would not normally expect Serpico to entertain this belief.

As a result of the presuppositions of the speaker, sentences like the above conversationally imply similar information and, if the listener's world view is similar to that of the speakers, he will receive this information just as he does the literal meanings of the sentences.

That the presuppositions discussed above are, in fact, included in sentences **(4)–(6)**, is evidenced by the following ungrammatical constructions:

(4a)   *Serpico discovered that the world is round, but it's really flat.

(5a)   *Serpico pretended that the world is flat, which he knows to be true.

(6a)   *Even Serpico believes that the world is round, but nobody else does.

(6b)   ? Even Serpico believes that the world is round, and I'm not the least bit surprised.

Notice that the working of presuppositions is not based on actual fact, but rather on the real world view of the conversational participants (and sometimes also the third person being referred to). For example, consider sentence **(7)**.

(7)   Serpico pretended that the world is round (in order to pass his exam).

Sentence **(7)** would be viewed, in most segments of modern society, as quite strange, if not downright ungrammatical, because the verb *pretend* presupposes that its complement is false. Nevertheless, **(7)** would be perfectly appropriate if uttered either in the days of Columbus or at a modern-day meeting of the Flat-Earth Society. On the other hand, if the speaker believes that the world is round and the hearer understands it to be flat, some problems in communication are going to occur.

Pragmatics proper came into focus when linguists began to look at sentences which appear to have both a literal meaning and a "conveyed meaning" which is often quite different from the basic meaning of the sentence. For example:

(8)   Can you turn off the bubble machine?

Sentence **(8)**, if taken literally, is a simple request for information; on the other hand, the speaker may be well aware that his addressee is capable of turning off the bubble machine, and a simple answer "Yes, I can" with no action might in this case result in an act of retribution from a well-bubbled questioner.

The complexity of the problem is widened if one observes that all or any of the following utterances (among others) can be used to request the opening of a window:

(9a)   I request that you open the window.
(9b)   Open the window!
(9c)   Will you open the window?
(9d)   Won't you open the window?
(9e)   It would be nice if you'd open the window.
(9f)   Is the window open?
(9g)   Oh boy, is it ever hot in here!
(9h)   Are you hot?

If we stuck to the traditional assumption of generative grammar that synonymous sentences are derived from identical deep structures (recall that this was one of the main motivations for postulating the existence of transformations in the first place), we would be forced to say that all of the above sentences are derived from the same deep structure. This solution, has, in fact, been proposed. However, in addition to such a solution being counterintuitive, it is evident that several new, extremely complex and powerful, and probably *ad hoc*, transformations would need to be added to the theory. In order to avoid this difficulty, the idea of pragmatics has been introduced. As was pointed out previously, pragmatics relates language to the "real-world situation of its use." In other words, a sentence like (9f), which is ambiguous (being either a simple request for information or a command to open a window), can only be interpreted by analyzing it in the light of the situation in which it is used, the relationship between the speaker and hearer, and other "extralinguistic" considerations. Notice that such a view necessarily enlarges the realm of competence, so that a speaker, in order to use his language appropriately, must have in his competence not only a knowledge of formal grammatical rules, but also ideas of how, where, and when different linguistic features may appropriately be used. Notice also that the demarcation between competence (underlying knowledge of structure of the language) and performance (actual use of the language) becomes more blurred. This has, in fact, been very much the trend in recent years, and particularly in related fields like psycholinguistics and sociolinguistics.

It might be interesting to look at a couple of the more interesting and radical proposals which have arisen in recent months from considerations like the above. The following are representative examples only; many similar ones could have been chosen with no less justification. The first example has to do with what Weiser (1974) has referred to as "deliberate ambiguity." Consider the following situation:

A runs into an acquaintance, B, who is a member of a committee making an investigation that is supposed to be closed to the public until it reaches a final conclusion. A knows that it would be unethical for B to talk about what went on in that day's hearing. But A *doesn't* know—this is the crucial uncertainty—how willing B is to stretch his ethics on occasion. To ask straight out ("What went on?") would show that A entertains the possibility that B might be dishonest, which would be insulting if B is not. But if A says nothing, he loses the chance to find out what went on in the hearing in case B *was* willing to talk. So A says—at the appropriate time, in the appropriate tone of voice—"I'm curious about what went on at the hearing." If B is willing to talk, he can treat this as a request for information. If B is going to stick by his ethics, all he has to do is say, "Yes, I guess a lot of people are. The reporters would love to get their hands on a transcript," and it becomes clear that A has not made a request, but a simple statement about his state of mind. If B suspects what A is up to, there is not much he can do about it. If confronted, A can back off with an innocent "Oh, but I wasn't asking you to *tell* me! I was just saying I'm curious." Although A would be willing, under favorable circumstances, for his statement to be taken as a request, he has not committed himself to anything more than a statement about his own curiosity.

Not only is Weiser's sentence ("I'm curious about what went on at the hearing") ambiguous, but it has two meanings at one and the same time. Under the traditional analysis, such an ambiguous sentence can be derived from one or the other of two distinct deep structures, but not both at the same time! On the other hand, the usual pragmatic analysis would require the meaning of such a sentence to be determined by joint considerations of form and context—but it has been assumed that context will *uniquely* determine the meaning. There is, then, no mechanism in linguistic theory at present to allow a sentence to have two meanings *at the same time*.

George Lakoff (1974) has recently considered another equally radical departure. As a preface, recall again that in the *Aspects* and later frameworks, a particular instance of a sentence is derived from a unique deep structure which represents its meaning. Lakoff, however, presents examples like the following:

(10) John invited *you'll never guess how many people* to his party.

(11) John is going to, *I'm sorry to say it's Chicago*, on Saturday.

The above sentences seem to involve an unusual type of embedding. It is not clear what classes of constituents are represented by the italicized expressions; they are, however, clearly related to complete sentences similar to the following:

(10a) You'll never guess how many people John invited to his party.

(11a) I'm sorry to say it's Chicago John is going to on Saturday.

At first glance it seems reasonable to claim that **(10)** and **(11)** are, in fact, derived from deep structures resembling **(10a)** and **(11a)**, respectively. However, such a proposal is contraindicated by such fantastic sentences as **(12)**.

> **(12)**   John invited *you'll never guess how many people* to *you can imagine what kind of a party* at *it should be obvious where* with *God only knows what purpose* in mind, despite *you can guess what pressures*.

What Lakoff has proposed (greatly simplified) is that sentence **(10)** is derived by an amalgation of two different deep structures! Prime candidates are the following:

> **(10b)**   John invited *a lot of people* to his party.
> **(10c)**   You'll never guess how many people John invited to his party.

Sentence **(10)** results from **(10c)**, at some point in the derivation, being substituted for the italicized portion of **(10b)**. Of course, certain deletion transformations must also apply to reduce **(10c)** to the appropriate form. Such a derivation, of course, would be disallowed in the *Aspects* framework.

That syntactic amalgams fall into the realm of pragmatics follows from the fact that certain amalgams, while being predicted by a purely syntactic analysis like the above, turn out to be ungrammatical.

> **(13)**   *John invited *Sam guessed how many people* to his party.
> **(14)**   *John is going to, *I'm sorry it's Chicago*, on Saturday.

Without going into detail, it is, according to Lakoff, "conversational entailment in context that determines which underlined [italicized] NP's can occur"—or, in other words, pragmatic considerations.

We see, then, that the development of pragmatic theory has had important implications for transformational theory, both respecting the role and functioning of deep structure and transformations, as well as the notion of linguistic competence. These ideas, basic to generative theory, are not, of course, proved incorrect, but are rather being increasingly refined and better understood. This is the nature of all new scientific discoveries, and there is no question but that the process will continue.

Contributions of Psycholinguistics

In contrast to linguistics in the narrow sense, which has in the past been mostly concerned only with determining the most economical description of language and its universal characteristics, the goal of psycholinguistics is to explain how a speaker attains this competence in the first place and how he uses it in actual discourse. In a sense, psychology might be said to be concerned with behavior (i.e., performance) rather than competence. However, since performance is necessarily based on competence, it has become increasingly difficult to separate the two. At any rate, psycholinguistic studies have much to contribute toward the crucial question of the processes involved in using language. While language acquisition is also an important subfield of psycholinguistics, it will not be possible to discuss it in detail. The latter sections of each chapter have quite a bit to say on this topic.

As has been emphasized previously in this book, Chomsky and other transformational grammarians have, since the publication of *Syntactic Structures*, pointed out repeatedly that transformational analyses do not necessarily mirror real processes used to produce and understand sentences. However, certain concepts promoted in the field, such as that of "explanatory adequacy," have, whether intentionally or unintentionally, tended to further such an unproven viewpoint. Early in the history of generative grammar, many educators jumped on the bandwagon and began teaching English and other languages by explicit formulation and memorization of complex transformational rules. At the same time, psychologists and psycholinguists, some of whom accepted the idea of the speaker/hearer explicitly applying transformations and others of whom considered the idea completely counter-intuitive, designed experiments to test the concept. (Much of the following is presented in much more detail in Greene (1972).) Early results turned out to be amazingly positive. The earliest experiments carried out by George Miller (1964) and others were based on the possibility that not only does a speaker utilize transformations in producing a sentence, but that a hearer must reverse these transformations in order to recover the deep structure and the meaning of the sentence. In addition, application of each transformation, either direct or reversed, should take time. Subjects were asked, for example, to change an active sentence into a passive or a passive into an active, and to locate the resulting sentence in a list. The results showed that direct and reversed transformations took approximately equal times, with the PASSIVE transformation taking longer than the NEGATION transformation. In addition, transformation of an active sentence to a Passive Negative results in a time quite close to the sum of the times taken for the PASSIVE and NEGATION transformations applied independently.

The excitement generated by experiments like the above waned rapidly, however, with the development of more sophisticated procedures. The difficulty with the above is that subjects were specifically instructed to perform transformations, which means that results pertain only to the possibly artificial experimental situation. It was found that differences in experimental design or in sample sentences resulted in unexplainable differences; for example, sometimes passives took longer than negatives and sometimes just the opposite. Especially when meaning, rather than syntax alone, was included in the experimental designs, results became vastly different. One example is Slobin's experiments (1966) involving reversible and non-reversible actives and passives (discussed on pages 112–113) as in the following:

(15a) The girl hit the boy.

(15b) The boy was hit by the girl.

(16a) The girl is watering the flowers.

(16b) The flowers are being watered by the girl.

The passive **(15b)** is reversible, since interchanging the subject and object results in a grammatical sentence; by the same token, **(16b)** is non-reversible.

(15c) The girl was hit by the boy.

(16c) *The girl is being watered by the flowers.

Slobin discovered that although a sentence like **(15b)** took longer to process than one like **(15a)**, subjects took no longer to determine the meaning of a passive sentence like **(16b)** than of an active one like **(16a)**. He proposed that this is because of the semantic constraints on the subject and object. In other words, it does not seem to be necessary to reverse the PASSIVE transformation to understand **(16b)**. These findings were elaborated on by later experiments which showed an analysis of this type is often involved even in reversible sentences, just in case "expected events" are depicted. This is exemplified by the following sentences:

(17a) The doctor treated the patient.

(17b) The patient was treated by the doctor.

(17c) The doctor was treated by the patient.

Processing time for the above three sentences was approximately equal; furthermore, subjects often misinterpreted **(17c)** to have the meaning of **(17b)**. The indication is that they were placing more importance on surface semantic cues than on syntactic concepts.

In contrast to the many experimental indications that transformations do not function in language use, it does seem that both surface and deep structure are regularly involved in speech production and interpretation. One psycholinguistic experiment which has become well-known was originated to demonstrate the psychological reality of phrase structure constituents in surface structure. In these experiments (e.g., Fodor and Bever, 1965) subjects heard a sentence in one ear and a click in the other and were asked to report at what point in the sentence the click had occurred. The click was often reported to be displaced from its actual position toward the location of constituent boundaries. Bever (1971) extended the technique and applied it to sentences for which deep structure constituents and surface structure constituents differ. His results bear out the hypothesis that not only surface structure, but deep structure as well, has an effect on click placement.

Levelt (1970) performed an experiment in which he asked his subjects to judge the syntactic relatedness between the words of a sentence. He found, as generative theory would predict, that in the sentence "The boy raises frogs," for example, "the" vs. "boy" and "raises" vs. "frogs" are judged to be more closely related than the pair "boy" vs. "raises." The suspected reason is the existence of a major constituent break between the *NP* and the *VP*. Levelt found, however, that not all judged relationships mirrored the surface structure so closely, but that some depended on reference to deep structure. An example is the sentence "Carla takes the book and goes to school," which Levelt presented to his subjects in Dutch. The two verbs "takes" and "goes" were judged to be equally closely related to the subject "Carla"; this can be explained directly by reference to a deep structure containing conjoined sentences, each of which has "Carla" as its subject (as discussed in Chapter 6).

Other studies are abundant which demonstrate that sentences are recalled in a form much nearer to their deep structure than to their surface structure; that is, meaning appears to be what is recalled, rather than surface form. All of these considerations indicate that deep structure, or at least something very similar to it, is represented in the mind of the listener and is used in interpreting linguistic input, as opposed to transformations, which seem to have no real counterpart in sentence interpretation. Notice, however, that psycholinguistic studies like the above have concentrated almost exclusively on the listener. They have little to say about the role of transformations in speech production. On the basis of physical limitations of the speaker and the ease and speed with which he speaks, however, it seems unlikely that transformations are applied one by one in a direct fashion here either. None of this rules out the possibility, though, that transformations figure somehow in the initial learning of linguistic structures and perhaps even indirectly in language use.

One interesting offshoot of evidence like the above has been the development by some psycholinguists, particularly Bever, Fodor, and Garrett (see Fodor and Garrett, 1967; Bever, 1970) of a linguistic theory based on cognition. Again, the theory has little to say about language production, but concentrates on the interpretation of linguistic input. Bever, Fodor, and Garrett claim that in processing sentences a listener, rather than recovering the deep structure of a sentence through reversed transformations, applies certain perceptual strategies based on syntactic and semantic relationships inherent in the surface structure. They point to structures like **(18b)** and **(19b)**, which, while transformationally derived from **(18a)** and **(19a)**, are "obviously not more complex to understand" than the **(a)** structures.

(18a) the house which is red
(18b) the red house
(19a) That John left the party angrily amazed Bill.
(19b) It amazed Bill that John left the party angrily.

While few specific perceptual strategies have been proposed, and while even these have not been formalized, two shall be presented here to demonstrate the theory. Consider the following two sentences:

(20a) The editor authors the newspaper hired liked laughed.
(20b) The editor the authors the newspaper hired liked laughed.

Both **(20a)** and **(20b)** are perfectly grammatical. Nevertheless, because of the depth of embedding, they are extremely difficult to process, and **(20a)** is much more so than **(20b)**. If the reader still finds difficulty in processing **(20a)**, possibly a representation of the embedding will help:

(20a) The editor authors the newspaper hired liked laughed.

Bever proposes the following perceptual strategy in explanation:

> The first N . . . V . . . (N) . . . clause . . . is the main clause, unless the verb is marked as subordinate.

That is, the listener (or reader), because he processes the sentence from left to right, first interprets "authors" as the verb of "the editor," and then "the newspaper" as its object (i.e., the first five words represent an N . . . V . . . N sequence). Of course, when he encounters the word "hired," he is forced to the realization that his interpretation is wrong, and that he must begin over again and try another interpretation. This accounts for the extreme difficulty of **(20a)**. The intrusion of the determiner "the" in **(20b)** forces the listener to interpret "authors" as a noun; therefore the strategy does not apply, and this results in **(20b)** being easier to understand than **(20a)**.

Another strategy proposed by Bever is the following:

> Any *Noun-Verb-Noun* (NVN) sequence within a potential internal unit in the surface structure corresponds to "*actor-action-subject*."

This strategy is closely related to the first presented above. Bever uses it to explain why passive sentences are more difficult to understand than active sentences. For example:

(21) The *center* was *tackled* by the *quarterback*.

Obviously the italicized words form an NVN sequence, which, according to Bever's strategy, tends to be interpreted as *actor-action-object*. The tendency would likely be even stronger when the natural roles are reversed, as in **(21)**. Of course, this is the wrong interpretation, and this tendency must be overcome by close examination of the syntactic cues indicating the passive ("was," "-ed," "by") if the proper meaning is to be extracted.

Bever and his colleagues have expanded the concept of perceptual strategies past the limited goal of explaining sentence processing to a more general goal requiring a radical revision of linguistic theory. Recall that one of the basic teachings of Chomsky and his followers is the concept of linguistic universals, which exist across languages, and which are present in the head of each language learner, enabling him to learn his language at the surprisingly rapid rate observed. A simple example of a linguistic universal is the existence of nouns and verbs in all languages. Bever feels that such universals are not linguistic, but cognitive universals; that is, innate capacities for language learning are not specific to language, but rather, ". . . specific properties of language structure and speech behavior reflect certain general cognitive laws." The noun/verb distinction, for example, results from a natural nonlinguistic distinction between substance on the one hand and action or attribute on the other. If true (and this has yet to be shown—many problem areas still remain), this hypothesis would invalidate one of Chomsky's strongest claims.

One final area for which psychological investigations have had something to say is that of grammaticality. Chomsky's original goal for a grammar was that it generate all grammatical sentences of a language and no ungrammatical ones. The implication is that there is a clear bipartite division in the language between grammatical and ungrammatical sentences. In addition, Chomsky assumed that competence is isomorphic with the intuitions of an ideal speaker-hearer in a homogeneous speech community. However, several difficulties arise with such a view.

First, certain sentences which the grammar naturally generates are judged "bad" by native speakers. One such example is **(20a)**, repeated below.

    (20a) The editor authors the newspaper hired liked laughed.

Second, a native speaker is not always able to make a clear choice between grammatical and ungrammatical sentences; one sentence may be "more grammatical" or "less grammatical" than the second. For some speakers, for example, the following sentences form a continuum as far as grammaticality is concerned. (We shall return to them shortly.)

    (22a) He figured out the answer.
    (22b) He figured out something.
    (22c) He figured out Ann.
    (22d) He figured out it.

Chomsky handles the first case by differentiating between "grammaticality" and "acceptability." Grammaticality, he says, is a function of competence; acceptability is a function of performance, and is affected by memory and storage limitations of the brain, context, etc. Thus, Chomsky argues that if a speaker is given sufficient time to process **(20a)** and possibly has it explained to him, he will eventually understand it and accept it as well-formed. Sentence **(20a)**, then, is grammatical, but unacceptable. Contrast this with a sentence like **(23)**, which is clearly ungrammatical.

(23)   *Laughed editor authors newspaper the hired liked the.

This distinction also has not proven to be as clear-cut as Chomsky would have liked. As competence assimilates more and more of what had previously been included in performance, the separation line between "grammatical" and "acceptable" becomes more and more hazy. The second concept of "degrees of grammaticality" thus increases in relevance. This concept was discussed in *Aspects* (pp. 148–153), but not formalized. Ross (1967) attempted a formalization by using question marks. His formalism has been employed to some extent in this text. Thus, the sentences in **(22)** are represented as follows:

(22a)   He figured out the answer.
(22b)   ? He figured out something.
(22c)   ?*He figured out Ann.
(22d)   *He figured out it.

In this notation, ? means "not quite grammatical," while ?* might be translated "barely grammatical, if at all." The only problem with Ross's notation is that the number of degrees of grammaticality is likely infinite, and four symbols obviously cannot represent all the fine distinctions (as in **(24a–i)** of the next paragraph). Finally, the fact that degrees of grammaticality are real can easily be seen in many recent linguistics papers, where one sentence is commonly referred to as being simply "better" or "worse" than another.

A more serious difficulty with grammaticality arises when one observes the wide range of judgments made by various speakers of a language. For example, consider the following sequence.

(24a)   John called the girl up.
(24b)   John called the pretty girl up.
(24c)   John called the pretty Belgian girl up.
(24d)   John called the pretty Belgian girl who visited the showroom up.
(24e)   John called the pretty Belgian girl who visited the showroom yesterday up.
(24f)   John called the pretty Belgian girl who visited the showroom yesterday while Mr. Smith was on the phone up.
(24g)   John called the pretty Belgian girl who visited the show-

room yesterday while Mr. Smith was on the phone long distance up.

(24h) John called the pretty Belgian girl who visited the showroom yesterday while Mr. Smith was on the phone long distance with his mother up.

(24i) John called the pretty Belgian girl who visited the showroom yesterday while Mr. Smith was on the phone long distance with his mother in Santa Ana up.

While most speakers will agree that **(24a)** is fully acceptable and **(24i)** fully unacceptable, they will likely not agree on the sentences in between, and may find it difficult to even make their own judgments on some of these sentences. Thus grammaticality is **relative.** This difficulty exists not only for long sequences such as this, but native speakers often disagree strongly as to the grammaticality of isolated sentences; readers of this book have almost surely encountered the problem when reading "grammatical" or "ungrammatical" sentences in the text. In fact, rarely is a linguistics paper presented for which listeners or readers agree 100 percent with the author's judgments. This has forced linguists into the argument that they are describing only *their own dialect*. It must be recalled that the purpose of the competence/performance distinction was originally to foster homogeneity in the linguistic corpus; it now seems that speakers' judgments are anything but homogeneous. And the problem becomes more serious when many linguists use their own intuitive judgments exclusively in determining grammaticality. It yet remains to be seen whether a highly trained linguist can make truly natural and neutral judgments about sentences. In addition, both linguists and psycholinguists have encountered difficulties not only in finding agreement between speakers on any one sentence, but even in replicating the findings of other investigators; it seems that even a single speaker may judge a sentence differently on two separate occasions.

Probably the best-known psychological studies in this area have been done by Greenbaum, Quirk, and Svartvik (see Greenbaum and Quirk, 1970). They have developed techniques for comparing subjects' judgments about acceptability against their actual usage elicited in controlled conditions. They found some discrepancies between judgments and usage, and determined that factors such as educational background and subjects' opinions about the tests affected the results.

All of the above, while presented somewhat pessimistically, does not negate all recent linguistic findings. Disagreement and difficulties of the above types appear mostly with relatively rare sentence types; agreement in other cases is quite uniform. An understanding of these facts, however, does lead to a healthy open mind when encountering new linguistic claims. Ross and others have proposed new ideas such as "fuzzy grammar," "output constraints," etc. which partially account for the difficulties. Sociolinguistics, on the other hand, has taken a completely different approach, as will be seen in the next section.

Sociolinguistics

In recent years, many linguists have become increasingly interested in the relationship of language to society. These linguists have stressed the "-linguistics" half of "sociolinguistics" and have concentrated on the form taken by language in differing contexts, both linguistic and social. Their studies have shown that variation is much more widespread, but also much more predictable, than had been thought previously.

The one outstanding characteristic of sociolinguistics is its concern for variation, and this at the same time serves to distinguish it from the traditional emphasis of linguistics proper. Linguists have, since the time of Saussure in the early part of the century at least, considered languages to be homogeneous systems. As we have seen in earlier sections of the text, this has had a strong effect on all aspects of language study, from basic theoretical assumptions to methods of formulating specific rules to account for the data, and the form of the rules themselves. As presented in the early chapters of this book, rules have been considered to be of two types: obligatory and optional. Obligatory rules apply whenever their environment is met, producing regular outputs. Optional rules, however, may or may not apply, and the assumption has been that it is not possible to predict in any given situation whether or not such a rule will apply, but that this is up to the free choice of the individual speaker. For example, the two following sentences are differentiated only according to whether or not an optional rule has applied.

(25a)   That Hitler was an egomaniac cannot be denied.

(25b)   It cannot be denied that Hitler was an egomaniac.

In cases such as this, the two variants **(25a)** and **(25b)** have been considered to be in free variation, and nothing further has been said. Proportions of use of each variant and differences in distribution based on region, social class, or style have not been considered to be linguistically relevant, or, in general, to be predictable. Such differences have generally been believed to be minor ones, and to a large extent not part of the speaker's underlying competence in the language. In addition, performance factors have been considered to be inaccessible to linguistic analysis, because of a large number of hesitations, false starts, and other errors in speaking. However, psycholinguistic and sociolinguistic studies have shown that such errors are not all that common: that variability is common in language use, but that it is systematic, and, in addition, that its study leads to important insights which are relevant both for linguistics and for education.

We have already dealt, in the sections on pragmatics and psycholinguistics, with the gradual incorporation of more and more "performance" phenomena into competence, and with the difficulties resulting from the use of intuitive judgments of grammaticality in linguistic descriptions. The actual formulation of rules themselves has also been in accordance with the above-mentioned concept of linguistic homogeneity. Rules are written with a single, unvarying output. However, since it is impossible to ignore variant forms completely, some rules have had to be made optional, and formulated in such a way that application will produce one variant, and non-application another. The theoretical assumption resulting from such a formulation would be that either variant is equally favored, and that variation is free: that is, variant choice has no significant results.

It is clear, however, from recent studies, that the choice of variant does have important consequences, particularly at the social level. It has also been proven for many cases that choice is not free even when social factors are ruled out; linguistic environment plays a much greater role than had been supposed. Finally, even in the absence of influencing linguistic environments, one variant is often clearly favored over another.

Sociolinguistics has achieved great insights as a result of its changes of emphasis. It has been concerned with language, not in reference to an abstract "idealized speaker-hearer," but rather with its actual use in real situations at specified times and locations. In addition, sociolinguists have shown that while variation is great, much of what linguists had previously considered to be unpredictable "free variation" was actually highly systematic and predictable. Most variation appears not to be idiosyncratic, but to occur with high probability in definable situations. Variation falls into at least three distinct categories:

1. Much linguistic variation is regional, and although regional dialects are an everyday topic of conversation, geographic variation is much more widespread than is generally recognized. Linguists do admit its existence but generally consider it irrelevant; this is likely one source of the idea of an "idealized" (or free from regional dialect features) speaker-hearer.

2. Social dialect, defined by a person's membership in various social classes, is also an important type of variation. Differences between social dialects, like those between regional dialects, are also not haphazard but quite predictable.

3. Stylistic variation is also a regularly occurring phenomenon. People speak or write very differently depending on their location, their subject-matter, and the group being addressed. Although lin-

guists have tended to place stylistic variation in with other "performance factors," it also has been shown to be highly systematic.

Some sociolinguists, by isolating regional variation from the other
two types, have achieved interesting insights into the latter two. Not
only have they shown extreme regularity, but they have also found that
the two are inseparably connected. Since a similar effect is produced
either by a higher social class or by a more formal situation, for example, a particular variant may display an identical distribution for the
two cases of (1) a lower-class speaker in a formal situation and (2) an
upper-class speaker in a casual speech situation.

As mentioned previously, linguistic and social context help to determine the frequencies of various forms. Sociolinguists have formalized
this notion so that it is possible to say, for example (hypothetically),
that in a particular environment, sentence **(25a)** will be used 20 percent
of the time and sentence **(25b)** 80 percent of the time. Standard generative theory, of course, would have to say that the probability of either
form being used is 50 percent. Of course, in a different context, the
probabilities may be quite different. Certain writers have argued that
not only does a native speaker know which rules are variable and
which constraints operate, but that he also knows "the probabilities
toward rule operation contributed by each constraint." Chomsky and
other linguists have often stated that our ultimate goal is an *explanatory* model of language, which will be able not only to describe
language, but also to explain and describe all that a speaker implicitly
knows about his language. And since speakers seem to know a great
deal about variable rules in their language, this knowledge needs to be
formalized and included in the makeup of linguistic rules.

Because of their different viewpoint, sociolinguists have avoided the
problems inherent in basing linguistic analyses on intuitions of the linguist. Instead, they have collected data directly from groups of native
speakers in the community, in normal use situations. In this way, direct
experimental data are available. And since actual speech is much more
consistent than has been claimed, sociolinguistic analyses are quite re-
liable. In addition, sociolinguists are able to elicit various styles of language dependent on situation: for example, the language of oral reading, the language of very formal situations, the language used in the
peer group, etc. Of these, analyses based on competence have tended
to treat only one homogeneous style, a relatively formal one.

Sociolinguists have stressed, as have linguists in other fields, that no
one dialect, either regional or social, is better than another. Many distinctions between dialects are not even noticed by most speaker-hear-
ers, and those which are are evaluated solely on the basis of social
biases and stereotypes. Of course, for socialization purposes, it may
sometimes be necessary to teach features of the Standard Dialect to

native speakers of nonstandard dialects, although there is still a great deal of debate on this subject. One interesting fact that has come about through sociolinguistic studies is the continuing widespread use of nonstandard features despite mass communication and attempts at corrective education. Use of "ain't" and multiple negatives, as in "We ain't never had no trouble about none of us pulling out no knife or nothing," have been present in English for hundreds of years and still persist, all efforts of well-meaning English teachers notwithstanding (see Labov, 1965). It seems that the influence of the peer group outweighs all other factors; only a strongly motivated desire for change will result in replacement of socially unacceptable variants of this type.

Glossary

This glossary is provided so that the reader might have easy access to technical terms used in the text. Most words which appear in boldface in the main text are defined below, as well as a few additional terms. Some of those which appear in boldface in the text are specifically defined there as well as here, but for others a complete definition appears only in the glossary. Included in the list below are traditional, structural, and transformational terms, as well as some nonlinguistic terms used in the research sections; many are probably familiar to the reader already, but they are included for the sake of completeness. On the other hand, no attempt has been made to exhaustively cover the language of linguistics; only words pertinent to this text are included. Also, definitions herein apply only to the English language. It should also be noted that many of the words below have nontechnical uses in English; these are ignored, and only technical definitions are included. Finally, the names of specific transformations are not listed; they can be easily located through the index, under the entry *transformations*.

A few standard abbreviations are used. *E.g.*, of course, refers to a following example; *Cf.* directs the reader to a related term in the glossary. Within a definition, terms which are defined elsewhere are followed by *q.v.* (one term immediately preceding) or *qq.v.* (more than one term). In some cases *q.v.* may refer to a single word preceding, and in others to a term consisting of several words.

242

Many of the following definitions are similar to those given in Pei and Gaynor (1967) which, while more traditional, is much more comprehensive than is this glossary.

abstract morpheme. A morpheme (q.v.) which at the deep structure (q.v.) level is similar to the form which appears in surface structure (q.v.) (E.g., PAST represents various spoken past tense morphemes.) (Cf. *concrete morpheme.*)

abstract representation. See *deep structure.*

active verb. 1. A verb used in the active (nonpassive) voice; that is, the surface subject (q.v.) of the sentence is the performer of the action indicated by the verb. 2. A verb which expresses activity (e.g., "scream") in contradistinction to *stative verbs* (q.v.), which describe a state or quality only (e.g., "know").

affix. A morpheme (q.v.) added to a root (q.v.) to change or alter its meaning. A *prefix, suffix,* or *infix* (qq.v.).

agent. 1. The person or thing performing the action expressed by the verb of the sentence. 2. The *deep subject* (q.v.) of the sentence.

agentive. An ending added to verbs to produce a meaning something like "one who does."

agreement rules. Inflectional rules (q.v.) which adjust the form of a verb to agree in number, person, case, or gender (qq.v.) with its subject.

allomorph. A variant shape of a morpheme (q.v.) occurring in certain environments. (E.g., [s], [z], and [əz] are allomorphs of the plural morpheme.)

ambiguous. Having two or more meanings.

antecedent. The noun phrase (q.v.) which is coreferent to a particular pronoun (q.v.); it is the antecedent which triggers Pronominalization.

anthropological linguistics. The study of language in its cultural setting.

applied linguistics. The application of linguistic research to practical areas, including language teaching, stylistics, and machine translation.

Aspect. A category indicating duration or completion of action or state of the verb; in English, *Perfective* or *Progressive* (qq.v.).

auxiliary. That phrase structure (q.v.) constituent which precedes the verb in deep structure (q.v.) and which consists of *Modals, Tense,* and/or *Aspect* (qq.v.).

babbling. The stage of language acquisition at which a child produces only meaningless concatenations of sounds.

base. That component of a grammar (q.v.) consisting of the *phrase structure* plus the *lexicon* (qq.v.).

base-and-modifier technique. One method of diagraming (q.v.) sentences; it emphasizes relationships between words and deemphasizes order.

(E.g., He| looked| number.)

bound morpheme. A morpheme (q.v.) which never occurs in isolation, but is always combined with at least one other morpheme in forming a word. (Cf. *free morpheme*.)

bracketing. A method of abbreviating tree (q.v.) structures by constituents within labeled brackets. (E.g., $[_S$ NP VP $_S]$.)

case. The grammatical function or syntactic relationships of a word. (E.g., subject, object of preposition, instrumental, etc.)

Case Grammar. A syntactic model developed by Fillmore. It is a variation of generative grammar (q.v.) whose deep structures (q.v.) emphasize case (q.v.) relationships between the verb and each noun. (E.g., Agentive, Instrumental, Dative, Factive, Locative, Objective, etc.)

clause. An embedded constituent of a sentence containing a subject and a predicate; clauses are embedded sentences in deep structure (q.v.).

cognitive universal. According to Bever, an innate capacity for learning of a certain type which may include as one of its features a *linguistic universal* (q.v.). (E.g., the noun/verb distinction which exists in all languages as the result of a natural cognitive distinction.)

command. In Langacker's terminology, a node *A* is said to command a node *B* if (1) neither *A* nor *B* dominates (q.v.) the other, and (2) the closest *S*-node dominating *A* also dominates *B*.

comparative. The form of an adjective or adverb which expresses a comparatively greater amount of the quality or characteristic indicated. (E.g., "bigger" is the comparative of "big"; "more friendly" is the comparative of "friendly.") (Cf. *superlative*.)

comparative linguistics. That branch of linguistics which deals with the comparison of two or more language systems, usually with the goal of determining historical or genetic relationships (q.v.), and of reconstructing earlier stages of these languages and ultimately the parent language from which they have developed.

competence. A speaker-hearer's implicit, perfect knowledge of the rules and functioning of his language. (Cf. *performance*.)

complement. An embedded sentence (q.v.) of a certain type, which is introduced by one of the complementizers "for-to," "POSS-ing," or "that."

complementizer. A morpheme (q.v.) or group of morphemes which introduces a surface *complement* (q.v.); the three English types are the "for-to," "POSS-ing," and "that" complementizers.

complex sentence. A sentence containing an independent clause (q.v.) and one or more embedded clauses. (Cf. *simple sentence, compound sentence.*)

compound sentence. A sentence consisting of two or more simple sentences (q.v.) joined by "and," "or," or "but." (Cf. *simple sentence, complex sentence.*)

conceptual structure. See *deep structure.*

concrete morpheme. A morpheme (q.v.) which appears in the deep structure (q.v.) in a form more or less similar to that which appears in the surface structure (q.v.). (Cf. *abstract morpheme.*)

conjunct. In conjunction (q.v.), each of the two or more constituents (q.v.) which are joined together by a conjunction "and," "or," or "but."

conjunction. 1. The joining of sentences by "and," "but," and "or." 2. A word used to form conjunction ("and," "or," or "but").

constative (sentence). According to Austin, a sentence which (1) can be either true or false, and (2) simply states a fact without performing the action of the verb, in contradistinction to a *performative sentence* (q.v.).

constituent. In a linguistic tree (q.v.), all the material dominated by a common node (E.g., *Det + N + S* is a constituent if dominated by *NP.*)

constructivist approaches. Van Uden's term for traditional approaches to teaching grammar to a deaf student which put parts of speech together into "baked" sentences which are rote-learned by the child.

controlled study. Cooper and Rosenstein's term for language acquisition studies in which carefully chosen tests and other techniques, such as memory recall, are used to elicit language performance from children. (Cf. *free study.*)

conversational implication. That which is implied by what is said.

coreference. The characteristic of referring to the same item or object. (E.g., In "John broke his tooth," "John" and "his" are coreferent.)

declarative sentence. A sentence which makes a statement or assertion. (Cf. *interrogative sentence, imperative sentence.*)

deep structure. The level of grammatical structure at which both meaning and grammatical relationships are preserved. Transformations (q.v.) apply to the deep structure to produce *surface structure* (q.v.).

deep subject. That noun phrase (q.v.) in a sentence which is its subject at the level of deep structure (q.v.). (Cf. *surface subject.*)

derivation. A sequence of trees (q.v.) resulting from the step-by-step application of linguistic rules (q.v.).

derivational rule. A rule which applies to a word or root (q.v.) to form a new word, by the addition of a prefix or suffix (qq.v.) or other means. Usually, but not always, derivational forms belong to different grammatical classes than the word from which they were derived. (E.g., "transformation" and "transformationally" are derived from "transformation.") (Cf. *inflectional rule.*)

descriptive linguistics. The branch of linguistics which deals with the scientific description of languages as discrete entities at a given point in time.

determiner. A word which precedes a noun and "determines" the definiteness, indefiniteness, location, or some other quality of the noun. Articles, demonstratives and genitives, for example, are determiners.

diagraming. A means of representing diagramatically the component parts of a surface structure (q.v.) sentence and their syntactic relationships.

dialect. A variety of language used by a particular speech group which differs in certain identifiable features from the forms used by other speech groups within the same language. All dialects, including the Standard Dialect, are equally useful in communicating within the speech group.

diminutive. A word derived from another word by the addition of a suffix (q.v.) of a certain type in order to signify a small object or animal of that kind.(E.g., "fishie," "doggie.")

direct object. The person or object in a sentence which is the direct receiver of the action of the verb. (Cf. *indirect object.*)

directly dominate. In Langacker's definition, a node *A* is said to directly dominate a node *B* if *A* dominates (q.v.) *B* and there are no intervening nodes.

dominate. According to Langacker, a node *A* is said to dominate a node *B* if it appears above it in the tree (q.v.) and is connected to it by a path of branches.

echo question. A question to repeat part of a statement made by someone else, and showing surprise or a request for additional information. In contrast to other question types, word order remains the same as for statements; only intonation (q.v.) differs. (E.g., "Zelda has done what?")

embedded question. A question which is embedded in a higher sentence. (E.g., "Bill wonders *who ate the porridge.*")

embedded sentence. A sentence which is embedded in a main sentence and appears in the surface structure (q.v.) as, for example, a relative clause or complement (qq.v.).

expansion. The rewriting of a node as two or more nodes lower in the tree; a shorthand version of a *node admissibility condition* (q.v.).

feature. A marking on a lexical item indicating its characteristics and restrictions on its capacity for lexical insertion (q.v.).

Fitzgerald Key. A means of representing surface sentence patterns; developed by Edith Fitzgerald and widely used in teaching deaf children.

frame. In structuralism (q.v.), a sentence with a space into which words can be inserted or substituted to test for class membership. (E.g., a *determiner* is any word which can be substituted for "the" in the frame "(The) bread is good.")

free morpheme. A morpheme (q.v.) that can stand by itself as a word in the language. (Cf. *bound morpheme.*)

free study. In Cooper and Rosenstein's terminology, a language acquisition study in which the investigator collects a sample of written or spoken language from children and analyzes it. (Cf. *controlled study.*)

free variation. Variation between forms which is considered to be unaffected by environment and therefore unpredictable.

gender. In pronouns, sex of the noun referred to: male, female, or neuter.

generate. A term used to refer to functioning of linguistic rules (q.v.) in the sense of "define" or "describe."

generalized transformation. In the earlier *Syntactic Structures* framework, a transformation (q.v.) which operates to combine two or more deep structures (q.v.) to produce compound or complex sentences (qq.v.). Generalized transformations have no place in the more recent theory. (Cf. *singulary transformation.*)

generative grammar. See *transformational generative grammar.*

Generative Semantics. A variation of generative grammar (q.v.) in which deep structure (q.v.) is identical to the underlying meaning of a sentence and is much more abstract than in the Standard Theory (q.v.). Semantics and phonology (q.v.), rather than being interpretive components (q.v.), are closely integrated with the syntax. (q.v.).

genetic relationship. Relationship between languages as the result of development from a common ancestral language.

governed rule. A rule whose application or non-application is determined by the presence or absence of a certain subset of a particular class of words, usually verbs.

grammar. The set of rules (q.v.) or statements which generate (q.v.) or describe the makeup and functioning of a language.

grammatical subject. See *surface subject.*

grammaticality. With reference to a sentence, the characteristic of being well-formed on the basis of the rules (q.v.) of the grammar (q.v.).

head noun phrase. A noun phrase (q.v.) immediately preceding an embedded sentence (q.v.) which, if identical to a noun phrase within the embedded sentence, triggers Relativization.

hierarchical arrangement. The characteristic of words in sentences falling into certain groups, with groups within groups to an indefinite depth of embedding.

historical linguistics. The branch of linguistics which is concerned with studying the relationship between the different stages of a language over long periods of time and the processes by which languages change through time.

holophrastic. The stage of language acquisition at which one-word utterances appear to have different semantic intentions, discernible in terms of the context of action of child and observer. (E.g., "Milk" can mean "That's my milk," "Give me milk!" or "Is that my milk?" depending on the stress and intonation.)

Immediate Constituent Analysis. A means of diagraming sentences which not only separates groups of words and shows their relationships, but also shows their hierarchical grouping.

(E.g., Hortense rides a broom.)

imperative sentence. A sentence which expresses a command or request. (Cf. *declarative sentence, interrogative sentence*.)

indefinite. A noun phrase which is used without reference to a certain person or object. (E.g., "any," "anything.")

indefinite noun phrase. A noun phrase (q.v.) which appears in deep structure (q.v.) but does not specify a unique item. Indefinite noun phrases have been represented as $[_{NP}WH\text{-some } N_{NP}]$.

indirect object. The noun phrase in a transitive (q.v.) sentence to or for whom or which the action of the sentence takes place. (E.g., "He gave *the girl* a ring.")

Indo-European. The family of languages which provided the major theoretical developments in linguistics throughout the 19th century. In addition to English and the other Germanic languages, it includes most of the European languages as well as some of those of the Indian subcontinent.

infix. An affix (q.v.) inserted within a root. (Cf. *prefix, suffix*.)

inflectional rule. A rule which changes the shape of a root (q.v.) to express syntactic functions and relationships. (E.g., the plural morpheme.) (Cf. *derivational rule*.)

internal reconstruction. The analysis of a single language to reconstruct its hypothetical parent language.

interpretive components. Those components of a grammar (q.v.) which serve to interpret the structures generated by the syntax (q.v.), the semantics, morphology, and phonology (qq.v.).

interrogative sentence. A sentence which asks a question. (Cf. *declarative sentence, imperative sentence*.)

intonation. The relative pitch heights of the voice throughout a sentence.

intransitive. With reference to a verb or a sentence, not taking a direct object (q.v.). (Cf. *transitive*.)

irregular verb. A verb which is inflected exceptionally. (Cf. *regular verb*.)

kernel sentence. In Chomsky's *Syntactic Structures* framework, a sentence resulting from the application of obligatory transformations (q.v.) only, and no optional transformations, to a deep structure (q.v.) representation.

lexical insertion. The insertion of morphemes (q.v.) into the deep structure (q.v.) of a sentence.

lexicon. A listing of the morphemes (q.v.) of a language, with their syntactic, semantic, and phonological characteristics.

linguistic tree. A notational device for representing the hierarchical arrangement (q.v.) and internal relationships of sentences by means of branching nodes.

linguistic universal. A category, feature, or characteristic which occurs in all or most of the languages of the world. (E.g., nearly all languages obey certain Ross Constraints (q.v.).)

linguistics. The scientific study of natural language (q.v.).

logical subject. See *deep subject*.

major rule. A rule that applies in the proper environment with few exceptions. (Cf. *minor rule*.)

mass noun. A noun whose singular and plural forms are identical. (E.g., "sheep.")

mathematical linguistics. That branch of linguistics which deals with the formal aspects of linguistic description and notation, and with the study of artificial languages.

minor rule. Lakoff's term for a rule which applies to only a small subclass of the appropriate environments. (E.g., Negative Transportation is restricted to verbs like "think," "hope," "seem," etc.) (Cf. *major rule*.)

modal. A particular type of auxiliary, which expresses mood or tense of the verb: "can," "may," "must," "ought," "shall," "should," "will," and "would."

morpheme. The minimal unit of grammatical structure and meaning, in most cases manifesting a single constant meaning. Each word consists of one or more morphemes.

morphology. The study of morphemes (q.v.) and their combinations.

natural approach. An approach to teaching language to deaf students, popularized by Groht, which deemphasizes formal language teaching and emphasizes language use in natural situations.

natural language. A language used by human beings, many of whom learned it in infancy without being formally taught.

node admissibility conditions. Those rules (q.v.) which determine the acceptability or unacceptability of the nodes in a deep structure tree (q.v.). Equivalent to *phrase structure rules* (q.v.).

nominal. A structuralist term defined by substitution in syntactic frames (q.v.), and roughly equivalent to a noun or noun phrase.

non-restrictive relative. A relative clause which simply elaborates on the characteristics of the head noun phrase, and is not essential to the meaning of the sentence. (E.g., "Elephants, which are enormous, have few enemies.") (Cf. *restrictive relative*.)

non-reversible passive. A passive sentence whose subject and object cannot be reversed without the creation of an ungrammatical sentence. (E.g., "The flowers were watered by the butler.") (Cf. *reversible passive*.)

noun phrase. A constituent (q.v.) which contains at least a noun, and optionally one or more determiners.

novel utterance. A sentence which is produced by a speaker for the first time. The common production of novel utterances is evidence against the view of language learning by memorization.

null string. A term used to refer to a $\emptyset$ constituent, that is, a constituent with no morphemes (q.v.).

number agreement. Grammatical agreement as to number between syntactically related words of the sentence, especially subject and verb.

Object-Object Deletion. A rule commonly used by deaf people, which deletes the object of an embedded sentence (q.v.) (or second conjunct (q.v.)) on identity with the object of the main sentence (or first conjunct). (E.g., "John chased the girl and he scared.")

Object-Subject Deletion. A rule commonly used by deaf people which deletes the subject of an embedded sentence (q.v.) (or second conjunct (q.v.)) on identity with the object of the main sentence (or first conjunct). (E.g., "The dog chased the girl had a red dress.")

obligatory transformation. A transformation (q.v.) which must be applied if its structural description (q.v.) is met. (Cf. *optional transformation*.)

open words. In the "Pivot-Open" hypothesis, words belonging to open classes, such as nouns and verbs, whose membership can be added to indefinitely. (Cf. *pivot words*.)

optional transformation. A transformation (q.v.) which may or may not be applied when its structural description (q.v.) is satisfied. (Cf. *obligatory transformation*.)

ordering. See *rule ordering*.

parsing. See *diagraming*.

partially ordered rules. A set of rules (q.v.) for which some ordering relationships are necessary to produce an acceptable output while others are nonsignificant. For example, if rule 1 must precede rule 2, but rule 3 may apply either before or after 2, the rules are partially ordered.

past participle. A verb form indicating past or completed action or time, usually ending in -*ed* or -*en*. (E.g., "hated," "eaten.") (Cf. *present participle*.)

past perfect. The verbal aspect which refers to an action which occurred previous to some point of time in the past—the point of reference is specified in the context. It consists of "had" plus the past participle. (E.g., "had gone," "had copied.") (Cf. *present perfect*.)

perception verb. A verb which expresses action of the senses. (E.g., "hear," "see.")

perfective. That verbal aspect which signifies a period of time in relation to some other time specified in the context: *present perfect* (q.v.) or *past perfect* (q.v.).

performance. The actual use of language by a speaker (or writer) in concrete situations, characterized by unintentional errors and ungrammaticalities. (Cf. *competence*.)

performative (sentence). A sentence which, in its utterance, actually performs the stated action. (E.g., a person who says "I order you to go" gives the order as he speaks.) (Cf. *constative sentence*.)

person. The grammatical distinction, in pronouns, between speaker, hearer, and non-speaker-hearer. A *1st-person* pronoun is one which refers to the speaker; a *2nd-person* pronoun refers to the person or persons he is speaking to; a *3rd-person* pronoun refers to some person or persons other than the speaker or hearer.

personal pronoun. A pronoun denoting first, second, or third person. (E.g., "he," "her," "it.") (Cf. *relative pronoun, reflexive pronoun*.)

phonetics. The study of the physical characteristics of speech sounds: articulatory, acoustic, and perceptual.

phonology. The study of the sound systems of language.

phrase structure. That component of a grammar (q.v.) which expands (q.v.) constituents (q.v.) to create the deep structure (q.v.).

pivot words. In the "Pivot-Open Hypothesis," a class of words of limited membership used by children to modify the meaning of open words (q.v.); roughly equivalent to adult function words like determiners and prepositions. (Cf. *open words*.)

pragmatics. The study of language as it is used in real-world situations and how its form is determined by these situations.

predicate. A traditional grammatical term, roughly equivalent to *verb phrase* (q.v.).

predicate adjective. An adjective which follows the verb *be* or a limited class of stative verbs (q.v.) and describes the subject. (E.g., "That dog seems smart.")

prefix. An affix (q.v.) added to the beginning of a root. (Cf. *suffix, infix.*)

prepositional phrase. A phrase consisting of a preposition plus a noun phrase (q.v.). (E.g., "to the dock," "at the hop.")

present participle. That form of the verb created by adding *-ing* to the stem. (E.g., "playing," "barking.") (Cf. *past participle.*)

present perfect. That verbal aspect (q.v.) which refers to an action which took place an unspecified number of times at any time previous to the present. It consists of the present tense of *have* plus the past participle (q.v.) form of the verb. (E.g., "has gone," "have copied.") (Cf. *past perfect.*)

presupposition. That which is inherently assumed to be true with the production of a certain sentence.

progressive. That verbal aspect which indicates continuing action; it is comprised of the verb *be* plus the present participle of the verb. (E.g., "is hoping," "was developing.")

pronoun. See *personal pronoun, relative pronoun, reflexive pronoun.*

psycholinguistics. The study of the connection between man's use of language and his psychological processes, as well as the study of language acquisition.

quantifier. A constituent which specifies some quantity of a following noun phrase. (E.g., "some," "many," "all.")

recursion. The process of generating (q.v.) sentences within sentences which allows for an indefinite number of possible sentences in a language.

reflective conversational approach. Van Uden's approach to teaching deaf children language, which emphasizes interactive conversation between adults and children, with the adults reflecting back the children's productions in a way that provides them necessary information for further improvement.

reflective method. See *reflective conversational approach.*

reflexive pronoun. A pronoun which is used as a direct object and is coreferent to the subject of the sentence. (E.g., "myself," "themselves.") (Cf. *personal pronoun, relative pronoun.*)

regional dialect. A dialect (q.v.) which is differentiated from others on the basis of geographic location of its speakers.

regular verb. A verb which is inflected according to regular rules (q.v.). (Cf. *irregular verb.*)

relative clause. A clause which contains one of the relative pronouns "who," "whom," "which," or "that."

Relative Copying. A rule commonly applied by deaf people, which "copies" the head noun phrase (q.v.) in a relative clause (q.v.) rather than simply replacing it by a relative pronoun (q.v.). (E.g., "*The boy who he* hit the ball ran home.")

relative grammaticality. The idea that all sentences are not clearly "grammatical" (q.v.) or "ungrammatical," but that some are more or less grammatical than others, with the degree of grammaticality differing from speaker to speaker.

relative pronoun. A pronoun which introduces a relative clause (q.v.): "who," "whom," "which," or "that." (Cf. *personal pronoun*, *reflexive pronoun*.)

relative word. See *relative pronoun*.

restrictive relative. A relative clause (q.v.) which defines or limits the head noun phrase (q.v.), and is essential to the meaning of the sentence. (E.g., "Elephants which are full-grown have few enemies.") (Cf. *non-restrictive relative*.)

reversible passive. A passive sentence whose subject and object can be interchanged to give an equally grammatical sentence. (E.g., "The man was kissed by the woman.") (Cf. *non-reversible passive*.)

rewriting rule. A *phrase structure* (q.v.) *rule* (q.v.).

root. The basic part of a word (often a free morpheme (q.v.)) to which affixes (q.v.) may be added.

Ross Constraints. A set of constraints on transformations (q.v.) first proposed by J. R. Ross.

rule. In transformational grammar, a statement which describes some aspect of language as it is, and *not* how it should be.

rule ordering. The necessity for certain rules (q.v.) to be applied in a certain order to produce the correct output.

selectional restriction. A specific type of lexical *feature* (q.v.).

semantic interpretation rules. Those rules (q.v.) which, when applied to the deep structure (q.v.) of a sentence, give its meaning.

semantic projection rules. See *semantic interpretation rules*.

sentence negation. Negation of the entire sentence rather than one of its subparts.

simple sentence. A sentence containing only one *S* node. (Cf. *complex sentence*, *compound sentence*.)

singulary transformation. In the *Syntactic Structures* framework, a transformation (q.v.) which applies to a single deep structure (q.v.), as opposed to a *generalized transformation* (q.v.), which applies to two or more deep structures. In more recent treatments all transformations are singulary.

social dialect. A dialect (q.v.) which is differentiated from others on the basis of social characteristics (e.g., class, race, sex) of its speakers.

sociolinguistics. The investigation of language in its social context.

Standard Theory. The theory of transformational grammar (q.v.) developed in Chomsky's *Aspects*, as opposed to Generative Semantics, Case Grammar (qq.v.), etc.

stative verb. A verb which expresses a state, rather than an action. (E.g., "know.") (Cf. *active verb*.)

strict subcategorization feature. A specific type of lexical *feature* (q.v.).

strong verb. A verb which forms the past tense in an irregular or exceptional way. (Cf. *weak verb*.)

structural change. Notation which specifies the manner in which the input constituents (q.v.) are changed by application of a rule (q.v.). (Cf. *structural description*.)

structural description. Notation which identifies the constituent (q.v.) structure necessary for application of the rule. (Cf. *structural change*).

structuralism. A field of linguistics developed in the early 20th century. It was strongly influenced by behaviorism and emphasized the structure of surface linguistic units.

suffix. An affix (q.v.) added at the end of a root (q.v.). (Cf. *prefix*, *infix*.)

superlative. The form of an adjective or adverb which expresses the greatest amount of the quality or quantity indicated. (E.g., "biggest" is the superlative of "big"; "most friendly" is the superlative of "friendly.") (Cf. *comparative*.)

surface structure. The output of the transformational (q.v.) component of a grammar (q.v.) to which the phonological rules (q.v.) apply to give the spoken form. (Cf. *deep structure*.)

surface subject. The subject of a sentence at the surface structure (q.v.) level. (Cf. *deep subject*.)

synonymous. Having the same meaning.

syntax. The study of the rules (q.v.) which determine the order and grouping of words in sentences.

tag question. A question which ends in a tag such as "isn't he?", "had it?".

telegraphic sentence. An abbreviated sentence type used by children, often consisting of only one or two words.

Tense. The grammatical category, part of the auxiliary (q.v.), which expresses the time (past or nonpast) of the verb.

textual pronominalization. Pronominalization across sentences. (E.g., "Bill wrote home. Then *he* went to bed.")

transformation. See *transformational rule*.

transformational component. That component of a grammar (q.v.) consisting of the transformational rules (q.v.) which apply to deep structure (q.v.) to create surface structure (q.v.).

transformational generative grammar. That model of linguistics which postulates an underlying deep structure (q.v.) which is related to the surface structure (q.v.) of a sentence via linguistic transformations (q.v.).

transformational grammar. See *transformational generative grammar.*

transformational rule. A rule which applies to a linguistic tree (q.v.) to delete, insert, or transpose elements to produce a new, different tree.

transitive. With reference to a verb or a sentence, taking a direct object (q.v.). (Cf. *intransitive.*)

tree. See *linguistic tree.*

tree-pruning. A procedure that deletes stranded, non-branching nodes from a tree (q.v.) after lower material has been moved.

underlying structure. See *deep structure.*

vacuous application. Application of a rule (q.v.) which results in no changes in the tree.

variable. In the formulation of transformational rules (q.v.), an abbreviatory device (X,Y,Z, etc.) used to represent indeterminate structure whose composition is irrelevant to the operation of the rule.

verb phrase. A constituent (q.v.) consisting of an auxiliary and a verb (qq.v.), and optionally noun phrases, embedded sentences, and prepositional phrases (qq.v.).

Vernacular Black English. The social dialect spoken by most working-class Blacks.

vocalization. That stage of language acquisition at which recognizable intonation contours appear, similar to those of adult sentences.

voiced. Pronounced with vibration of the vocal cords. (Cf. *voiceless.*)

voiceless. Pronounced with no vibration of the vocal cords. (Cf. *voiced.*)

weak verb. A verb which forms its past tense according to regular rules. (Cf. *strong verb.*)

WH-Question. A question which begins with a WH-word ("what," "who," "when," or "where") and is answered with a noun phrase or a prepositional phrase. (Cf. *Yes-No Question.*)

Wing Symbols. A structuralist based (q.v.) set of symbols developed by George Wing of the Minnesota School for the Deaf for representing form and function of elements of a sentence.

Yes-No Question. A question which can be answered either "yes" or "no." (Cf. *WH-Question.*)

References

Austin, J. L. *How to do things with words*. New York: Oxford University Press, 1965.

Bateman, D., and Zidonis, F. *The effect of a study of transformational grammar on the writing of ninth and tenth graders*. Champaign, Ill.: National Council of Teachers of English, 1966.

Bellugi, U. The roots of language in the sign talk of the deaf. *Psychology Today*, 1972, *6* *(1)*, 60-64, 76.

Berko, J. The child's learning of English morphology. *Word*, 1958, *14*, 150-177. Reprinted in A. Bar-Adon and W. Leopold (Eds.), *Child language: A book of readings*. Englewood Cliffs, N.J.: Prentice-Hall, 1971.

Bever, T. G. The influence of speech performance on linguistic structure. In G. B. Flores d'Arcais and W. J. M. Levelt (Eds.), *Advances in psycholinguistics*. Amsterdam: North Holland, 1970.

Bever, T. G. The cognitive basis for linguistic structures. In J. J. Hayes (Ed.), *Cognition and the development of language*. New York: Wiley, 1971.

Bloom, L. *Language development: Form and function in emerging grammars*. Cambridge, Mass.: M.I.T. Press, 1970.

Borkin, A., et al. *Where the rules fail: A student's guide*. Bloomington, Ind.: Indiana University Linguistics Club, 1972.

Brown, R. *Psycholinguistics: Selected papers*. New York: Free Press, 1970.

Brown, R. *A first language: The early stages*. Cambridge, Mass.: Harvard University Press, 1973.

Brown, R., Cazden, C., and Bellugi, U. The child's grammar from I to III. In J. P. Hill (Ed.), *Minnesota Symposium on Child Psychology*. Vol. 2. Minneapolis: University of Minnesota Press, 1969.

Brown, R., and Hanlon, C. Derivational complexity and order of acquisition in child speech. In J. R. Hayes (Ed.), *Cognition and the development of language*. New York: Wiley, 1971.

Cazden, C. The acquisition of noun and verb inflections. *Child development*, 1968, *39*, 433-438.

Cazden, C. *Child language and education*. New York: Holt, Rinehart, and Winston, 1972.

Charrow, V. R. *Deaf English: An investigation of the written English competence of deaf adolescents*. Psychology and Education Series, Institute for Mathematical Studies in the Social Science. Stanford University. Technical report No. 236, September 30, 1974.

Chomsky, C. *The acquisition of syntax in children from 5 to 10*. Cambridge, Mass.: M.I.T. Press, 1969.

Chomsky, N. *Syntactic structures*. The Hague: Mouton, 1957.

Chomsky, N. *Aspects of the theory of syntax*. Cambridge, Mass.: M.I.T. Press, 1965.

Cooper, R. The ability of deaf and hearing children to apply morphological rules. *Journal of Speech and Hearing Research*, 1967, *10*, 77-86.

Cooper, R, and Rosenstein, J. Language acquisition of deaf children. *The Volta Review*, 1966, *68*, 58-67.

Davis, O., Gladney, M., and Leaverton, L. *I be scared* (1969). Referred to in W. Wolfram and R. W. Fasold *The study of social dialects in American English*. Englewood Cliffs, N.J.: Prentice-Hall, 1974.

Diller, K. C. *Generative grammar, structural linguistics, and language teaching*. Rowley, Mass.: Newbury House, 1971.

Ervin-Tripp, S. Discourse agreement: How children answer questions. In J. R. Hayes (Ed.), *Cognition and the development of language*. New York: Wiley, 1970.

Ferguson, C. A., and Slobin, D. I. (Eds.). *Studies of child language development*. New York: Holt, Rinehart, and Winston, 1972.

Fillmore, C. J. The position of embedding transformations in a grammar. *Word*, 1963, *19*, 208-231.

Fillmore, C. J. The case for case. In E. Bach and R. T. Harm (Eds.), *Universals in linguistic theory*. New York: Holt, Rinehart, and Winston, 1968.

Fitzgerald, E. *Straight language for the deaf*. Washington, D.C.: The Volta Bureau, 1949.

Fodor, J. A., and Bever, T. G. The psychological reality of linguistic segments. *Journal of Verbal Learning and Verbal Behavior*, 1965, *4*, 414-20. Reprinted in L. A. Jakobovits and M. S. Miron (Eds.), *Readings in the psychology of language*. Englewood Cliffs, N.J.: Prentice-Hall, 1967.

Fodor, J. A., and Garrett, M. Some syntactic determinants of sentential complexity. *Perception and Psychophysics*, 1967, *2*, 289-96.

Fraser, C., Bellugi, U., and Brown, C. Control of grammar in imitation, comprehension and production. *Journal of Verbal Learning and Verbal Behavior*, 1963, *2*, 121-135.

Fries, C. C. *The structure of English*. New York: Harcourt, Brace, 1952.

Greenbaum, S., and Quirk, R. *Elication experiments in English: Linguistic studies in use and attitude*. (Miami Linguistics Ser., No. 10) Miami: U. of Miami Press, 1970.

Greene, J. *Psycholinguistics: Chomsky and psychology*. Harmondsworth, Eng.: Penguin Education, 1972.

Groht, M. *Natural language for deaf children*. Washington, D.C.: A. G. Bell Association for the Deaf, 1958.

Gruber, G. Topicalization in child language. *Foundations of language*, 1967, *3*, 37-65.

Hamel, C. A. *Language curriculum: Based on concept formation and transformational grammar*. Providence: Rhode Island School for the Deaf, 1971.

Harris, Z. Co-occurrence and transformation in linguistic structure. *Language*, 1957, *33*, 283-340. Reprinted in J. A. Fodor and J. J. Katz (Eds.), *The structure of language: Readings in the philosophy of language*. Englewood Cliffs, N.J.: Prentice-Hall, 1964.

Hatch, E. Four experimental studies in syntax of young children. Southwest Regional Laboratory for Educational Research and Development Tech. Rpt. 11, Inglewood, California, 1969.

Hayhurst, H. Some errors of young children in producing passive sentences. *Journal of Verbal Learning and Verbal Behavior*, 1967, *6*, 634-639.

Hunt, K. W. Grammatical structures written at three grade levels. Champaign, Ill.: National Council of Teachers of English, 1965.

Huxley, R. The development of the correct use of subject personal pronouns in two children. In G. B. Flores d'Arcais and W. J. M. Levelt (Eds.), *Advances in psycholinguistics*. Amsterdam: North Holland, 1970.

Jakobovits, L. A. *Foreign language learning*. Rowley, Mass.: Newburg House, 1970.

Kessel, F. S. The role of syntax in children's comprehension from ages six to twelve. *Monographs of the Society for Research in Child Development*. 1970, *35* (6 whole No. 139).

Klima, E. Negation in English. In J. A. Fodor and J. J. Katz (Eds.), The *structure of language: Readings in the philosophy of language*. Englewood Cliffs, N.J.: Prentice-Hall, 1964.

Klima, E., and Bellugi-Klima, U. Syntactic regularities in the speech of children. In J. Lyons and R. J. Wales (Eds.), *Psycholinguistic papers*. Edinburgh: Edinburgh University Press, 1966.

Labov, W. Stages in the acquisition of standard English. In R. Shuy (Ed.), *Social dialects and language learning*. Champaign, Ill.: National Council of Teachers of English, 1965.

Labov, W. Some sources of reading problems for Negro speakers of non-standard English. In Alexander Frazier (Ed.), *New Directions in Elementary English*. Champaign, Ill.: National Council of Teachers of English, 1967.

Labov, W. *The study of non-standard English*. Champaign, Ill.: National Council of Teachers of English, 1970.

Labov, W. Methodology. In W. D. Dingwall (Ed.), *A survey of linguistic science*. College Park, Maryland: Linguistic Program, University of Maryland, 1971(a).

Labov, W. Variation in language. In C. E. Reed (Ed.), *The learning of language*. New York: Appleton-Century-Crofts, 1971(b).

Labov, W., Cohen, P., and Robins, C. *A preliminary study of the structure of English used by Negro and Puerto Rican speakers in New York City*. Final Rept. Coop. Res. Proj. No. 3091 (Eric ED 003819) Washington, D.C.: Office of Education, 1965.

Lakoff, G. *Irregularity in syntax*. New York: Holt, Rinehart, and Winston, 1970.

Lakoff, G. Syntactic amalgams. In M. W. LaGaly, R. A. Fox, and A. Bruck (Eds.), *Papers from the tenth regional meeting: Chicago Linguistic Society*, 1974.

Lakoff, R. A syntactic argument for negation transportation. In R. I. Binnick, et al. (Eds.), *Papers from the fifth regional meeting: Chicago Linguistic Society*, 1969.

Lakoff, R. Passive resistance. *Papers from the seventh regional meeting: Chicago Linguistic Society*, 1971.

Langacker, R. Pronominalization and the chain of command. In D. A. Reibel and S. A. Schane (Eds.), *Modern studies in English*. Englewood Cliffs, New Jersey: Prentice-Hall, 1969.

Lee, L. L. Developmental sentence types: A method for comparing normal and deviant syntactical development in children's language. *Journal of Speech and Hearing Disorders*, 1966, *31*, 311-330.

Lee, L. L., and Canter, S. M. Developmental sentence scoring: A clinical procedure for estimating syntactic development in children's spontaneous speech. *Journal of Speech and Hearing Disorders*, 1971, *36*, 315-334.

Levelt, W. J. M. A scaling approach to the study of syntactic relations. In G. B. Flores d'Arcais and W. J. M. Levelt (Eds.), *Advances in psycholinguistics*. Amsterdam: North Holland, 1970.

Limber, J. Genesis of complex sentences. In T. E. Moore (Ed.), *Cognitive development and acquisition of language*. New York: Academic Press, 1973.

Loban, W. *The language of elementary school children*. Champaign, Ill.: National Council of Teachers of English, 1963.

McCarr, J. E. *Lessons in syntax: Teacher's manuals*. Lake Oswego, Oregon: Dormac, 1973(a).

McCarr, J. E. *Lessons in syntax: Student workbook*. Lake Oswego, Oregon: Dormac, 1973(b).

McCawley, J. D. Concerning the base component of a transformational grammar. *Foundations of Language*, 1968, *4*, 243-369.

McKee, P., Harrison, M. L., McCowen, A., Lehr, E., and Durr, W. K. *Reading for meaning* (4th ed.). Boston: Houghton Mifflin, 1966.

McNeill, D. *The acquisition of language: The study of developmental psycholinguistics*. New York: Harper and Row, 1970.

Mellon, J. *Transformational sentence combining*. Champaign, Ill.: National Council of Teachers of English, 1969.

Menyuk, P. Syntactic structures in the language of children. *Child Development*, 1963, *34*, 407-422.

Menyuk, P. Syntactic rules used by children from pre-school through first grade. *Child Development*, 1964, *35*, 533-546.

Menyuk, P. *Sentences children use*. Cambridge, Mass.: M.I.T. Press, 1969.

Miller, G. A., and McKean, K. E. A chronometric study of some relations between sentences. *Quarterly Journal of Experimental Psychology*, 1964, *16*, 297-308. Reprinted in C. Oldfield and J. C. Marshall (Eds.), *Language: selected readings*. Harmondsworth, Eng.: Penguin, 1968.

Moog, J. Approaches to teaching pre-primary hearing-impaired children. *AOEHI Bulletin: Education of the hearing impaired*, 1970, *1*, 52-59.

Moores, D. *Applications of "Cloze" procedures to the assessment of psycholinguistic abilities of the deaf*. Unpublished doctoral dissertation, University of Illinois, 1967.

Nida, E. *A synopsis of English*. Norman, Oklahoma: Summer Institute of Linguistics, 1960. Republished, The Hague: Mouton, 1966.

O'Donnell, R. C., Griffin, W. J., and Norris, R. C. *Syntax of kindergarten and elementary school children: A transformational analysis*. Champaign, Ill.: National Council of Teachers of English, 1967.

O'Neill, M. *The receptive language competence of deaf children in the use of the base structure rules of transformational-generative grammar*. Unpublished doctoral dissertation, University of Pittsburgh, 1973.

Pei, M., and Gaynor, F. *A dictionary of linguistics*. Totowa, N.J.: Littlefield, Adams & Co., 1967.

Power, D. J. *Deaf children's acquisition of the passive voice*. Unpublished doctoral dissertation, University of Illinois, 1971.

Power, D. J. Deaf children's acquisition of sentence voice and reversibility. In D. Reigel (Ed.), *Language development and disorders*. Melbourne: Australian College of Speech Therapists, 1973.

Power, D. J., and Quigley, S. P. Deaf children's acquisition of the passive voice. *Journal of Speech and Hearing Research*, 1973, *16*, 5-11.

Quigley, S. P., Montanelli, D. S., and Wilbur, R. B. *An examination of negation in the written language of deaf children*. Unpublished manuscript, Institute for Research on Exceptional Children, University of Illinois at Urbana-Champaign, 1974.

Quigley, S. P., Montanelli, D. S., and Wilbur, R. B. *Some aspects of the verb system in the language of deaf students*. Unpublished manuscript, Institute for Research on Exceptional Children, University of Illinois at Urbana-Champaign, 1975.

Quigley, S. P., and Power, D. J. *The development of syntactic structures in the language of deaf children*. Urbana, Ill.: Institute for Research on Exceptional Children, 1972.

Quigley, S. P., Smith, N. L., and Wilbur, R. B. Comprehension of relativized sentences by deaf students. *Journal of Speech and Hearing Research*, 1974, *17* (3), 325-341.

Quigley, S. P., Wilbur, R. B., and Montanelli, D. Question formation in the language of deaf students. *Journal of Speech and Hearing Research*, 1974, *17*(4), 699-713.

Quigley, S. P., Wilbur, R. B, and Montanelli, D. S. *Complement structures in the language of deaf children*. Unpublished manuscript, Institute for Research on Exceptional Children, University of Illinois at Urbana-Champaign, 1975.

Quigley, S. P., et al. *Syntactic structures in the language of deaf children*. Final Rept. National Institute of Education Project 232175. Urbana, Ill.: Institute for Child Behavior and Development, 1976.

Rosenbaum, P. S. *The grammar of English predicate complement constructions*. Research Monograph No. 47. Cambridge: M.I.T. Press, 1967.

Ross, I. R. *Constraints on variables in syntax*. Unpublished doctoral dissertation, M.I.T., 1967.

Ross, J. R. On declarative sentences. In R. A. Jacobs and P. Rosenbaum (Eds.), *Readings in English transformational grammar*. Waltham, Mass.: Ginn & Co., 1970.

Schiefelbusch, R. L. (Ed.) *Language of the mentally retarded*. Baltimore, Maryland: University Park Press, 1972.

Schmitt, P. Language instruction for the deaf. *The Volta Review*, 1966, *68*, 85-105, 123.

Schmitt, P. *Deaf children's comprehension and production of sentence transformations and verb tenses*. Unpublished doctoral dissertation, University of Illinois, 1968.

Simmons, A. Motivating language in the young child. *Proceedings of the International Conference on Oral Education of the Deaf* (Vol. 2). Washington, D.C.: A. G. Bell Association for the Deaf, 1967.

Slobin, D. Grammatical transformations and sentence comprehension in childhood and adulthood. *Journal of Verbal Learning & Verbal Behavior*, 1966, *5*, 219-27.

Stokoe, W. C., Jr. Sign language structure: An outline of the visual communication systems of the American deaf. *Studies in Linguistics*. Occasional Paper No. 8, 1960. Reissued, Washington, D.C.: Gallaudet College Press.

Stokoe, W. C., Jr. *Semiotics and human sign language*. The Hague: Mouton, 1972.

Streng, A. *Syntax, speech & hearing*. New York: Grune & Stratton, 1972.

Taylor, L. *A language analysis of the writing of deaf children*. Unpublished doctoral dissertation, Florida State University, 1969.

Tervoort, B. T. Esoteric symbolism in the communication behavior of young deaf children. *American Annals of the Deaf*, 1961, *106*, 436-480.

Tervoort, B. T., and Verberk, A. J. A. *Analysis of communicative structure patterns in deaf children*. Final Rept. Vocational Rehabilitation Administration Project RD-467-64-65. Groningen, Netherlands, 1967.

Turner, E., and Rommetveit, R. The acquisition of sentence voice and reversibility. *Child Development*, 1967, *38*, 649-660.

van Uden, A. *A world of language for deaf children. Part I, Basic principles*. St. Michielsgestel, Netherlands: Institute for the Deaf, 1968.

Weiser, A. Deliberate ambiguity. In M. W. LaGaly, R. A. Fox, and A. Bruck (Eds.), *Papers from the tenth regional meeting: Chicago Linguistic Society*, 1974.

Wilbur, R. B., Montanelli, D. S., and Quigley, S .P. *Pronominalization in the language of deaf students*. Unpublished manuscript, Institute for Research on Exceptional Children, University of Illinois at Urbana-Champaign, 1975.

Wilbur, R. B., Quigley, S. P., and Montanelli, D. S. Conjoined structures in the language of deaf students. *Journal of Speech and Hearing Research*, 1975, *2*, 319-335.

Wolfram, W., and Fasold, R. W. *The study of social dialects in American English*. Englewood Cliffs, N.J.: Prentice-Hall, 1974.

Index